THE GREAT CANADIAN HOLIDAY PUZZLE BOOK

DELUXE GIFT EDITION

ALSO AVAILABLE

THE GREAT CANADIAN COTTAGE PUZZLE BOOK
THE GREAT CANADIAN ROAD TRIP PUZZLE BOOK

THE GREAT CANADIAN HOLIDAY PUZZLE BOOK

DELUXE GIFT EDITION

DAN LIEBMAN,
GENERAL EDITOR

DUNCAN McKENZIE,
SENIOR PUZZLE CONSTRUCTOR

ZOË McKENZIE,
PUZZLE CONSTRUCTOR

Collins

The Great Canadian Holiday Puzzle Book, Deluxe Gift Edition

Published by Collins,
an imprint of HarperCollins Publishers Ltd

First published by Collins in an original trade paperback edition: 2015
This Deluxe Gift Edition: 2016

HarperCollins books may be purchased for educational, business,
or sales promotional use through our Special Markets Department.

HarperCollins Publishers Ltd.
2 Bloor Street East, 20th Floor
Toronto, Ontario, Canada
M4W 1A8

www.harpercollins.ca

Library and Archives Canada Cataloguing in Publication
information is available upon request.

ISBN: 978-1-44345-348-6

Printed and bound in the U.S.A.
RRD 9 8 7 6 5 4 3 2 1

INTRODUCTION

We hope you enjoy this collection of puzzles and quizzes. They are, as you will have noticed, Canadian. Some are proudly, "flag-wavingly" Canadian—with questions about uniquely Canadian geography, quotes by Canadian comics, and quizzes about Canadian culture. In other puzzles, what makes them Canadian is something more subtle.

You'll still find references here to Hollywood films and US celebrities. After all, we share much of our culture with our southern neighbours (that's *neighbours*, not *neighbors*—you'll discover that this book also favours Canadian spelling). But these are all puzzles written by Canadians, for Canadian solvers—so maybe that's why these pages have more mentions of ice and winter than you'd find in the usual puzzle book, and less about the desert. There's more about Canadian trivia, more about Canadian people and places, and, of course, more about hockey. You'll also find lots of puzzles with holiday themes, and we hope they'll put you in a merry mood.

These puzzles have been designed to suit different levels of skill and also different occasions. Some, such as crosswords, word searches, and sudokus, are a perfect pastime for when you're trapped indoors on a cold winter day. Others, like stinkety pinkety and many of the quizzes, were included because they're great for playing together as a group.

You'll find fresh material here. Some puzzles, such as our unique antlergrams and maple leaf puzzles, put a lighthearted Canadian spin on anagram puzzles. Others, such as triple meanings, word jigsaw, and before and after, were invented especially for this book. You'll find other original creations throughout.

And if you're *not* a Canadian, we sympathize. We realize you may be stumped by the clues about loonies, toques, and Chicken Bones (the candy, of course). We could have offered tips. But maybe it's best if you give this book as a gift to your Canadian friends—or, better yet, ask them, very politely, to help you with the answers.

So, grab a pencil, put on your thinking cap, and have fun over the holidays—or whenever you have some time for an enjoyable challenge!

Solutions are coded by puzzle number and begin on page 343.

1.

ANAGRAMS

The following items are all anagrams of words or phrases describing winter activities. See how many you can solve.

1. O, SCURRYING ON STICKS

   _ _ _ _ _ - _ _ _ _ _ _ _
   _ _ _ _ _ _

2. HALF STING BLOW

   _ _ _ _ _ _ _ _   _ _ _ _ _

3. TAKES IF URGING

   _ _ _ _ _ _   _ _ _ _ _ _ _

4. GOING TO BANG

   _ _ _ _ _ _ _ _ _ _ _

5. ON SINEW HOGS

   _ _ _ _ _ _ _ _ _ _ _

6. AN AMUSING, BOLD WIN

   _ _ _ _ _ _ _ _   _   _ _ _ _ _ _ _

7. I SIGN CHIEF

   _ _ _   _ _ _ _ _ _ _

8. RIDE COLD GANGS

   _ _ _ _ _ _ _   _ _ _ _ _ _

2.

ANTLERGRAM

The goal of antlergrams is to form as many words as you can using the letters in the moose's nose and antlers. Each letter can be used only once, which means you can form a word with two Ts only if there are two Ts in the puzzle. Each word must be three or more letters long and must contain the letter in the nose, along with any combination of the letters from the antlers. For the ultimate challenge, see if you can find the one 9-letter word that contains ALL the letters in the puzzle.

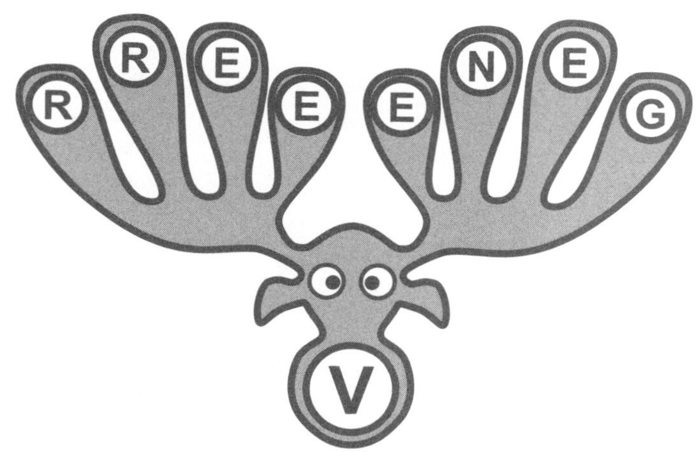

3.

CHRISTMAS PUNS 1 CROSSWORD

ACROSS

1. Tall tale cowboy Bill
6. Made a barking sound
11. Ng of They Might Be Giants song
14. Saudi's neighbour
15. It makes you blush
16. "___ Air" (Nicolas Cage film)
17. Weighed down
18. Where do polar bears keep their money?
20. Take out, slangily
21. Comedian Tim
23. Echoing song
24. What do you call a condition you get from eating ornaments?
27. Dust bug
28. To ___ their own
29. Matthew's Spanish cousin
30. Cat-headed Egyptian goddess
31. Mount
33. Some sibilant sounds
35. Lecture inits.
36. Paddle
39. Rocky hill
40. Unruly crowd
43. Gossip featurer
45. Stadium
47. Kind of wrestling
50. Under way
53. "You can say that again!"
54. Online patron
55. What do you call a vagabond who wraps gifts for the poor?
57. Rears
59. Like a busybody (var.)
60. Genetic stuff
61. What do you get if you cross a snowman with a vampire?
63. Negative particle
65. Always, to a poet
66. Wild water buffaloes
67. Tropical vine
68. Wine descriptor
69. Venetian officials
70. Gear shafts

DOWN

1. Most socially graced
2. Make starve
3. Rhythmic
4. Type of Xbox
5. Red Sea peninsula
6. Plant also known as spikenard
7. Ornate Gothic window
8. Like a top comic
9. Id's partner
10. ___-eyed
11. Former French colony
12. Medium-sized musical groups
13. Type of footwear
19. Flunks
22. Advanced law deg.
25. "___ loves you yeah, yeah, yeah . . ."
26. Acceptable
32. John or Jane
34. Victorian or Elizabethan
37. Banned orchard spray
38. Civilizing
40. Commemorative
41. Private, like a conversation
42. Some head ties
43. Military unit
44. South African dish
46. "Go team!"
47. Used the Net
48. Loan shark
49. "Cats" song
51. Worry too much (over)
52. What a ballerina stands on
56. Type of antelope
58. Dutch city
62. Buddy
64. Rule out

1	2	3	4	5		6	7	8	9	10		11	12	13
14						15						16		
17						18					19			
20				21	22					23				
24			25						26		27			
28					29						30			
31				32			33			34				
35				36	37	38		39				40	41	42
			43				44			45	46			
47	48	49			50			51	52		53			
54					55					56				
57				58		59						60		
61					62					63	64			
65				66						67				
68				69						70				

4.

TRIPLE MEANINGS

Many English words have multiple meanings. Here, we've given three different definitions that each describe the same word. Can you figure out the words?

1.	ENTERTAINMENT SPOT	BEAT	GOLF EQUIPMENT	________
2.	LINE	RECORD	SMOOTHING TOOL	________
3.	TIED	JUMP	CERTAIN	________
4.	ABRUPT MOVEMENT	DRIED MEAT	ANNOYING PERSON	________
5.	CORRECTLY	WATER HOLE	HEALTHY	________
6.	INSECT	ANNOY	LISTENING GADGET	________
7.	DISCARDED	NOT RIGHT	DEPARTED	________
8.	SCRAPE	YELP	TREE PART	________
9.	CREATE FAKE	WORK METAL	MOVE FORWARD	________

HOLIDAY MOVIES

1. In this movie, a young boy who questions his belief in Santa takes a train trip to the North Pole.
2. Who starred in the movie *The Bishop's Wife*? (Bonus points for naming all three stars)
3. Name the Christmas movie in which a young character tells her father, "Teacher says, every time a bell rings an angel gets his wings."

[Answers: 1. *The Polar Express*; 2. Cary Grant (as the angel), David Niven (as the bishop), and Loretta Young (as the bishop's wife); 3. *It's a Wonderful Life*]

PARTY GAME—
THE YEAR THAT WAS

This is a good game to play following a holiday dinner or on New Year's Eve.

Number of players: Five or more

What you'll need: The Internet and perhaps some magazines (for the emcee); a pen and a sheet of paper for each player

Object of the game: To see who remembers the dates on which specific events took place

To begin: The emcee writes down 15 to 20 events that took place in the past year. He or she should mix different topics, such as politics, humour, sports, and culture. Some events can be serious, but others should be funny. (Alternative play: select events from the past ten years.)

The play: The emcee reads out the events on the list (not in chronological order). The players write down the name of each event and their best guess for the day and month it happened.

After all the events have been read out, the emcee reveals their exact dates. The person with the closest date gets one point for each event. Players keep track of their own scores. The person with the highest total of points wins the game.

5.

PYRAMID POWER

The pyramid is made up of a series of words, each one containing the letters used in the word directly above it (the order of the letters may be changed) plus one new letter. Solve the clues to fill in the pyramid!

1. Rupees symbol ___
2. Referring to ___ ___
3. Salesperson ___ ___ ___
4. South American country ___ ___ ___ ___
5. Less contaminated ___ ___ ___ ___ ___
6. Media tycoon Murdoch ___ ___ ___ ___ ___ ___
7. Bliss ___ ___ ___ ___ ___ ___ ___
8. Hole for light ___ ___ ___ ___ ___ ___ ___ ___
9. Leaving on a jet plane ___ ___ ___ ___ ___ ___ ___ ___ ___
10. Escapee brought back ___ ___ ___ ___ ___ ___ ___ ___ ___ ___

FOOD, GLORIOUS FOOD!

1. What is the name of the cake traditionally eaten in Italy on Christmas?
2. What is the name of the fruitcake that has tapered ends, has a ridge down the centre, and is traditionally eaten in Germany on Christmas?
3. What is the name of the potato dish traditionally served on Hanukkah?

[Answers: 1. panettone; 2. stollen; 3. latke (potato pancake)]

6.

PYRAMID POWER

The pyramid is made up of a series of words, each one containing the letters used in the word directly above it (the order of the letters may be changed) plus one new letter. Solve the clues to fill in the pyramid!

1. Between D and F ___
2. Half an em ___ ___
3. Fishing gear ___ ___ ___
4. Housing payment ___ ___ ___ ___
5. Radio knob ___ ___ ___ ___ ___
6. Not male or female ___ ___ ___ ___ ___ ___
7. Professor with job security ___ ___ ___ ___ ___ ___ ___
8. Came back ___ ___ ___ ___ ___ ___ ___ ___
9. Value too low ___ ___ ___ ___ ___ ___ ___ ___ ___
10. Indiana Jones type ___ ___ ___ ___ ___ ___ ___ ___ ___ ___

ALBUM OF THE YEAR

The first holiday album to win a Juno Award for Album of the Year was

A. *Christmas* (Michael Bublé)
B. *Anne Murray's Christmas Album*
C. *An Oscar Peterson Christmas*
D. *Christmas Songs* (Diana Krall)
E. *Under the Mistletoe* (Justin Bieber)

[Answer: A. *Christmas* (Michael Bublé)]

7.

CHRISTMAS CAROLS

All the words in the list below are hidden somewhere in the grid of letters. See if you can find them! Words may run in any direction, including diagonally, and spaces are ignored. When you've crossed off all the words, read the leftover letters in the grid (running left to right, from top to bottom) to reveal a hidden quote related to the puzzle's theme. Strings of streetlights even stop lights blink bright red and green

DECK THE HALL
FELIZ NAVIDAD
FIRST NOEL
GREENSLEEVES
HURON CAROL
JINGLE BELLS

LET IT SNOW
MUST BE SANTA
O HOLY NIGHT
RATAPAN
SANTA BABY
SILENT NIGHT

SILVER BELLS
SLEIGH RIDE
WASSAIL
WE THREE KINGS
WHITE CHRISTMAS

8.

REBUS

In these puzzles, the arrangement of the letters and symbols suggests a common word or expression. For example, this combination

COVER
GOING

is "going undercover" (the word GOING is under the word COVER—literally). See how many you can figure out.

1. O NIGHT

2. NEW YEAR'S COUNT

3. W S N O W S N O W S N O (letters arranged in a circle)

4. WE HEARD HAVE ANGEL ANGEL ANGEL

5. RES OLU TI ON

9.

SKILLATHON

The goal is to find as many words as possible made up of the letters in the word or phrase below. Words must be made of four or more letters. No plurals allowed. Only one tense or form of a verb is permitted (if you find WALK, you can't also have WALKS, WALKED, WALKING, etc.). The exception is when two forms have different meanings—e.g., BORE and BORED.

ICE CREAM

Try to beat our experts. They found 28 words.

10.

MAPLE LEAF

The goal of this puzzle is to form as many words as you can using the letters contained in the leaf. Each letter can be used only once, so you can create a word with two Ts only if there are two Ts in the leaf. Each word must be three or more letters long, and all words must contain the large central letter of the leaf, along with any mix of the letters around the outside. For the ultimate challenge, see if you can find the one 10-letter word that contains ALL the letters in the leaf.

11.

WORDS × FIVE

This puzzle is similar to a crossword, but the five-letter answer to each clue is written twice—both across and down. So, if the solution to clue 1 is FLAME, you would write FLAME into the grid twice, from left to right and from top to bottom.

1	2	3	4	5
2				
3				
4				
5				

1. Christmas song
2. Proof of innocence
3. Had gotten up
4. Chunky
5. Flax fabric

12.

WORDS × FIVE

This puzzle is similar to a crossword, but the five-letter answer to each clue is written twice—both across and down. So, if the solution to clue 1 is FLAME, you would write FLAME into the grid twice, from left to right and from top to bottom.

1. Beeches and ashes
2. Take pleasure
3. Each one
4. Creepy
5. More sneaky

13.

WORD JIGSAW

The words in these quotes and quips have been sliced up into pieces, so you can no longer see where one word begins and another ends. The order of the letters inside each piece is unchanged. Can you reassemble the word pieces and figure out the original phrase?

1. ____ ____ ________ _____
   __ ___ ____ ______ ___
   ____ ____ __ ____ ___
   _________. —______ ______

   ACKA ARSON GESEAR HEM HEPO ICECAN ILYO INTI LOSET LYSOT MA MASJOH MEF NNYC ORCH RIST STOFF URP

2. ________ __ ___ ___ ____
   ______ ______ ____ ___
   _____ ____. —______ ____

   ACEV ATDRIVE ERFRO HTER ICTO ISTHES LAUG MTHEH RHUGO SWINT UMANF UNTH

3. ___ __ __ ____ __ __
   ________ _________, ___
   _____ ______ ____ __
   _________, ____ ___ ______
   _______ ___ _ _____
   _______. —_______ _______

   ANATCH CHAR DERWA ELF ERBET FORI HENIT HILD HIMS ILD KENS LESDIC MASW MESAND METI NEV OBEC ODT RENSO RIST SACH SMIGHT TERTH TISGO YFOUN

4. ______ ___ __ ____ _ __
   __ ______ ____ _____'_
   __ ________. _'__ ____ ___
   ____ _ __. _ _____ ___
   ___ ______ ___ ____ ___
   ______. —_______ _______

ALLILL ASEB DWAIT FORSP GERSHO HATID HATIDO HENTHE INDOWAN INWIN KMEW OISTA OUW PEO PLEAS REO RESNOB RINGRO RNSBY TELLY TERW UTTHEW

5. _ _ _ _ _ _ _ _ _ _ _ _ _ _ _ _ _ _ _
_ _ _ _ _ _ _ _ _ _ _ _ _ _ _ _ _ _
_ _ _. _ _ _ _ _ _ _ _ _ _ _ _ _ _ _
_ _ _ _ _ _ _ _ _ _ _ _ _ _ _ _ _ _ _
_ _
_ _ _ _ _ _ _ _ _. _ _ _ _ _ _ _ _ _ _ _ _ _ _

EDFORM EMPLE GINSAN HEASK HERTO IRLEYT ISTOP IXMOT LIEVIN MENTS MINADE NIWASS OGRA OKMETO PART PEDBE PHSH SEEHI TACLA TOREAND USWHE YAUT

6. _
_ _ _ _ _ _ _ _ _ _ _ _ _ _ _ _ '_
_ _ _ _ _ _! _ _ _ _ _ _ _ _ _ _ _ _ _ _ _,
_ _ _ _ _ _ _ _ _, _ _ _ _ _ '_ _ _ _ _
_ _ _ _ _ _ _ _ _ _. _ _ _ _ _ _
_ _ _ _ _ _ _ _ _ . . . _ _ _ _ _ _ _ . . . _ _ _ _ _
_ _ _ _ _ _ _ _ _ _ _ _ _ _! _ _ _.
_ _ _ _ _

ANSAL CHTHO DOE HAPSME HATIFCH HEGRIN HEHADN ITMO ITTLEB MASPER METHING OMEF OREW OREWHA OUGHT RED RIST RISTMA ROMAST RSE SHETH SNTC TBEF THENT TIFCH TOFSO UGH USS

WINTER PLACES

Which of these is *not* a real place?

A. Snowflake, Manitoba
B. Sled Lake, Alberta
C. Tinsel Town, Nova Scotia
D. Reindeer Station, Northwest Territories
E. Holly, Ontario

[Answer: C. Tinsel Town, Nova Scotia]

14.

SUDOKU: VERY EASY

A sudoku puzzle is a type of logic puzzle. Although it uses numbers, no mathematics is involved. The grid below is divided into nine large squares, each of which is divided into nine smaller squares. Each large square contains all the digits from 1 to 9, with each digit appearing exactly once. Each horizontal row of the puzzle also contains each digit exactly once, and so does each vertical row. By carefully observing which numbers are missing from each row, column, or square, see if you can figure out which numbers go where. There's only one possible solution to each puzzle.

	2	5				1		
1	6			9	2		8	4
					5		3	
4		1	6			3		5
	9	6	3		8	7	4	
7		2			4	9		8
	5		9					
6	1		8	4			5	7
		8				4	9	

15.

SUDOKU: VERY EASY

A sudoku puzzle is a type of logic puzzle. Although it uses numbers, no mathematics is involved. The grid below is divided into nine large squares, each of which is divided into nine smaller squares. Each large square contains all the digits from 1 to 9, with each digit appearing exactly once. Each horizontal row of the puzzle also contains each digit exactly once, and so does each vertical row. By carefully observing which numbers are missing from each row, column, or square, see if you can figure out which numbers go where. There's only one possible solution to each puzzle.

7	1			4	5			
	6				9		3	
	8			3	6			4
	2	1						9
4		8		6		1		3
6						5	8	
8			6	9			5	
	3		8				4	
			3	5			2	1

16.

ONE STEP AT A TIME

Change the word at the top to the word at the bottom by altering one letter at a time. Each change should produce a new word. We've provided clues to help you on your way.

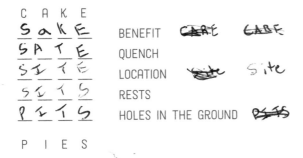

C A K E

_ _ _ _ BENEFIT
_ _ _ _ QUENCH
_ _ _ _ LOCATION
_ _ _ _ RESTS
_ _ _ _ HOLES IN THE GROUND

P I E S

C O L D

_ _ _ _ PEN FOR SHEEP
_ _ _ _ NOURISHMENT
_ _ _ _ SILLY PERSON
_ _ _ _ UNPLEASANT
_ _ _ _ SPIRIT
_ _ _ _ BROTH
_ _ _ _ WASHING MATERIAL

S N A P

TONGUE TWISTERS

Say each phrase quickly, three times.

1. I saw a kitten eating chicken in the kitchen.
2. Unique New York
3. If a dog chews shoes, whose shoes does he choose?
4. Tom threw Tim three thumbtacks.
5. Knapsack straps
6. Red lorry, yellow lorry, red lorry
7. Black bug bit a big black bear.
8. An ape hates grape cakes.
9. Please pay promptly.
10. How can a clam cram in a clean cream can?

17.

SYLLABLANK

The solution to each of the following puzzles is a single six-letter word. We've chopped each word up into the smaller words listed below. Place the smaller words into the right positions on the blanks to discover the original words.

A A A A A A AN ANY AT BAN BOW DIG ERR HOT I I IN IN ITS LED LED LET LIT MAR MU ON OR PAT POT SO TOR UPS

1. YELLOW FRUIT B A N   A N   A
2. THREW A BALL _ _ _   _ _ _
3. FINAL RESULT _ _ _   _ _ _
4. DIRTY S O   I   L E D
5. YACHT SPOT _ _ _   _ _   _
6. ENCHANTED DRINK P O T   I   O N
7. LONG LIST _ _ _   _ _ _
8. FILM ON METAL _ _ _   _ _   _
9. MAGICAL CHARM _   _ _   _ _ _
10. CORRECTIONS _ _ _   _ _   _
11. FINGERS _ _ _   _ _ _
12. SPEAKER _ _   _ _ _ _

18.

CROSS-CANADA CROSSWORD

ACROSS

1. CN Tower locale
8. Most eastern Great Lake
15. Toronto university
16. Read to the rowdy
17. Formerly Stelco
18. Rapid fall
19. Satellite broadcast to house (abbr.)
20. Stitch with a hook
22. Food preservative E320
23. US antidiscrimination agency
25. Sitar tunes
26. Work land
27. "___ with a View"
29. "Delta of Venus" author Anais
30. One-eyed "Futurama" woman
31. Big trip for Canadian bands
33. Sea-Wolf's surname
34. "Jungle Book" python
35. Dog breeder's group
36. Droopy
39. Former MP in green stetson
43. Flying through
44. Spanish hero El ___
47. Chatty sounding African explorer
48. Belted one out
49. Animal holders
51. "I ___ I taw a puddy tat!"
52. Sceptre's counterpart
53. Official order
55. Battle of Britain org.
56. "Maid of the Mist" home
58. Gaylord ___, "Show Boat" gambler
60. One who decorates with wood patterns
61. Libyan city
62. Stampede city
63. Nova Scotia capital

DOWN

1. 1970s PM
2. Walrus and Carpenter's walking companions
3. Film again
4. Food scrap
5. Billionth of a clock tick
6. "___ is human"
7. With a library patron
8. Waif
9. Frasier's brother
10. Promote
11. Cash machine
12. Saunters
13. Place to get a cold fish
14. Capital dweller
21. Movie effects
24. Kitchen activity
26. Mental impression
28. ___ Thai (Thailand's official name)
30. Indian hundred-thousands
32. Hound jokingly
33. Judge's expertise
36. Shriners, e.g.
37. "Legend of Zelda" instrument
38. Wizard's game in "Tommy"
40. Hear about
41. Aboriginals of Baja California
42. Web movie service
44. Yellow
45. Antibody type
46. Short supply
49. Nurse or parent
50. ___ Zagora, Bulgaria
53. Yucatan civilization
54. Noxious
57. Joke
59. Prefix with pen, gram, or centre

1 T	2 O	3 R	4 O	5 N	6 T	7 O	■	8 O	9 N	10 T	11 A	12 R	13 I	14 O
15 R	Y	E	R	S	O	N	■	16 R	I	O	T	A	C	T
17 U	S	S	T	E	E	L	■	18 P	L	U	M	M	E	T
19 D	J	H	■	20 C	R	O	21 C	H	E	T	■	22 B	H	A
23 E	E	O	24 C	■	25 R	A	G	A	S	■	26 P	L	O	W
27 A	R	O	O	28 M	■	29 N	I	N	■	30 L	E	E	L	A
31 U	S	T	O	U	32 R	■	■	■	33 L	A	R	S	E	N
■	■	■	34 K	A	A	■	■	■	35 A	K	C	■	■	■
36 M	37 O	38 P	I	N	G	■	■	■	39 W	H	E	40 L	41 A	42 N
43 A	C	I	N	G	■	44 C	45 I	46 D	■	47 S	P	E	K	E
48 S	A	N	G	■	49 C	A	G	E	50 S	■	51 T	A	W	T
52 O	R	B	■	53 M	A	N	D	A	T	54 E	■	55 R	A	F
56 N	I	A	57 G	A	R	A	■	58 R	A	V	59 E	N	A	L
60 I	N	L	A	Y	E	R	■	61 T	R	I	P	O	L	I
62 C	A	L	G	A	R	Y	■	63 H	A	L	I	F	A	X

19.

CRYPTOGRAM

Each of the quotes below has been encrypted, with each letter of the alphabet substituted for a different letter. The substitutions are different for each puzzle. Use your code-breaking skills to discover the original quotation! (Hints: Start with short words—a one-letter word is usually A or I. Count the number of each letter—the most common letter in English is E, followed by T, A, O, I, and N, while the most common three-letter word is THE.)

1. X AOQOYQ SXNO-XHYCTEHZO EROHQY:
QBOW ESKEWY ETRCO QBEQ X YBESS
YDPOAEW AXO, KBXZB XY HDQ YD.—
YQOJBOH SOEZDZM

2. ILGOZYU KBU AO YIO AOZY ELTQSU,
AXY QY'Z QKELVYBGY YL VOKOKAOV
YIBY BEEBVOGYTU, AU OTQKQGBYQLG,
MQZILGOZYU QZ YIO ZOSLGM-AOZY
ELTQSU.—NOLVNO SBVTQG

3. A CXBH HR G HLXIGFW DIRTF HR LXEF YX JRFX CAHL ERBXEABXQQ, OTH BR RBX XEQX HTIBXP TF. —QHXCGIH UIGBJAQ

4. SQL RIIA MSQ MCFUFMFKJ, MIQPJHQ, SQP MIHWASFQ, SQP HIOU RIIAO PI. —TJQDSHFQ RCSQBAFQ

5. CSJHYHFE HE YQP EAHJJPG DEP ST MJDLY SMOPFYE. —JPEYPW M. CPKWESL

6. FYNK UQ VCXI ONHEUN FCSX PKX RKARSQ, C RIN P KCHN, IPZN TSPQTNK. FYNK GYNQ'AN ZCKCIYNX, C HSCUO ERG. —NAUP OEUONHV

20.

STINKETY PINKETY

In this game, you are given the clues to a two-word rhyming phrase, along with some version of the words STINKETY PINKETY, which tells you how many syllables are in the answer.

Example: Giant hog (Stink Pink)
Answer: Big pig

1. Even-handed panda (Stink Pink)
2. Naval dessert (Stink Pink)
3. Weaker sewer (Stinky Pinky)
4. Guardsman's unease (Stinky Pinky)
5. Petite ghost (Stinky Pinky)
6. Impostor mallard (Stink Pink)
7. Rocky globe (Stinky Pinky)
8. Ape businessman (Stinky Pinky)
9. Tragic hearsay (Stinky Pinky)
10. Hefty fee for kidnappers (Stinky Pinky)

CHICKEN BONES

"Chicken bones" are a hot-pink candy with a spicy cinnamon crust and a bittersweet-chocolate core. Invented in 1885 in St. Stephen, New Brunswick, they continue to be made by which company?

A. Rowntree
B. Laura Secord
C. Ganong
D. Lowney
E. Mars Canada

[Answer: C. Ganong]

EASY 1

DOUBLE-DOUBLE TAKE

Spot the difference: can you find the 6 changes?

© Valengilda/iStock

Q. I'm standing at the North Pole, facing the South Pole. The East is on my left hand. What is on my right hand?

A. Fingers.

LIMERICK FUN

Limerick Shuffle

Limericks are five-line poems with a strict rhyming scheme: AABBA. Here are some shuffled holiday limericks. Rearrange the five lines of each so that the order is correct:

1. "I don't think that I'm going to bed.
I never can sleep
On the night before Christmas I said:
Or while sugarplums dance in my head."
When I hear reindeer creep

2. And now when it sings
It can croon Christmas carols on key.
Looked a little bit shopworn to me.
So I dusted its wings
The angel on top of the tree

Limerick Scramble

The last word or words of each line have been scrambled. Unscramble the word(s) to complete the limerick:

1. Each year on the first of BCDEEEMR
I jot down some things to BEEEMMRR.
Not words of ECIVDA
Or what's naughty and ECIN
But what presents to buy next BEEMNORV.

2. The elf said to Santa, "It's ITEM
To prepare for your next chimney BMICL.
Take a towel and PASO
To give you some PEOH
Of washing away all the MIGER."

3. Each year I resolve something EWN
As I look at my life in EWIVER.
Should I go on a TIDE?
Or not even YTR TI
Or, better yet, MIAIRUTS.

SOLUTION EASY 1

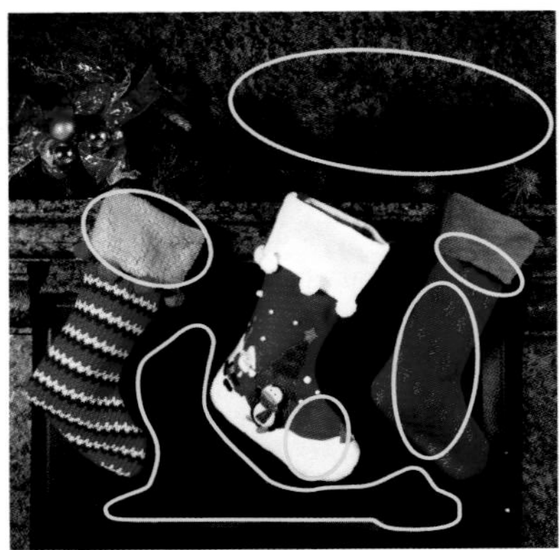

Answer: Limerick Shuffle
1. *On the night before Christmas I said:*
"I don't think that I'm going to bed.
I never can sleep
When I hear reindeer creep
Or while sugarplums dance in my head."
2. *The angel on top of the tree*
Looked a little bit shopworn to me.
So I dusted its wings
And now when it sings
It can croon Christmas carols on key.

Answer: Limerick Scramble
1. *December; remember; advice; nice; November;*
2. *time; climb; soap; hope; grime;*
3. *new; review; diet; try it; tiramisu*

21.

WORDPLAY: ALPHABET SOUP

Below are a few of the dog breeds recognized by the Canadian Kennel Club. One copy of each letter of the alphabet has been removed from the list. Fill in the blanks to restore the names, using each letter of the alphabet only once (cross out each letter as you use it).

1. ___ A S ___ I F ___
2. B A ___ E N ___ I
3. ___ ___ G
4. H O ___ A ___ A R T
5. ___ O R ___ O I
6. ___ A ___ M A T I A ___
7. B ___ ___ E R
8. P E ___ ___ N ___ E S E
9. B R A ___ U E F ___ A N ___ ___ I S
10. G R ___ ___ ___ O U N D

ARCTIC QUIZ

The land in the Arctic Circle is divided among all but one of the following:

A. Norway
B. Sweden
C. Russia
D. China
E. Iceland
F. Finland
G. Canada
H. The United States
I. Greenland

[Answer: D. China]

22.

TRIPLE MEANINGS

Many English words have multiple meanings. Here, we've given three different definitions that each describe the same word. Can you figure out the words?

1.	OCCURRENCE	CONTAINER	MYSTERY	____________
2.	RETAIN	TOWER	CONTINUE	____________
3.	FOREMOST	MATURITY	PREPARE	____________
4.	PLAN	TILT	CATCH FISH	____________
5.	COMPUTER PART	PITCH	TEST ANSWERS	____________
6.	REAR	SUPPORT	IN THE PAST	____________
7.	CLOTH STRIP	RING	MUSICAL ENSEMBLE	____________
8.	WOODEN STICK	FLYING CREATURE	FLUTTER EYELID	____________
9.	ARCHED ROOF	STRONGHOLD	LEAP	____________

TRUE OR FALSE?

1. The world's first UFO landing pad was built in Alberta in 1967.
2. About 77 percent of the world's maple syrup comes from Quebec.
3. Ontario's lakes contain about one-fifth of the world's fresh water.
4. In total area, the Northwest Territories are smaller than Nunavut but larger than Quebec.

[Answers: 1., 2., and 3. are true. 4. is false—the Northwest Territories are smaller than Nunavut and smaller than Quebec.]

23.

TRIPLE MEANINGS

Many English words have multiple meanings. Here, we've given three different definitions that each describe the same word. Can you figure out the words?

1.	SEED HOLDER	WHALES	FUEL HOLDER	________
2.	MAKE HOLE	FAST WAVE	DULL ONE	________
3.	IRISH MONEY	SHALLOW BOAT	KICK BALL	________
4.	SMALL ARROW	FABRIC ROLL	METAL FASTENER	________
5.	BANNER	LOSE ENERGY	FLAT STONE	________
6.	CHANGE MOOD	GET BIGGER	CAR COATING	________
7.	DANCE	GREAT TIME	INFLATABLE TOY	________
8.	STAKE	PLACE NOTICE	MAIL	________
9.	IMMORALITY	SUBSTITUTE	CLAMP	________

SNOWFLAKES AND ICICLES

1. True or false: Snowflakes are just frozen raindrops.
2. On what side of a building do icicles most often form?

[Answers: 1. false—snowflakes are frozen molecules of water that have joined together; 2. the southern side]

24.

THE INTERNET

All the words in the list below are hidden somewhere in the grid of letters. See if you can find them! Words may run in any direction, including diagonally, and spaces are ignored. When you've crossed off all the words, read the leftover letters in the grid (running left to right, from top to bottom) to reveal a hidden quote related to the puzzle's theme.

G E S T T I D I G I T A L I C
F N O G I N F O E L R M C N H
A R C T I O N M I O M F R S A
F C T T H E E A O O I N A T T
T Y A E E M M R C N S N W A R
E B L T N E I T S L L P L N O
I E N C S D O K E T A I A T O
K R E O E D I I L I N K N M M
V S T O R O N N B R O W S E R
I P W K V M G F G A B D R S G
R A O I E A I N O K F L R S O
A C R E R I O M A R S F O A O
L E K I R N W E H Y U U D G G
H O M E P A G E R A N M R E L
A D D R E S S T B H T M L F E

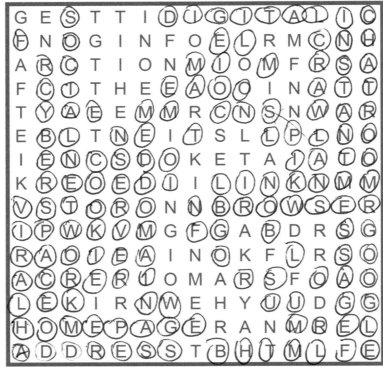

ADDRESS
BLOG
BROWSER
CHAT ROOM
COOKIE
CRAWL
CYBERSPACE
DIGITAL
DOMAIN
DOT COM
EMAIL
FORUM
FRIENDING
GOOGLE
HOME PAGE
HTML
INSTANT MESSAGE
LINK
MEME
ONLINE
SERVER
SOCIAL NETWORK
SPAM
SURF
VIRAL
WEB

25.

BEFORE AND AFTER

The words in each group have one thing in common: they all frequently appear either immediately before or immediately after the solution word. For example, if the group includes CHRISTMAS, APPLE, TRUNK, HOUSE, and FAMILY, the solution might be TREE (CHRISTMAS TREE, APPLE TREE, TREE TRUNK, TREE HOUSE, FAMILY TREE). When you've figured out all the solutions, read the first letter of each to discover the puzzle's secret theme.

1. AIR COAT COFFEE FRUIT MEAT PRINCE SNOW START WATER — F R E S H

2. AUTUMN BURNING DEAD DRY GREEN OAK RAKING RUSTLING TEA — L E A V E S

3. BLOSSOM BOWL CLOCKWORK GLOW GRATED JUICE PEEL RIND ZEST — O R A N G E

4. BATH BOTTLED COLD DRINKING HEATER RUNNING SALT SUPPLY TAP — W A T E R

5. ARTISTIC BLANK CREATIVE FACIAL FREE GRIM MUSICAL PAINED PUZZLED — e x p r e s s i o n

6. BUDDING HISTORICAL LANGUAGES NOVEL OFFICE SUMMER TRUE WHIRLWIND WRITER — R O M A N C E

26.

ANTLERGRAM

The goal of antlergrams is to form as many words as you can using the letters in the moose's nose and antlers. Each letter can be used only once, which means you can form a word with two Ts only if there are two Ts in the puzzle. Each word must be three or more letters long and must contain the letter in the nose, along with any combination of the letters from the antlers. For the ultimate challenge, see if you can find the one 9-letter word that contains ALL the letters in the puzzle.

CHRISTMAS RICH
CHRIST
CHASM
CRASH
CARS
CAMS
CASH
CATS

27.

SKILLATHON

The goal is to find as many words as possible made up of the letters in the word or phrase below. Words must be made of four or more letters. No plurals allowed. Only one tense or form of a verb is permitted (if you find WALK, you can't also have WALKS, WALKED, WALKING, etc.). The exception is when two forms have different meanings—e.g., BORE and BORED.

BOB AND DOUG

Try to beat our experts. They found 26 words.

28.

PYRAMID POWER

The pyramid is made up of a series of words, each one containing the letters used in the word directly above it (the order of the letters may be changed) plus one new letter. Solve the clues to fill in the pyramid!

1. Alphabet starter ___
2. Sun god ___ ___
3. Circle part ___ ___ ___
4. Farm portion ___ ___ ___ ___
5. Water bird ___ ___ ___ ___ ___
6. Divine drink ___ ___ ___ ___ ___ ___
7. Positive ___ ___ ___ ___ ___ ___ ___
8. Chemical change ___ ___ ___ ___ ___ ___ ___ ___
9. "Au ______" (quite the opposite) ___ ___ ___ ___ ___ ___ ___ ___ ___
10. Pastime ___ ___ ___ ___ ___ ___ ___ ___ ___ ___

TOQUE TRIVIA

The word *toque* is thought to have come from the Spanish word *toca*, which means

A. a woollen covering
B. a man's wig
C. a disguise
D. a woman's headdress
E. a French hat

[Answer: D. a woman's headdress]

29.

PYRAMID POWER

The pyramid is made up of a series of words, each one containing the letters used in the word directly above it (the order of the letters may be changed) plus one new letter. Solve the clues to fill in the pyramid!

1. D and F separator
2. Editor cut down
3. Finished
4. Email button
5. Requires
6. Stiffened
7. Stands for
8. Began to melt
9. Bedecked

ELVIS

Elvis Presley said that his favourite Christmas song was

A. "Jingle Bell Rock"

B. "Blue Christmas"
C. "Silver Bells"
D. "I'll Be Home for Christmas"

[Answer: B. "Blue Christmas"]

30.

CATCH A WORD: MYTHICAL CREATURES

In this type of puzzle, the answer appears in its correct order but may begin in the middle of a word and be interrupted by spaces and punctuation. For example: The Canadians were victorious in hockey once again. Can you find the names of ten mythical creatures hidden in the sentences below?

1. Our juice bar serves only the finest mango lemonade.
2. The bland rag on the counter really needed replacement.
3. Diego blinked in the bright sunlight.
4. Though ostensibly a vegetarian, Olaf scarfed down steaks from time to time.
5. For all his hard work, she only gave Levi a thank you note.
6. The hard war fought against the enemy turned out to have been in vain.
7. There are many interesting organisms in a forest besides trees, including fungi, ants, birds, and mosses.
8. Transit prices just aren't fair, you know.
9. Remembering his safety protocol, Matt rolled on the floor to extinguish the fire.
10. Not only did the waiter splatter me with ketchup, a cab raced past me and doused my clothes.

PARTY GAME—WHO AM I?

This game can be played with people of different ages. Try to pick someone that everyone will be familiar with.

Number of players: Four to ten

What you'll need: Sticky notes and pens

Object of the game: To guess the name of someone known to everyone in the group (a movie star, a politician, or a character from fiction—or even a friend)

To begin: Decide on a category. Each player then writes a person's name on a sticky note and passes it to another member of the group. Without looking at the note, each player sticks it to his or her forehead.

The play: Form a circle. The first player asks one yes-or-no question to determine the name on his or her forehead. Anyone in the group may answer. (Example: Am I a real-life celebrity?) Continue moving around the circle, with players asking questions about "their" identity, until someone figures out the name on his or her own sticky note. You'll probably have to go around the circle several times before you narrow down who you are. Play until there are second- and third-place winners.

31.

WORDS × FIVE

This puzzle is similar to a crossword, but the five-letter answer to each clue is written twice—both across and down. So, if the solution to clue 1 is FLAME, you would write FLAME into the grid twice, from left to right and from top to bottom.

1	2	3	4	5
2				
3				
4				
5				

1. Pack with four suits
2. Conscious
3. Poe's "Nevermore" bird
4. Put on clothing
5. Sight, for one

32.

WORDS × FIVE

This puzzle is similar to a crossword, but the five-letter answer to each clue is written twice—both across and down. So, if the solution to clue 1 is FLAME you would write FLAME in the grid two times, from left to right and from top to bottom.

1	2	3	4	5
2				
3				
4				
5				

1. Light wood ~~CEDAR~~ CEDAR BIRCH ASPEN
2. Steer clear avoid
3. With rounded projections CURVE
4. Assault on a castle SWARM
5. Poisonous snake COBRA

33.

CRYPTOGRAM

Each of the quotes below has been encrypted, with each letter of the alphabet substituted for a different letter. The substitutions are different for each puzzle. Use your code-breaking skills to discover the original quotation! (Hints: Start with short words—a one-letter word is usually A or I. Count the number of each letter—the most common letter in English is E, followed by T, A, O, I, and N, while the most common three-letter word is THE.)

1. J YLC CSJSNEK NC UOZHZ J YLC CSERC. J SHJNK CSJSNEK NC UOZHZ J SHJNK CSERC. EK AT DZCF, N OJQZ J UEHF CSJSNEK.

2. XLR MLDF QYGSXZYI DCDA IDS MLYD QS SXD PEPPND RAQO JQWSLAG?

3. P VKBX K LFJ RNUKBPBH OPGGFGZ. PX PZ ZFOUXCPBH P RFANY GUKNNS ZUU OSZUNE YFPBH.

4. W N T   F U N I   W N T ' S H   A H J J Y U A   N X L

_ _ _   _ _ _ _   _ _ _ ' _ _   _ _ _ _ _ _ _   _ _ _

I O H U   W N T   R Y U F   W N T S   J H H J O   Y U J N

_ _ _ _   _ _ _   _ _ _ _   _ _ _ _   _ _ _ _ _   _ _ _ _

M   R J H M F - M U L   J O H W   R J M W   J O H S H .

_   _ _ _ _ _ - _ _ _   _ _ _ _   _ _ _ _   _ _ _ _ _ .

5. L C N   H C   K C P   F Y C G   Q U T C B   J V C E

_ _ _   _ _   _ _ _   _ _ _ _   _ _ _ _ _   _ _ _ _

T P V W R B D   R B   Y L A   J V K R B D   G U B ?

_ _ _ _ _ _ _   _ _   _ _ _   _ _ _ _ _ _   _ _ _ ?

Y U Z A   U N U K   Y L A R V   Q V C C E F .

_ _ _ _   _ _ _ _   _ _ _ _ _   _ _ _ _ _ _ .

THE FALLS

What is the name of the frozen waterfall in Banff National Park—one of the park's most difficult ice-climbing routes?

A. the Terminator
B. the Last Resort
C. the Annihilator
D. the Ejector
E. the Disruptor

[Answer: A. the Terminator]

34.

LETTER DROP

The quotation by Eric Morecambe below has been written into a grid. Words run left to right, and each line wraps around to the line below. Sadly, the letters have all dropped out of the puzzle. All the letters are in the correct columns, but their order may have changed. Can you restore the letters to their proper places and discover the quote? Punctuation is still in its original position, and spaces between words are marked by black boxes. Remember, words don't end at the end of a line unless there's a black box there.

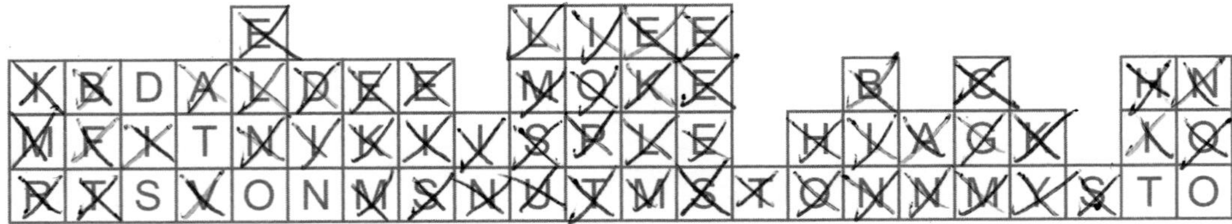

35.

REBUS

In these puzzles, the arrangement of the letters and symbols suggests a common word or expression. For example, this combination

COVER
GOING

is "going undercover" (the word GOING is under the word COVER—literally). See how many you can figure out.

1. 

2. 

3. 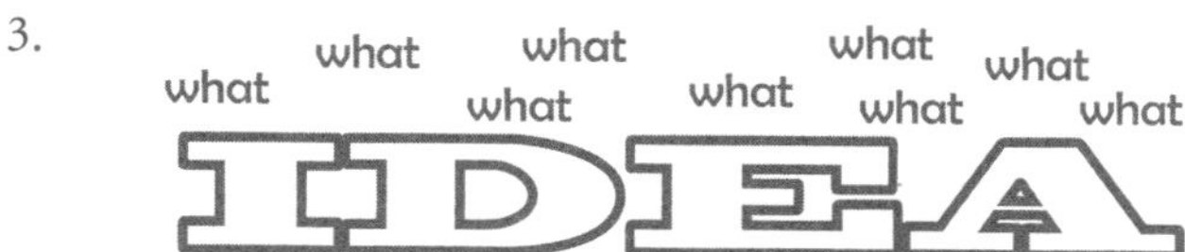

4. 

5. TUNN-EL-

36.

13 × 13 CROSSWORD

ACROSS

1. Indian wrap
5. Purloin
10. Seat of power
12. "And if that ___ enough . . ."
14. In the vicinity
15. Acid neutralizer
16. Thorn in one's side
17. By ___ of (due to)
19. Former record man
20. Cinderella task
22. Denuded
23. Hi-___ graphics
24. Trimmed during haircut
25. Piece of armour
29. The best
30. Islamic festival
31. Absorbed
32. English or French
37. Screenplay abbr. when not outside
38. Weaken
39. Punch hard
40. Film cutter
42. Eagle constellation
44. Great sorrow
45. Skulked
46. Of late
47. They sometimes have it

DOWN

1. Tiny insect eater
2. Got to one's feet
3. Way to go?
4. Tavern
5. Swinged slang
6. Injury
7. Bother
8. Field worker
9. Add to
10. Bugle tune
11. Whirlpools
13. Runner's statistics
18. Alternatively
21. Nanny's buggy
22. Meadow call
24. Edifice: Abbr.
25. Manitoba city
26. Turtle or snake
27. Nosh on
28. Gland between the eyes
29. Screamed
32. A Stooge
33. Crime of great interest
34. As peas in a pod are
35. Heraldry's red
36. "Zounds!"
38. Baseball call
41. Pull behind
43. "Sine ___ non"

	1	2	3	4			5	6	7	8	9	
10					11		12					13
14							15					
16					17	18				19		
20				21					22			
				23				24				
	25	26	27				28					
29						30						
31					32				33	34	35	36
37				38					39			
40			41				42	43				
44							45					
	46							47				

37.

SUDOKU: VERY EASY

A sudoku puzzle is a type of logic puzzle. Although it uses numbers, no mathematics is involved. The grid below is divided into nine large squares, each of which is divided into nine smaller squares. Each large square contains all the digits from 1 to 9, with each digit appearing exactly once. Each horizontal row of the puzzle also contains each digit exactly once, and so does each vertical row. By carefully observing which numbers are missing from each row, column, or square, see if you can figure out which numbers go where. There's only one possible solution to each puzzle.

9		3			1			
2	6					4	1	9
4					5	8	3	2
	4	6		5			8	
	9	8	1		4	3	6	
	2			6		5	9	
7	1	4	5					8
8	5	9					7	3
			8			1		5

38.

SUDOKU: VERY EASY

A sudoku puzzle is a type of logic puzzle. Although it uses numbers, no mathematics is involved. The grid below is divided into nine large squares, each of which is divided into nine smaller squares. Each large square contains all the digits from 1 to 9, with each digit appearing exactly once. Each horizontal row of the puzzle also contains each digit exactly once, and so does each vertical row. By carefully observing which numbers are missing from each row, column, or square, see if you can figure out which numbers go where. There's only one possible solution to each puzzle.

	5	8		9			4	2
9			2					1
4					5		7	9
			5	8		2		7
3		9			2	5		6
			3		1			
7		6			4			3
	2			1		9	6	
	1			2	6			

39.

WORD JIGSAW

The words in these quotes and quips have been sliced up into pieces, so you can no longer see where one word begins and another ends. The order of the letters inside each piece is unchanged. Can you reassemble the word pieces and figure out the original phrase?

1. _ _ _ _ _ _ _ _   _ _ _   _ _ _   _ _ _ _ _ _ _ _ _
   _ _ _ _ _ _ _ _ _   _ _   _ _ _   _ _ _ _ _ _ _
   _ _ _   _ _ _ _   _ _   _ _ _ _   _ _ _ _. —
   _ _ _ _ _ _ _   _ _ _ _ _ _ _ _

   AGHAN AYSA ECOM EDOMI ENDING ENTDEP EOFYO FER HOLID LLDIF NICMON ONTH PANYAND REA TIM URLIF

2. _ _ _ _ _ _   _ _ _   _ _ _ _ _   _ _ _ _   _ _ _
   _ _ _ _ _ _ _ _ _   _ _ _ _   /   _ _ _ _ _ _   _ _
   _ _ _ _ _ _ _'_   _ _ _ _ _ _ _ _   _'_ _   _ _ _
   _ _ _ _ _,   _ _ _   _ _ _   _ _ _ _   _ _ _ _ _
   _   _ _ _ _ _ _   _ _ _ _   _ _ _ _   /   _ _
   _ _ _ _ _ _ _ _ _   _ _ _ _ _ _ _ _   _ _ _ _ _
   _ _ _ _ _   _ _ _   _ _ _ _ _ _. — _ _ _ _
   _ _ _ _ _ _ _

   ABO ACHNIG ADDE ARUS EADO EART ERLIK ERTHE ETAP ETHES ETILLA EVEN FARANE FASTS FOLDS FOREH HAND HEAR HTAL IGHT INGS KIND LAZEON LETH MALAZ PLENDO RSHINE TARAB TEAD THEM USTR VETHY

3. _ _ _   _ _   _ _ _   _ _ _ _ _ _   _ _   _ _ _

_ _ _ _ _ _ _ _ _ _   _ _ _ _   _ _ _ _ _ _ _ _

_ _ _ _ _ _   _ _   _ _ _ _   _ _ _   _ _   _ _ _ _. —

_ _ _ _ _ _ _   _ _ _ _ _ _ _ _ _ _ _

EGLOR ENTMAD FOURD HAKES HEW INTERO IOUSS ISCONT LIAMS NOWIST ORKWIL PEARE SUNOFY UMMERB YTHIS

4. _ _ _ _   _ _ _   _ _ _   _ _ _ _ _ _ _ _   _ _ _ _ _

_ _ _ / _ _   _ _ _ _   _ _ _ _ _ _ _   _ _ _

_ _ _ _   _ _ _ _ / _ _ _ _ _ _ _   _ _ _   _ _ _ -

_ _ _ _ _   _ _ _ _ _ _ _ _,   _ _ _'_ _   _ _

_ _ _ _   _ _   _ _ _ _ _ _ _! — _ _ _ _ _ _

_ _ _ _ _

DEERL DOUTWI EERUD GODO HEREDNO HEREIN HEYS HIMAST HIST HOUTE INDEE NALLT OHNN OLPHT ORYJ OVED RYOULL SEDRE THE THGL WNIN YMARKS

5. _ _   _ _ _ _ _ _   _ _ _ _   _ _ _ _   _ _ _

_ _ _ _ _ _ _ _ _.   _   _ _ _ _ _ _ _ _

_ _ _ _ _ _   _ _ _ _ _ _ _   _ _   _ _ _ _   _ _ _

_ _ _ _ _ _   _ _ _. — _ _ _ _ _ _   _ _ _ _ _ _ _ _

ANNO BRESCO DFI FELL HEN ITHOUR LYFORO RYMEL NNEC OUSAN OWMEN TLI TUSW URSEL VEON VESATH VILL WEC

6. _ _ _   _ _ _ _ _   "_ _ _ _   _ _   _ _ _ _ _ _"

_ _ _   _ _ _ _ _   _ _ _ _ _ _ _ _ _   _ _ _ _?

_ _ _ _ _'_   _ _ _ _ _ _   _ _ _ _ _

ERAND ETEND ING MAK TLEEL MASTO RIST SLOVEM TASLIT ESCH VIS WHOS YSSAN

40.

AROUND THE RINK

All the words in the list below are hidden somewhere in the grid of letters. See if you can find them! Words may run in any direction, including diagonally, and spaces are ignored. When you've crossed off all the words, read the leftover letters in the grid (running left to right, from top to bottom) to reveal a hidden quote related to the puzzle's theme.

hockey players wear numbers because you cant always identify the body with dental records

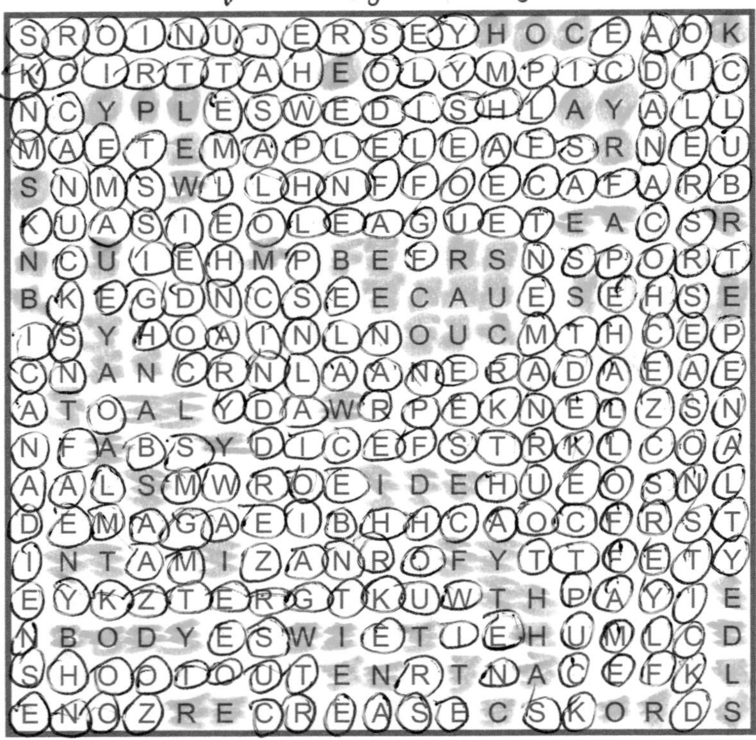

```
S R O I N U J E R S E Y H O C E A O K
K O I R T T A H E O L Y M P I C D I C
N C Y P L E S W E D I S H L A Y A L L
M A E T E M A P L E L E A F S R N E U
S N M S W L L H N F F O E C A F A R B
K U A S I E O L E A G U E T E A C S R
N C U I E H M P B E F R S N S P O R T
B K E G D N C S E E C A U E S E H S E
I S Y H O A I N L N O U C M T H C E P
C N A N C R N L A A N E R A D A E A E
A T O A L Y D A W R P E K N E L Z S N
N F A B S Y D I C E F S T R K L C O A
A A L S M W R O E I D E H U E O S N L
D E M A G A E I B H H C A O C F R S T
I N T A M I Z A N R O F Y T T F E T Y
E Y K Z T E R G T K U W T H P A Y I E
N B O D Y E S W I E T I E H U M L C D
S H O O T O U T E N R T N A C E F K L
E N O Z R E C R E A S E C S K O R D S
```

AMATEUR
ARENA
BODYCHECK
BRUINS
CANADA
CANADIAN
CANADIENS
CANUCKS
CLUB
COACH
CREASE
CZECH
DEKE
FACEOFF
FAN
FLAMES
FLYERS
FRANCHISE
GAME
GOALIE
GORDIE HOWE
GRETZKY
HALL OF FAME
HAT TRICK
HELMET
ICE
JERSEY
JUNIORS
LEAGUE
LINESMAN
MAPLE LEAFS
NHL
OILERS
OLYMPIC
OPEN NET
PENALTY
PUCK
RINK
SEASON
SHOOTOUT
SKATE
SLAPSHOT
SPORT
STICK
SWEATER
SWEDISH
TEAM
TOURNAMENT
ZAMBONI
ZONE

41.

SYLLABLANK

The solution to each of the following puzzles is a single nine-letter word. We've chopped each word up into the smaller words listed below. Place the smaller words into the right positions on the blanks to discover the original words.

A ACTS AID AM AN ART ART AT ATE BAR BAR BE BUS COAL COL CON CUR CURT EM END HE HE HERS HO I I I IF IT LED ON OR PEN PER RAM RED RED SING SLIT TAG US

1. ROUGH MAN ___ ___ ___   ___ ___ ___   ___   ___ ___
2. GOVERNMENT ALLIANCE ___ ___ ___ ___   ___ ___   ___   ___ ___
3. MOVED LIKE A SNAKE ___ ___ ___ ___   ___ ___   ___ ___ ___
4. BUBBLE UP ___ ___ ___   ___ ___ ___   ___ ___ ___
5. MAGICAL SYMBOL ___ ___ ___   ___ ___ ___   ___ ___ ___
6. PULSE ___ ___   ___ ___ ___   ___ ___   ___ ___
7. GIVING SUPPORT ___ ___ ___   ___ ___   ___ ___ ___ ___
8. PEOPLE LYING IN WAIT ___ ___   ___ ___ ___   ___ ___ ___ ___
9. ARCHEOLOGIST'S FINDS ___ ___ ___   ___ ___   ___ ___ ___ ___
10. CLEANER ___ ___   ___ ___   ___ ___   ___ ___ ___
11. AGREED ___ ___ ___   ___ ___ ___   ___ ___ ___
12. BROUGHT TO AN END ___ ___ ___ ___   ___   ___   ___ ___ ___

42.

PYRAMID POWER

The pyramid is made up of a series of words, each one containing the letters used in the word directly above it (the order of the letters may be changed) plus one new letter. Solve the clues to fill in the pyramid!

1. Me, myself
2. Contained
3. Cotton machine
4. Saggitarius, e.g.
5. Bell sounds
6. Cereals
7. Scratchy
8. Shorting out
9. Carbonated

HOLIDAY SONGS

1. Who popularized the New Year's song "Auld Lang Syne"?
2. What popular holiday song did Judy Garland sing in the movie *Meet Me in St. Louis*?
3. In the song "White Christmas," what line follows "With every Christmas card I write"?

[Answer: 1. Guy Lombardo and His Royal Canadians; 2. "Have Yourself a Merry Little Christmas"; 3. "May your days be merry and bright"]

43.

PYRAMID POWER

The pyramid is made up of a series of words, each one containing the letters used in the word directly above it (the order of the letters may be changed) plus one new letter. Solve the clues to fill in the pyramid!

1. Roman one	I
2. Spanish yes	S I
3. Knight's title	S I R
4. Get up	R I S E
5. Emergency wail	S I R E N
6. Quit	R E S I G N
7. Digits	F I N G E R S
8. Turning down	R E F U S I N G
9. Statuettes	F I G U R I N E S

HOLIDAY FLOWERS

Where were poinsettias originally grown?

A. Spain
B. Venezuela
C. Guatemala
D. Sicily
E. Mexico

[Answer: E. Mexico]

44.

SKILLATHON

The goal is to find as many words as possible made up of the letters in the word or phrase below. Words must be made of four or more letters. No plurals allowed. Only one tense or form of a verb is permitted (if you find WALK, you can't also have WALKS, WALKED, WALKING, etc.). The exception is when two forms have different meanings—e.g., BORE and BORED.

NOVA SCOTIA

Try to beat our experts. They found 67 words.

45.

ONE STEP AT A TIME

Change the word at the top to the word at the bottom by altering one letter at a time. Each change should produce a new word. We've provided clues to help you on your way.

F I R E

_ _ _ _ TOWARDS THE FRONT

_ _ _ _ INNER PART

_ _ _ _ CABBAGE

_ _ _ _ EMBRACE

C O A L

S N U G

_ _ _ _ BRITISH KISSING

_ _ _ _ MUCUS

_ _ _ _ CHARRED REMNANTS

_ _ _ _ FOOLISH PERSON

_ _ _ _ ABBR. AT THE END OF A PAGE

_ _ _ _ RABBIT, IN HERALDRY

C O Z Y

A STAR IS BORN

Who was the first non-human to be inducted into the Canadian Sports Hall of Fame?

[Answer: racehorse Northern Dancer, in 1965]

SPELLING BEE

Below is a list of commonly misspelled words. Read it to someone, or have someone read it to you, as a test of spelling skills.

1. accommodate
2. accessible
3. asinine
4. cemetery
5. embarrass
6. existence
7. independent
8. lightning
9. misspell
10. mischievous
11. niece
12. occurrence
13. practically
14. potatoes
15. weird

46.

STINKETY PINKETY

In this game, you are given the clues to a two-word rhyming phrase, along with some version of the words STINKETY PINKETY, which tells you how many syllables are in the answer.

Example: Giant hog (Stink Pink)
Answer: Big pig

1. Decent grain (Stink Pink)
2. Matrimonial vehicle (Stinky Pinky)
3. Where Parisians sit (Stink Pink)
4. Discord among alpacas (Stinky Pinky)
5. Tree cat's turn (Stinky Pinky)
6. Badly dressed henchman (Stinky Pinky)
7. Course adjustment (Stinkety Pinkety)
8. Ill will in the king's house (Stinky Pinky)
9. Snake-based paint thinner (Stinkety Pinkety)
10. Lively pottery (Stinkety Pinkety)

FIGURE SKATING

Match the figure skating term in the first column to its description in the second column.

A. axel jump
B. back flip (banned in competition)
C. back spin
D. camel spin
E. sizzle
F. twizzle

1. a spin performed on the back outside edge of a skate
2. a jump where the takeoff is from a forward outside edge of a skate
3. an exercise done by beginning skaters
4. multi-rotational one-foot turns that move a skater down the ice
5. a spin position where the free leg is extended into the air in an arabesque position parallel to the ice
6. a reverse somersault in the air

[Answers: A = 2; B = 6; C = 1; D = 5; E = 3; F = 4]

47.

TRIPLE MEANINGS

Many English words have multiple meanings. Here, we've given three different definitions that each describe the same word. Can you figure out the words?

1.	SAKE	INTRIGUE	MONEY PRICE	______________
2.	EXCITE	FLUID MOVER	SHOE	______________
3.	MC	ARMY	CHURCH BREAD	______________
4.	STRIKE	PASTE FOR FRYING	BASEBALL PLAYER	______________
5.	VESSEL	ROB	FACE	______________
6.	STUFF	NOTEBOOK	HOME	______________
7.	CASTING CONTAINER	FUNGUS	EARTH	______________
8.	SET UP	THROW	TAR	______________
9.	LEFT	HARBOUR	WINE	______________

WHO STAYS UP LATER?

1. According to the *Daily Mail*, what percentage of Canadians are awake at midnight on New Year's Eve?

A. 52 percent
B. 68 percent
C. 79 percent

2. According to the *Daily Mail*, what percentage of Americans are awake at midnight on New Year's Eve?

A. 61 percent
B. 71 percent
C. 81 percent

[Answers: 1. = C. 79 percent; 2. = B. 71 percent]

EASY 2

DOUBLE-DOUBLE TAKE

Spot the difference: can you find the 6 changes?

Gift Idea with a Twist

If you're part of a gift-giving group, one idea is for each person to write down his or her name and year of birth. Everyone draws a name. The idea is to find a gift that relates to the year in which the person was born.

HOLIDAY HUMOUR

Judge: "What are you charged with?"
Prisoner: "Doing my Christmas shopping early."
Judge: "That's not a crime. How early were you shopping?"
Prisoner: "Before the store opened."

What do you call an elf wearing ear muffs?
Anything you want. He can't hear you.

This holiday season,
instead of gifts, I've decided to give
everyone my opinion.
— Anonymous

What does a reindeer say before
telling a joke?
This one will sleigh you.

What do you call Santa living at the South Pole?
A lost Claus.

SOLUTION EASY 2

48.

TRIPLE MEANINGS

Many English words have multiple meanings. Here, we've given three different definitions that each describe the same word. Can you figure out the words?

1.	LUCK	PARASITE	ANCHOR PART	________
2.	HOLE MAKER	STRIKE	DRINK	________
3.	BALL FOR LAWN	DISH	THROW	________
4.	PUFF	STRIKE	DISAPPOINTMENT	________
5.	THIGH	ROSE FRUIT	COOL	________
6.	SMALL CARRIAGE	MUSICAL BOOKING	ROWING BOAT	________
7.	REST SIDEWAYS	TILT	FAT-FREE	________
8.	DISMOUNT	SETTLE	BURNING	________
9.	AVERAGE	POOR	INTEND	________

REINDEER QUIZ

1. Name the eight reindeer in "A Visit from St. Nicholas" (also known as "'Twas the Night Before Christmas") in alphabetical order.
2. Why do biologists think Santa's reindeer are female?

[Answers: 1. Blixem (Blitzen), Comet, Cupid, Dancer, Dasher, Dunder (also known as Donner), Prancer, and Vixen; Rudolph came later. 2. Both male and female reindeer have antlers, but males generally shed theirs in November while females keep theirs until the spring.]

49.

REBUS

In these puzzles, the arrangement of the letters and symbols suggests a common word or expression. For example, this combination

COVER
GOING

is "going undercover" (the word GOING is under the word COVER—literally). See how many you can figure out.

1. UP
HOUSE

2. BREAD

3. SANTA CLAUS L A N E

4. 

5. BOY
DRUMMER

50.

ANTLERGRAM

The goal of antlergrams is to form as many words as you can using the letters in the moose's nose and antlers. Each letter can be used only once, which means you can form a word with two Ts only if there are two Ts in the puzzle. Each word must be three or more letters long and must contain the letter in the nose along with any combination of the letters from the antlers. For the ultimate challenge, see if you can find the one 9-letter word that contains ALL the letters in the puzzle.

51.

BEFORE AND AFTER

The words in each group have one thing in common: they all frequently appear either immediately before or immediately after the solution word. For example, if the group includes CHRISTMAS, APPLE, TRUNK, HOUSE, and FAMILY, the solution might be TREE (CHRISTMAS TREE, APPLE TREE, TREE TRUNK, TREE HOUSE, FAMILY TREE). When you've figured out all the solutions, read the first letter of each to discover the puzzle's secret theme.

1. ATTRACTION DESTINATION FOREIGN INFORMATION OFFICE RESORTS SEASON SHOPS TRAP _ _ _ _ _ _ _

2. DIRT GRAVEL MAP NARROW RUNNER SIGNS TOLL TRIP WINDING _ _ _ _

3. BAG CONDITIONER DRY FRESH HOT MATTRESS PRESSURE QUALITY STRIKE _ _ _

4. ANNUAL CHRISTMAS DREAM EXTENDED FAMILY PAID SPOTS SUMMER TOGETHER _ _ _ _ _ _ _ _

5. ACCOUNT BUSINESS EXTRA INCURRED MEDICAL OPERATING RECEIPTS REPORT TAXPAYER _ _ _ _ _ _ _

6. CENTRAL GEOGRAPHIC PRECISE REMOTE SCOUT SECRET SHOOTING UNDISCLOSED UNKNOWN _ _ _ _ _ _ _ _

52.

CANADIAN BANDS

All the words in the list below are hidden somewhere in the grid of letters. See if you can find them! Words may run in any direction, including diagonally, and spaces are ignored. When you've crossed off all the words, read the leftover letters in the grid (running left to right, from top to bottom) to reveal a hidden quote related to the puzzle's theme.

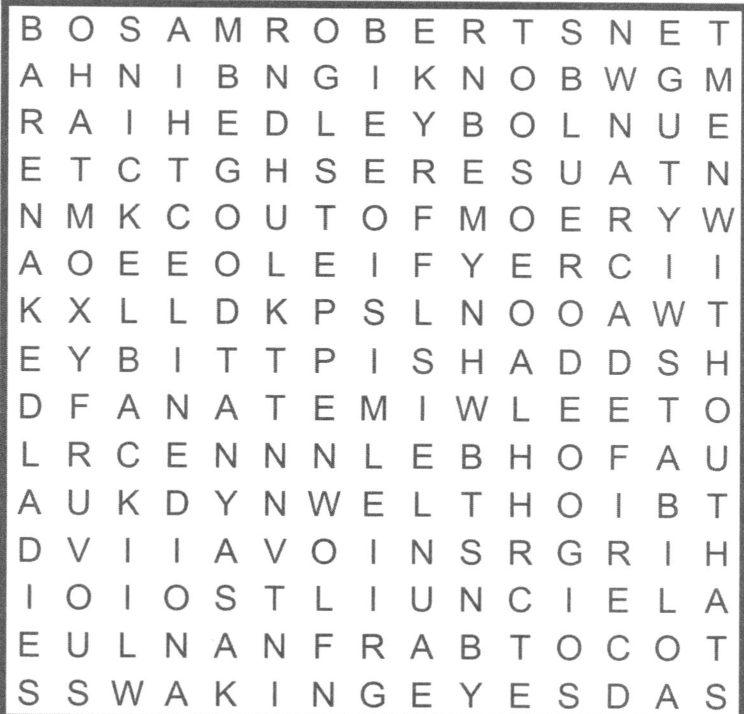

B O S A M R O B E R T S N E T
A H N I B N G I K N O B W G M
R A I H E D L E Y B O L N U E
E T C T G H S E R E S U A T N
N M K C O U T O F M O E R Y W
A O E E O L E I F Y E R C I I
K X L L D K P S L N O O A W T
E Y B I T T P I S H A D D S H
D F A N A T E M I W L E E T O
L R C E N N N L E B H O F A U
A U K D Y N W E L T H O I B T
D V I I A V O I N S R G R I H
I O I O S T L I U N C I E L A
E U L N A N F R A B T O C O T
S S W A K I N G E Y E S D A S

ARCADE FIRE
BARENAKED LADIES
BE GOOD TANYAS
BLUE RODEO
BTO
CELINE DION
GUESS WHO
HEDLEY
MEN WITHOUT HATS
METRIC
MOXY FRUVOUS
NEIL YOUNG
NICKELBACK
RUSH
SAM ROBERTS
SLOAN
STABILO
STEPPENWOLF
WAKING EYES

53.

WORDPLAY: INSIDERS 1

The words in the right-hand column can each be placed inside the blank spaces in the left-hand column to produce a new word. Can you figure out which word goes where?

A U _ _ _ _ _ _ N	ACHING
B U _ _ _ _ _ _ S	ANKLES
F O _ _ _ _ _ _ I N G	AVENGE
P _ _ _ _ _ _ E D	EARFUL
R E _ _ _ _ _ _ E S S	MORSEL
R E _ _ _ _ _ _ T	RAMBLE
S C _ _ _ _ _ _ D	RANGES
S C _ _ _ _ _ _ R	RECAST
S T _ _ _ _ _ _ T	RESENT
T _ _ _ _ _ _ L Y	SHINES
T E _ _ _ _ _ _ S	SULTAN
T H _ _ _ _ _ _ S	TOMATO

54.

ANAGRAMS

The following items are all anagrams of words or phrases describing items that might be found on the Christmas dining table. See how many you can solve.

1. SPICE IN 'EM

   _ _ _ _ _ _   _ _ _ _ _

2. DISCARDING THUMPS

   _ _ _ _ _ _ _ _ _ _ _   _ _ _ _ _ _ _ _ _

3. SEEK A DRY TUTOR

   _ _ _ _ _ _ _ _ _   _ _ _ _ _ _ _ _

4. CAN BURY CAREERS

   _ _ _ _ _ _ _ _ _ _ _   _ _ _ _ _ _ _

5. GREASED NEIGHBOUR

   _ _ _ _ _ _ _ _ _ _ _ _ _   _ _ _ _ _ _ _

6. PIPE UP MINK

   _ _ _ _ _ _ _ _ _   _ _ _ _

7. ASCENDANCY

   _ _ _ _ _ _   _ _ _ _ _ _ _

8. MADE A HOT SPOT

   _ _ _ _ _ _ _ _   _ _ _ _ _ _ _ _

55.

CRYPTOGRAM

Each of the quotes below has been encrypted, with each letter of the alphabet substituted for a different letter. The substitutions are different for each puzzle. Use your code-breaking skills to discover the original quotation! (Hints: Start with short words—a one-letter word is usually A or I. Count the number of each letter—the commonest letter in English is E, followed by T, A, O, I, and N, while the most common three-letter word is THE.)

1. WMO ETOBWOPW USOBPITO VJ B FVE CP WMBW RVI ZBR ZBAO B JVVS VJ RVITPOSJ QCWM MCZ, BKF KVW VKSR QCSS MO KVW PXVSF RVI, NIW MO QCSS ZBAO B JVVS VJ MCZPOSJ, WVV.—PBZIOS NIWSOT

2. CTDGEGZGPE PD XE TEHGETTO: NPFTPET BYP NPVLTN X UOPJVTF RPQ CGCE'Z AEPB RPQ YXC, GE X BXR RPQ CPE'Z QECTONZXEC.

3. UXT QWJT DWK TZU, UXT ATBB
HAZPWKJ; UXT ATBB DWK TZU, UXT
QWJT HAZPWKJ. —LXGSTBT RJWPTJO

4. FZYYUP DQP ZR NVPH JGT XVGGRP
JGTK XPKPDU AGK MVP AZEKP, HGM
MVP MGJ. —DTMVGK THOHGNH

5. KMU RNTK HUREHJEPIU KMCAO EPNWK
RZ RNKMUH CT KMEK DNH KMCHKZ
ZUEHT TMU TUHQUX KMU DERCIZ
ANKMCAO PWK IUDKNQUHT. KMU
NHCOCAEI RUEI VET AUQUH DNWAX. —
FEIQCA KHCIICA

6. HEP QYTW RTI T NXPTH IKLLPII,
SKH HEP TKZVPBLP RTI T
ZVITIHPX. —MILTX RVYZP

56.

MAGIC CROSSWORD

ACROSS

1. Certain cetacean
5. Cable inits.
8. Make-believe
12. What to do at a bee or in a coven
13. Sault Ste. Marie sch.
14. Root meaning "doctor"
16. Corolla attachment
17. Lacking emotion
19. Change the appearance of
21. Bio or chem, e.g.
22. Tailor's tool
23. Chaotic goddess
24. Ode title opening
26. However
31 Oohs' accompaniments
35. Extract from
38. Whether by land ___
39. Santana song featuring the lyric "don't turn your back on me, baby . . ."
42. Wish a plague on both houses, e.g.
43. "There ___ 'I' in 'team'"
44. Yemen's capital
45. House panels
47. Thing that's taken
49. Munches, colloquially
52. Appetites
57. Pic producer
60. Charm
62. "___ I Take You Home" (Lisa Lisa song)
64. Falcon's home
65. Chicken skewer
66. Cheerleader's request
67. It might deal you a bad hand
68. Longings
69. Always, poetically
70. Enthusiasm

DOWN

1. ___ citato
2. Smooth over
3. Bell noise
4. Ready to go
5. Ninja's toe shoes
6. Protrude
7. Search or clean
8. Bob of "The Simpsons"
9. Dave's computer
10. Vaudeville comic Roscoe
11. Wife at the Pole, for short
12. Gym subjs.
15. "Six Million Dollar Man" org.
18. "Either it is, ___ isn't"
20. German social psychologist Erich
25. "Super Monkey Ball" monkey
27. Spanish medals
28. West Point, briefly
29. Sweet cherry
30. Japanese flower
31. The basics
32. Tolouse's "to him"
33. A real stumper
34. Computer port standard
36. Some linemen, for short
37. Papua New Guinean coin
40. Famous presidential family
41. Projecting corner
46. Disappeared
48. Change form
50. Jazz singer Carmen
51. Take a liking (to)
53. Feminist Eleanor
54. Sci-fi home planet
55. Ring interior
56. Leave in, to an editor
57. Post-USSR inits.
58. Gone fishing
59. Bit of dust
61. Over yonder
63. Nickname for Agnes

	1	2	3	4		5	6	7		8	9	10	11	
12						13				14				15
16						17			18					
19					20							21		
22							23							
				24		25			26		27	28	29	30
31	32	33	34		35		36	37		38				
39				40					41					
42						43					44			
45					46			47		48				
				49		50	51		52		53	54	55	56
57	58	59		60				61						
62			63							64				
65						66				67				
	68					69				70				

57.

WORDS × SIX

This puzzle is similar to a crossword, but the six-letter answer to each clue is written twice—both across and down. So, if the solution to clue 1 is GOBLIN you would write GOBLIN in the grid two times, from left to right and from top to bottom.

1	2	3	4	5	6
2					
3					
4					
5					
6					

1. Collision
2. Swiss cereal
3. Man, woman, or child
4. Belongings
5. Dress
6. Glittery strips

58.

WORDS × SIX

This puzzle is similar to a crossword, but the six-letter answer to each clue is written twice—both across and down. So, if the solution to clue 1 is GOBLIN you would write GOBLIN in the grid two times, from left to right and from top to bottom.

1	2	3	4	5	6
2					
3					
4					
5					
6					

1. Get at
2. Tight garment
3. Impact site
4. Lord's land
5. Fume
6. Road

59.

SUDOKU: VERY EASY

A sudoku puzzle is a type of logic puzzle. Although it uses numbers, no mathematics is involved. The grid below is divided into nine large squares, each of which is divided into nine smaller squares. Each large square contains all the digits from 1 to 9, with each digit appearing exactly once. Each horizontal row of the puzzle also contains each digit exactly once, and so does each vertical row. By carefully observing which numbers are missing from each row, column, or square, see if you can figure out which numbers go where. There's only one possible solution to each puzzle.

4	9	5	1	3	7	2	6	8
8	7	3	2	5	6	9	4	1
2	1	6	4	8	9	7	5	3
5	6	9	8	2	1	4	3	7
3	8	4	7	6	5	1	2	9
7	2	1	9	4	3	6	8	5
9	4	2	3	7	8	5	1	6
6	3	7	5	1	4	8	9	2
1	5	8	6	9	2	3	7	4

60.

SUDOKU: VERY EASY

A sudoku puzzle is a type of logic puzzle. Although it uses numbers, no mathematics is involved. The grid below is divided into nine large squares, each of which is divided into nine smaller squares. Each large square contains all the digits from 1 to 9, with each digit appearing exactly once. Each horizontal row of the puzzle also contains each digit exactly once, and so does each vertical row. By carefully observing which numbers are missing from each row, column, or square, see if you can figure out which numbers go where. There's only one possible solution to each puzzle.

5	9			7	6	1	4	3
3	6			9				
1		4		3	5			
	7	3			2			
	8						5	
			7			3	1	
			4	5		8		9
				2			3	
2	4	5	9	8			6	

61.

THREE-WAY ANAGRAMS

These sets of three common words or phrases are all anagrams of each other. We've given you the definitions. Can you figure out the words?

Example

S K A T I N G — WINTER ACTIVITY

S T A K I N G — PLACING A BET

T A K I N G S — MONEY MADE

1.	_ _ _ _ _ _ _ STANCE	_ _ _ _ _ _ _ LAY AWAY (5, 2)	_ _ _ _ _ _ _ ACTING GROUPS
2.	_ _ _ _ _ KILLED	_ _ _ _ _ WOOD FASTENERS	_ _ _ _ _ MOLLUSC
3.	_ _ _ _ _ TRAP	_ _ _ _ _ MAKES MONEY	_ _ _ _ _ COMES CLOSER
4.	_ _ _ _ _ _ 3.26 LIGHT YEARS	_ _ _ _ _ _ HIJINKS	_ _ _ _ _ _ ABRASION
5.	_ _ _ _ _ _ _ COMEDIAN ADAM	_ _ _ _ _ _ _ SPEAK ILL	_ _ _ _ _ _ _ GROWLED
6.	_ _ _ _ _ _ U.S. PRESIDENT JIMMY	_ _ _ _ _ _ IMPACT MARK	_ _ _ _ _ _ GLOWING BULLET
7.	_ _ _ _ _ GLOSSY FABRIC	_ _ _ _ _ HOLY PERSON	_ _ _ _ _ DIRTY MARK
8.	_ _ _ _ _ _ VOCALIST	_ _ _ _ _ _ WHAT A KING DOES	_ _ _ _ _ _ QUIT
9.	_ _ _ _ _ POINTED WEAPON	_ _ _ _ _ HARVESTS	_ _ _ _ _ LEFTOVER
10.	_ _ _ _ _ _ HOURGLASSES	_ _ _ _ _ _ GOOD POINTS	_ _ _ _ _ _ MALE SALUTATION

62.

MAPLE LEAF

The goal of this puzzle is to form as many words as you can, using the letters contained in the leaf. Each letter can be used only once, so you can create a word with two Ts only if there are two Ts in the leaf. Each word must be three or more letters long, and all words must contain the large central letter of the leaf, along with any mix of the letters around the outside. For the ultimate challenge, see if you can find the one 10-letter word that contains ALL the letters in the leaf.

63.

REBUS

In these puzzles, the arrangement of the letters and symbols suggests a common word or expression. For example, this combination

COVER
GOING

is "going undercover" (the word GOING is under the word COVER—literally). See how many you can figure out.

1. NING **STRIKE**

2. 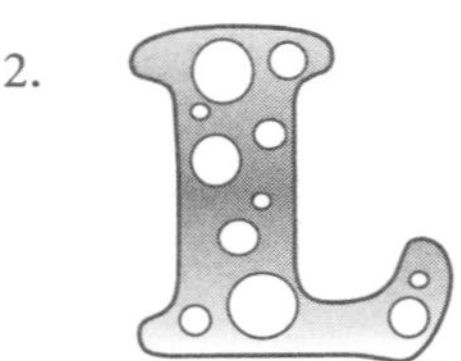

3. Due

   ————————→ Long

4. frontfrontfrontfrontfrontfrontfrontfrontfrontfront
   frontfrontfrontfrontfrontfrontfrontfrontfrontfront
   frontfrontfrontfrontfrontfrontfrontfrontfrontfront

5. AMOUNT AMOUNT

64.

SKILLATHON

The goal is to find as many words as possible made up of the letters in the word or phrase below. Words must be made of four or more letters. No plurals allowed. Only one tense or form of a verb is permitted (if you find WALK, you can't also have WALKS, WALKED, WALKING, etc.). The exception is when two forms have different meanings—e.g., BORE and BORED.

ALGONQUIN

Try to beat our experts. They found 31 words.

65.

WORDPLAY: INSIDERS 2

The words in the right-hand column can each be placed inside the blank spaces in the left-hand column to produce a new word. Can you figure out which word goes where?

C O _ _ _ _ _ S	AWARD
D I _ _ _ _ _ T	INTER
D U _ _ _ _ _ N	OTTER
F O _ _ _ _ _ S	RATIO
M I _ _ _ _ _ D	ROUTE
M O _ _ _ _ _ D	SCREE
N O _ _ _ _ _ S	SHEAR
P L _ _ _ _ _ S	SINES
P O _ _ _ _ _ S	THERE
R O _ _ _ _ _ S	UNDER
S E _ _ _ _ _ S	UNDER
S P _ _ _ _ _ D	UNTIE

MARK YOUR CALENDAR

1. What day is St. Stephen's Day?
2. True or false: The traditional plum pudding recipe contains no plums.
3. In what country do children await the arrival of Sinterklaas?

[Answers: 1. December 26; 2. true; 3: the Netherlands]

BASEBALL TRIVIA

1. Only two major league players (in various sports) have had their numbers retired *league-wide.* One was hockey player Wayne Gretzky, whose number was 99. The other was a legendary baseball player, whose number was 42. Who was he?

2. The Montreal Expos were awarded the first Major League Baseball franchise outside the United States. In 2004, the league moved the team. Where was the team moved and what was its new name?

3. The Toronto Blue Jays were the first Canadian-based Major League Baseball team to compete in and win a World Series. What embarrassing event took place in Atlanta before the second game of the series?

[Answers: 1. Baseball great Jackie Robinson, the first African-American player in the modern era of Major League Baseball, had his number retired from the league. 2. The Expos moved to Washington, D.C., and became the Washington Nationals. 3. The Canadian flag was flown upside down.]

66.

WORD JIGSAW

The words in these quotes and quips have been sliced up into pieces, so you can no longer see where one word begins and another ends. The order of the letters inside each piece is unchanged. Can you reassemble the word pieces and figure out the original phrase?

1. _ _   _ _ _   _ _ _ ' _   _ _ _   _ _ _ _ _ _ _ _ _ _
_ _ _   _ _ _ _ ,   _ _ _ _ _   _ _   _ _ _
_ _ _ _ _ _   _ _ _   _ _ _ ' _   _ _ _   _ _ _ _
_ _ _   _ _ _ ' _   _ _ _ _ . — _ _ _ _ _   _ _ _ _ _

CARW HATYO HETHING HINGY IFYO ILDE INKOFT NTTH OUWA SYO TGETE TGETT UDON UDON UDONT VERYT WANTOS

2. _ _   _ _ _ _ _ _ _ _ _ _ _   _ _   _ _ _ _   _ _
_ _ _ _ _ _ _ .   _ _   _ _ _ _ _   _ _   _ _ _ _
_ _ _ _ .   _   _ _ _ ' _   _ _ _ _   _ _ _
_ _ _ _ _ _ _   _ _ _ _ ,   _ _ _   _ _
_ _ _ _   _ _ _   _ _   _ _ _ _ _   _ _ _ _ _ _
_ _ _ _ _ _ _ _ _ _ _ _ . — _ _ _ _ _   _ _ _ _ _

ADLIP ARINGH ATHER BRIA DINGLI DOFHE ENEED EOFTH ESON HLIGH ISHAR LLO MINDHI MREA MYGRA NDF NKILEY OSEYE PSBU SIDONT STORE TERS THEUS WHIG

3. _ _   _ _ _   _ _ _ _ _ _ _ _   _ _ _ _   _ _ _
_ _ _ _   _ _ _ _ _ _   _ _   _ _ _ _ _ _ _
_ _ _   _ _ _   _ _ _   _ _ _ _ _ _ _   _ _ _
_ _ _ _ _ _ _ . — _ _ _ _ _ _ _   _ _ _ _ _ _

ASTCANNO DGAHLIN DHASN EVEST HANGE HATTHEP HEWH MOIRST NHISME OBELI ORVAL OTYETW RITTE TBEC

4. _ _ _ _   _ _   _ _ _   _ _ _ _

_ _ _ _ _ _ _ _ _ _ ;   _   _ _ _   _ _ _ _   _ _ _

_ _ _   _ _ _ _ _ _ . — _ _ _ _   _ _ _   _ _ _ _ _

AMAEB CANF DMENO EWA INDTH LEA LFRIT OTEM PTA ROWN TINT TIONI YMYSE

5. _ _ _   _ _ _ _ _   _ _ _ _ _   _ _ _ _ _ _ ,

_ _ _   _ _ _   _ _ _ _ _   _ _ _ _ _   _ _ _ _ _ _

_ _ _ _ . — _ _ _   _ _ _ _ _

AKETH AWAYT HESMAL INTGI LPRINTT OMWAITS RGEPR THELA VETHBUTT

6. _   _ _ _ _ _   _ _ _   _ _ _ _ _ _ ,   " _ _   _ _ _

_ _ _ _   _ _ _ _ _ _ _ _   _ _ _   _ _ _ _ ? "

_ _   _ _ _ _   _ _   _   _ _ _ _ .

AKITE DHEGA EANYTH EDTHED IASK INGFO OCTO RDOYO RWIN UHAV VEME

CHRISTMAS STORIES

1. In Charles Dickens's novel *A Christmas Carol*, who was Scrooge's dead business partner?
2. Who wrote *How the Grinch Stole Christmas!*?
3. Who wrote the short story "The Gift of the Magi"?

[Answers: 1. Joseph Marley; 2. Dr. Seuss; 3. O. Henry]

67.

CHRISTMAS PUNS 2 CROSSWORD

ACROSS

1. First name in baseball
5. Airplane class
9. Dean of medicine on "House"
14. Well-ripened
15. "Royal Canadian Air Farce"'s Goy
16. See eye to eye
17. Where do seals go to the movies?
19. Biblical queen
20. Makes an attempt
21. "Aladdin" prince
23. Lbs., e.g.
24. 27 Down composition
26. Not fair
28. What is a mummy's favourite part of Christmas gifts?
33. Imply
34. 0.0000001 joules
35. Andrews Sisters song "___ Mir Bist Du Schoen"
38. Supplement type
39. Shoe bottoms
41. "M*A*S*H" star
43. Also
44. Life force
45. Roman ___
46. What does a gingerbread man make his bed with?
50. Finalizes a comic page
53. "Fashion Emergency" model host
54. Karate rank
55. Poor grade
57. On the scale of the sea
62. Word before "change"
64. What do they call Baked Alaska in Alaska?
66. Fire leftover
67. Blue-black (Scots)
68. Really bad
69. '70s music
70. Articulates
71. Fail to notice

DOWN

1. Type of tub
2. Turkish leader
3. Hive residents
4. Norse poet
5. "Spin Off" host Kurt
6. It's chalked in pool
7. ___-Wan Kenobi
8. "Peter Pan" dog
9. Outer shell
10. Noise of annoyance
11. University in New Jersey
12. They're paid back
13. Rising agent
18. "It's pretty, but is ___?"
22. Breathers
25. Simian
27. Baroque composer
28. Letters before F in an end-of-week phrase
29. Juno's Greek equivalent
30. English prep school
31. Rockabilly singer Jackson and others
32. Bad temper
36. "Vogue" alternative
37. French thought
39. Breakfast baked good
40. "I see!"
42. Towards the stern
45. "Faith in ___" (Thoreau)
47. Roman philosopher
48. What you might say after falling down
49. Hosts, as an event
50. Left one's car running
51. One of the Judds
52. Door handles
56. Opposite of "flows"
58. Throat-clearing sound
59. Birthmarks
60. Part of a camera
61. Animation panels
63. Mo
65. Chicken ___ king

1	2	3	4	■	5	6	7	8	■	9	10	11	12	13
14				■	15				■	16				
17				18					■	19				
20							■	21	22		■	23		
■	■	■	■	24			25	■	26		27			
28	29	30	31					32				■	■	■
33					■	■	34			■	35	36	37	■
38				■	39	40				■	41			42
■	43			■	44			■	■	45				
■	■	■	46	47				48	49					
50	51	52				■	53				■	■	■	■
54			■	55		56	■	57			58	59	60	61
62			63		■	64	65							
66					■	67				■	68			
69					■	70				■	71			

68.

CRYPTOGRAM

Each of the quotes below has been encrypted, with each letter of the alphabet substituted for a different letter. The substitutions are different for each puzzle. Use your code-breaking skills to discover the original quotation! (Hints: Start with short words—a one-letter word is usually A or I. Count the number of each letter—the commonest letter in English is E, followed by T, A, O, I, and N, while the most common three-letter word is THE.)

1. I D G B S W ' M G P X D T S V S Z M T V P Y S B M G K
N P A W N M P M D T Q S M D V P P O ? Q T B S X F T
M D T Z A F F A K T W M .

2. F C M T X U X W X F D X A M D S R N M A N F P S A
L M J B N F D K O S Q M B S S T S W U X M D A F D K
L M J B W M D Q X K S D W S F Q U S B .

3. I L G Z Y J L M G P Z S M Y S M P G ; L Z ' M
S G P W W H D S Z L P G . — S J L M Z P Z F Y

4. YMPI YIMMWM AE YW GBCI PD WRI
HWMRARN BRX XAEKWSIM YJBY QWPM
JANJ EKJWWO KOBEE AE MPRRARN
YJI KWPRYMQ.—CPMY SWRRINPY

5. JVF DHW ELXS HP DCSHTEQ HP FWS,
HWN JCSQ USWSMHEEQ CHXS JF.

6. AILWJ GE Q UISHYDTLM WJGSO.
UJQW Q BDGKY WI UQEWY GW IS
BJGMHDYS.—OYIDOY XYDSQDH EJQU

HISTORY QUIZ

The first English colony in Canada turned 400 years old in 2010. It is

A. Cupids, Newfoundland and Labrador
B. Saint John, New Brunswick
C. Baddeck, Nova Scotia
D. Quebec City, Quebec

[Answer: A. Cupids, Newfoundland and Labrador]

69.

SYLLABLANK

The solution to each of the following puzzles is a single nine-letter word. We've chopped each word up into the smaller words listed below. Place the smaller words into the right positions on the blanks to discover the original words.

AN ANT AT COMB COPE DISH DRAG FAT FEAT FLY GOD HE HER HO HUM IS IS KIND LATE LEG MIME MODE NEW ON ON OR OUR PAN PENT PER PER RAT RED SPA TO USE

1. MAFIA BOSS ___ ___ ___
2. CHILDREN'S CHRISTMAS PLAY ___ __ ____
3. TOP APARTMENT ____ __ ___
4. PEOPLE EVERYWHERE ___ __ ____
5. BRING TO SHAME ____ __ ___
6. PASS LAW ___ __ ____
7. PLUMED ____ __ ___
8. HOST OR DISPUTE SETTLER ____ ___ __
9. POND DARTER ____ __ ___
10. TABLOID ___ ___ ___
11. UNDERSEA VIEWER ___ __ ____
12. SIDE IN A FIGHT ____ __ ___

70.

SANDWICHES

All the words and phrases below contain the letters for various types of bread. Every other letter has been removed. Using the clues, see if you can restore the missing letters to make a tasty stack of word sandwiches.

1. LOAD	B U _ _ _ N
2. PUTTING IT MILDLY	T O _ A _ _ _ _ _ _ _ S T
3. DEER LEATHER	B U _ _ _ _ _ N
4. HATLESS	B _ R _ _ E A _ _ D
5. CASINO SPINNER	R O _ L _ _ _ _ _ _ _ _ L
6. *39 STEPS* WRITER	B U _ _ _ _ _ N
7. *PILGRIM'S PROGRESS* WRITER	B U _ _ _ N
8. IGNORED CONTRACT	B R E A _ _ _ D
9. TREE WITHOUT NEEDLES	B R _ _ _ _ E A _ _ D
10. DESERT NOMAD	B _ _ _ U _ N
11. RIGGING SUPPORT	T O _ _ A S T
12. MAKE OVER	R _ _ _ Y _ E
13. SENIOR OFFICER	B _ _ _ A _ _ _ _ G E _ _ _ _ L
14. MILITARY FOOTHOLD	B R _ _ _ E _ _ A D
15. OVERCOOK	B U _ N
16. STYLIST	B _ _ U _ _ _ _ _ N

TRADITION!

In a Christmas tradition celebrated in Newfoundland and Labrador, kids often wear masks, make noise, ring bells, and go door to door for treats. This tradition is known as

A. humbugging
B. lumbering
C. bumbling
D. mummering

[Answer: D. mummering]

71.

ONE STEP AT A TIME

Change the word at the top to the word at the bottom by altering one letter at a time. Each change should produce a new word. We've provided clues to help you on your way.

G O L D

F O L D — BEND IN HALF

F O N D — AFFECTIONATE

F I N D — LOCATE

R I N D — OUTER PART OF A FRUIT

R I N G

G I F T

G I R T — BOUND AT THE WAIST

D I R T — EARTH

D A R T — POINTED PROJECTILE

C A R T — OX-DRAWN VEHICLE

C A R D

ARE WE THERE YET?

Which distance is greater: the distance between Toronto and the equator or that between Toronto and the North Pole?

[Answer: The distance between Toronto and the equator is greater, at 4,865 kilometres. The distance between Toronto and the North Pole is 4,694 kilometres.]

72.

STINKETY PINKETY

In this game, you are given the clues to a two-word rhyming phrase, along with some version of the words STINKETY PINKETY, which tells you how many syllables are in the answer.

Example: Giant hog (Stink Pink)
Answer: Big pig

1. Hideaway for money (Stink Pink)
2. Observance of rebel sailors (Stinkety Pinkety)
3. Traitorous topographer (Stinkety Pinkety)
4. Nitpicking love-lover (Stinkety Pinkety)
5. Grassland fruit (Stinkety Pinkety)
6. Bet between military men (Stinky Pinky)
7. Silver officer (Stinky Pinky)
8. Fishy witch doctor (Stinky Pinky)
9. Oddly coloured adhesive (Stink Pink)
10. Sarcastic noble (Stinky Pinky)

HAIL!

Canada's heaviest known hailstone hit Cedoux, Saskatchewan, on August 17, 1973. It weighed

A. 115 grams (about the same as a quarter-pound burger)
B. 170 grams (about the weight of a hockey puck)
C. 225 grams (about the same as a half pound of butter)
D. 290 grams (about the weight of three decks of cards)

[Answer: D. 290 grams (about the weight of three decks of cards)]

73.

PYRAMID POWER

The pyramid is made up of a series of words, each one containing the letters used in the word directly above it (the order of the letters may be changed) plus one new letter. Solve the clues to fill in the pyramid!

1. Indefinite article __
2. Near, towards __ __
3. Rested __ __ __
4. Food additive __ __ __ __
5. Purloin __ __ __ __ __
6. Stronghold __ __ __ __ __ __
7. Red __ __ __ __ __ __ __
8. Most obvioius __ __ __ __ __ __ __ __
9. Handcuffs __ __ __ __ __ __ __ __ __
10. Rejoices __ __ __ __ __ __ __ __ __ __

I'LL DRINK TO THAT

The Sourtoe Cocktail, created in 1973, is a cherished local tradition in

A. Yellowknife, Northwest Territories
B. Dawson City, Yukon
C. Whitehorse, Yukon
D. Prince George, British Columbia
E. Guelph, Ontario

[Answer: Dawson City, Yukon]

EASY 3

DOUBLE-DOUBLE TAKE

Spot the difference: can you find the 6 changes?

The Night before the Night before Christmas

On the South Coast of the island of Newfoundland, the first "official" day of the Christmas season is December 23, locally known as:

A. Mummer's Night
B. Tibb's Eve
C. Hermitage
D. Night of the Safe Harbour
E. St. Stephen's Eve

Answer: B. Tibb's Eve (sometimes also known as Tipsy Eve)

WINTER WONDERLAND

1. The average February snowfall in Charlottetown, Prince Edward Island, is 58 cm. The record-breaking February 2015 snowfall in that city was:

   A. 57.5 cm
   B. 90.2 cm
   C. 222.8 cm
   D. 144 cm
   E. 154.4 cm

2. On February 16, 2016, Ottawa was hit with a record-breaking one-day total snowfall of:

   A. 28 cm
   B. 38 cm
   C. 46 cm
   D. 51 cm
   E. 62 cm

SOLUTION EASY 3

3. This city hosts an annual winter festival, stringing more than three million lights along a 5-kilometre route:

   A. Fredericton, New Brunswick
   B. Calgary, Alberta
   C. Niagara Falls, Ontario
   D. Quebec City, Quebec
   E. Halifax, Nova Scotia

4. According to Environment Canada data, this city has the best odds of having a "perfect Christmas"—defined as snow on the ground of 2 cm or more on Christmas morning, and snow in the air sometime Christmas Day:

   A. Montreal, Quebec
   B. Sault Ste. Marie, Ontario
   C. St. John's, Newfoundland and Labrador
   D. Dartmouth, Nova Scotia
   E. Prince Rupert, British Columbia

Answers:
1. C. 222.8 cm;
2. D. 51 cm;
3. C. Niagara Falls, Ontario;
4. B. Sault Ste. Marie, Ontario

74.

PYRAMID POWER

The pyramid is made up of a series of words, each one containing the letters used in the word directly above it (the order of the letters may be changed) plus one new letter. Solve the clues to fill in the pyramid!

1. Euro letter ___
2. Type of dash ___ ___
3. Fisherman's aid ___ ___ ___
4. Adolesescent ___ ___ ___ ___
5. Gone from plate ___ ___ ___ ___ ___
6. Defeated ___ ___ ___ ___ ___ ___
7. Hard to debunk ___ ___ ___ ___ ___ ___ ___
8. Small piece of furniture ___ ___ ___ ___ ___ ___ ___ ___
9. Snow-covered ___ ___ ___ ___ ___ ___ ___ ___ ___

TOP OF THE WORLD

Thor Peak, the world's tallest purely vertical drop, measures 1,250 metres (the top of the CN Tower's antenna reaches 533 metres) and is located in

A. Baffin Island, Nunavut
B. Banff National Park, Alberta
C. Bear Glacier Provincial Park, British Columbia
D. Torngat Mountains National Park, Newfoundland and Labrador
E. Richards Island, Northwest Territories

[Answer: A. Baffin Island, Nunavut]

75.

CRYPTOGRAM

Each of the quotes below has been encrypted, with each letter of the alphabet substituted for a different letter. The substitutions are different for each puzzle. Use your code-breaking skills to discover the original quotation! (Hints: Start with short words—a one-letter word is usually A or I. Count the number of each letter—the most common letter in English is E, followed by T, A, O, I, and N, while the most common three-letter word is THE.)

1. Q N O G E L Y : W J Z N D W T M Y Z W W E L Y

Q K T R Z D W T L N W A D Z H J E K Z Y Z W W E L Y

M N D W J Z D N H N B M D T O W J Z L Z N D Z R W

Q T K F V Z S Z D N Y Z , J T W R J T H Z D , N L F

M K A R J W T E K Z W .

2. S J M U I S S J ' K J C J X X A U C I G F S P J U

X P J I U G B X P A U C S J S Z U X H I K I E K

V A K X P F Z B A T U I X X I V J K J R A U F J F

I H A X .

3. KIWPUR KDMEIV: CIUXS MZU WMA

______ ______: _____ ___ ___

KXSMMDXSYDHAPV, PKOPXYIDDR YW

______________, __________ __

USPR IAP HAYJYVE XIAK.

____ ___ _______ ____.

4. QPZM: W XVCZRV OLU OZMXZMA

____: _ ______ ___ _______

ONUMZYNUV ZM YPV XWUF.

_________ __ ___ ____.

5. LVXCDKU MVC NESUC VMVC HCSHYC

_______ ___ _____ ____ ______

FES MUJ ESF OSB MVC MDK NECD

___ ___ ___ ___ ___ ___ ____

FMXN LSV NEC MDUFCV.

____ ___ ___ ______.

6. YZPF SFZSTF GFVA JZDQFY. YZPF

____ ______ ____ ______. ____

YFF DKJDYDITF SFZSTF. ZRGFAY

___ _________ ______. ______

GVJF KZ DPVMDKVRDZK OGVRYZFJFA.

____ __ ___________ __________.

76.

ANTLERGRAM

The goal of antlergrams is to form as many words as you can using the letters in the moose's nose and antlers. Each letter can be used only once, which means you can form a word with two Ts only if there are two Ts in the puzzle. Each word must be three or more letters long and must contain the letter in the nose, along with any combination of the letters from the antlers. For the ultimate challenge, see if you can find the one 9-letter word that contains ALL the letters in the puzzle.

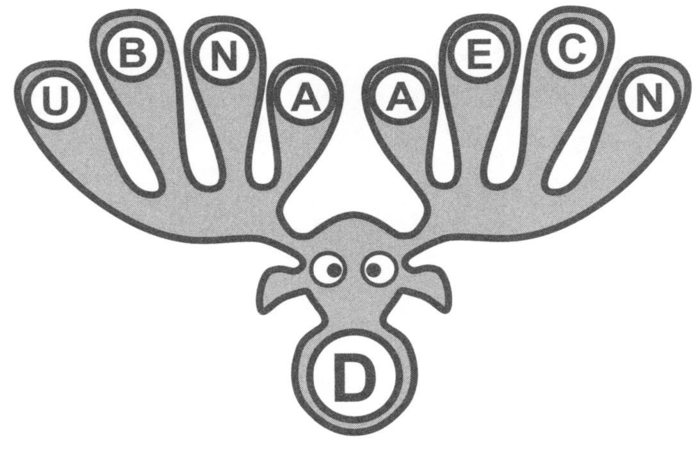

77.

ANAGRAMS

The following items are all anagrams of well-known Christmas songs. See how many you can solve.

1. RUDE HERD SNEERED HORNED PILOT

2. SHHH! GOD IN HEAVEN! LARGE AWE!

3. LISTEN THING

4. FLIRTATIOUS WOMAN HAS LYRICS

5. ACTUAL SNOW! TONS! IT'S MAGIC, NO?

6. THUD OR TIMELY TREMBLE

7. INNER WORLD WANTED

8. WORTHY MAN SOFTENS

78.

SUDOKU: EASY

A sudoku puzzle is a type of logic puzzle. Although it uses numbers, no mathematics is involved. The grid below is divided into nine large squares, each of which is divided into nine smaller squares. Each large square contains all the digits from 1 to 9, with each digit appearing exactly once. Each horizontal row of the puzzle also contains each digit exactly once, and so does each vertical row. By carefully observing which numbers are missing from each row, column, or square, see if you can figure out which numbers go where. There's only one possible solution to each puzzle.

			4	3				
	1		5					2
		3			1		6	
				2	9		5	1
	2	1				7	8	
9	5		1	4				
	7		3			2		
6					4		1	
				7	5			

79.

SUDOKU: EASY

A sudoku puzzle is a type of logic puzzle. Although it uses numbers, no mathematics is involved. The grid below is divided into nine large squares, each of which is divided into nine smaller squares. Each large square contains all the digits from 1 to 9, with each digit appearing exactly once. Each horizontal row of the puzzle also contains each digit exactly once, and so does each vertical row. By carefully observing which numbers are missing from each row, column, or square, see if you can figure out which numbers go where. There's only one possible solution to each puzzle.

6		1	5		7		3	
	8					2		
5			3					7
	3			9				
1	6						8	9
				4			1	
4					9			1
		8					9	
	5		4		3	8		2

80.

CHRISTMAS DELIVERY CROSSWORD

ACROSS

1. Unkempt person
5. "___ of Our Lives"
9. Hector's dad
14. Ask around
15. Greeks' Mars
16. What to do with an undone shoe
17. Fruit that isn't pretty
18. Setting for a Christie "Death"
19. Drummond's flower
20. Poisonous mushroom
22. Ill will
23. American letters
24. Ages ago
25. Life calling
28. It's repetetive
32. Ravens, maybe
33. Big estate
34. Potpourri
35. Bleating sound
36. Partner of the Brain
37. Firefighter's tool
38. Suffix with persist
39. Shopping wheels
40. Good looker
42. Coffee liqueur
44. Not too bad
45. "So say we all!"
46. Unable to
47. Historical party
50. Hot dog toppings
54. Stench
55. Photographer Lawless
56. Someone you go steady with
57. Peter's Spanish cousin
58. One of five lakes
59. Den
60. City near Dusseldorf
61. Video format
62. "If all ___ fails . . ."

DOWN

1. Bud, in a Stompin' Tom Connors song
2. VIP seat
3. Earthen pot
4. Portland country band ___ Trapper
5. Astaire or Rogers
6. Opera numbers
7. Restaurant site
8. Dir. opposite a Hitchcock classic
9. One who skips about
10. Entry in a film magazine
11. A couple
12. Native of Japan
13. Type of hall
21. Giggles
22. Pester
24. Sounds of 55 Down
25. It makes your teeth turn green, in a children's song
26. Swahili for "peace"
27. Spanish lasso
28. Owner of the team hidden in this puzzle
29. Flabbergast
30. Foxy lady?
31. Make an effort
33. Japanese condiment
36. Apple pie tool
39. Journalist Crowe
40. Fella
41. Possible to perform
43. Fertilizer
44. Person in a hurry
46. Fellow with a bow and arrow
47. "The straight" info
48. Tributes
49. Non-verbal agreements
50. TV host Griffin
51. The ___ deal
52. Speaker's platform
53. "Anything you say"
55. Caesar's "but"

1	2	3	4	■	5	6	7	8	■	9	10	11	12	13
14				■	15				■	16				
17				■	18				■	19				
20				21				■	22					
■	■	■	23				■	24				■	■	■
25	26	27				■	28					29	30	31
32					■	33					■	34		
35			■	■	36					■	■	37		
38			■	39					■	40	41			
42			43					■	44					
■	■	■	45				■	46				■	■	■
47	48	49				■	50					51	52	53
54					■	55				■	56			
57					■	58				■	59			
60					■	61				■	62			

81.

REBUS

In these puzzles, the arrangement of the letters and symbols suggests a common word or expression. For example, this combination

COVER
GOING

is "going undercover" (the word GOING is under the word COVER—literally). See how many you can figure out.

1. BELL BELL BELL

2. TOY BABE BABE BABE BABE LAND

3. CAME
   MIDNIGHT

4. R O
   CHRISTMAS
   N C
   TREE
   I K

5.

HOCKEY TRIVIA

1. Early hockey games featured stones, lumps of coal, or frozen cow or horse dung as pucks. What are today's pucks made of?

2. Why is a hockey rink's centre red line broken?

3. Between 1942–43 and 1967, there were only six teams in the National Hockey League. Can you name the "Original Six"? They're all still part of the NHL.

[Answers: 1. vulcanized rubber; 2. In the days of black-and-white television, viewers at home found it difficult to differentiate between the red and blue lines on the ice; hence, the broken red line. 3. Boston Bruins, Chicago Black Hawks, Detroit Red Wings, Montreal Canadiens, New York Rangers, Toronto Maple Leafs]

COUNTRY COUSINS

In addition to Canada, how many countries can you name that start with the letter *C* and end with the letter *A*? We came up with six.

[Answer: Cambodia, China, Colombia, Costa Rica, Croatia, and Cuba]

82.

TRIPLE MEANINGS

Many English words have multiple meanings. Here, we've given three different definitions that each describe the same word. Can you figure out the words?

1.	CLIMB	HORSE	MOUNTAIN	________
2.	KNIGHT	ADD SOUND	MAKE WATERPROOF	________
3.	VOLCANO DUST	TREE	BURNT REMAINS	________
4.	FAST	TRIM	MOVIE PART	________
5.	STAMP	EXPIRE	ROLLING CUBE	________
6.	REST ROOST	CROUCH	FRESHWATER FISH	________
7.	INFORMAL DANCE	BEER INGREDIENT	JUMP LIGHTLY	________
8.	CARRIER	ALE	GATEKEEPER	________
9.	CONTINUE	FINAL	PREVIOUS	________

CHRISTMAS IN CANADA

1. Which city is known as the Christmas capital of Canada?
2. Hollowed-out turnips (or other vegetables) with a candle inside are a holiday tradition observed in
   - **A.** Northern Ontario
   - **B.** the Yukon Territory
   - **C.** Labrador

[Answers: 1. Winnipeg, because of the many snowfalls it gets in December, almost always has snow on December 25. 2. = C. Labrador]

83.

TRIPLE MEANINGS

Many English words have multiple meanings. Here, we've given three different definitions that each describe the same word. Can you figure out the words?

1.	SMALL DOOR	DRAW LINES	INCUBATE	____________
2.	SUM	ARISTOCRAT	BE SIGNIFICANT	____________
3.	CHEWABLE CANDY	GLUE	MOUTH TISSUE	____________
4.	PLAYING PIECE	HOCK	DUPE	____________
5.	PUB	EXCLUDE	PRESSURE UNIT	____________
6.	ABOUT A FOOT	PROPEL BIKE	FLOOR LEVER	____________
7.	PROTRACTED	YEARN	FAR	____________
8.	NOSE PART	CARD GAME	OVERPASS	____________
9.	LOW IN PITCH	HOLE	SOLEMN	____________

CARNIVORE QUIZ

The world's biggest land-based carnivore is the

A. grizzly bear
B. polar bear
C. brown bear
D. black bear
E. bison

[Answer: B. polar bear]

84.

MAPLE LEAF

The goal of this puzzle is to form as many words as you can, using the letters contained in the leaf. Each letter can be used only once, so you can create a word with two Ts only if there are two Ts in the leaf. Each word must be three or more letters long, and all words must contain the large central letter of the leaf, along with any mix of the letters around the outside. For the ultimate challenge, see if you can find the one 10-letter word that contains ALL the letters in the leaf.

85.

HANUKKAH

All the words in the list below are hidden somewhere in the grid of letters. See if you can find them! Words may run in any direction, including diagonally, and spaces are ignored. When you've crossed off all the words, read the leftover letters in the grid (running left to right, from top to bottom) to reveal a hidden quote related to the puzzle's theme.

L B L E S S I N G S R O E C E
A M U S I C H D R A E C I H I
T S F A M I L Y D D U E L E G
K C U D R E I N D A E S L E H
E E D F R E E I S D E H L S T
S L C I G L G E M A D A E E D
Y E A O A A L A N U O M U T A
O B N C F P N W M C L A B A Y
M R D Y P A O I N E D S U W S
E A L A H D K E Y N S H N K Y
N T E O N U I G R A E R U U D
O I S U R Y S I A N H A E G D
R O S R E A L F D Y O B L E H
A N D R E I E T D E L B O L W
H E S H A L V S L P L I S A Y

APPLESAUCE
BLESSINGS
BUNUELOS
CALENDAR
CANDLES
CELEBRATION
CHEESE
EIGHT DAYS
FAMILY
GAMES
GIFTS
KISLEV
KUGEL
LATKES
MENORAH
MUSIC
RABBI
SHAMASH
SUFGANIYAH
SUNDOWN

86.

SKILLATHON

The goal is to find as many words as possible made up of the letters in the word or phrase below. Words must be made of four or more letters. No plurals allowed. Only one tense or form of a verb is permitted (if you find WALK, you can't also have WALKS, WALKED, WALKING, etc.). The exception is when two forms have different meanings—e.g., BORE and BORED.

SKATING

Try to beat our experts. They found 34 words.

87.

LETTER DROP

The quotation by Stephen Fry below has been written into a grid. Words run left to right, and each line wraps around to the line below. Sadly, the letters have all dropped out of the puzzle. All the letters are in the correct columns, but their order may have changed. Can you restore the letters to their proper places and discover the quote? Punctuation is still in its original position, and spaces between words are marked by black boxes. Remember, words don't end at the end of a line unless there's a black box there.

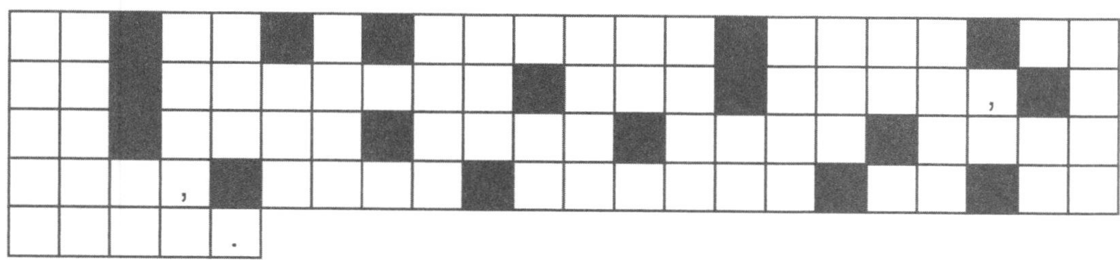

H	R																				
I	T		C			A		C			A		C		S			C			B
S	T		E	H	E	C		L	I	C	C	H	E		T	H	A	E		I	C
T	T	S	I	L	I	H	A	T	L	I	E	I	M	H	T	R	I	S		M	N
U	É	U	T	S	T	N	H	É	S	K	L	R	É	O	É	T	U	T	L	U	O

88.

THREE-WAY ANAGRAMS

These sets of three common words or phrases are all anagrams of each other. We've given you the definitions. Can you figure out the words?

Example

S K A T I N G	S T A K I N G	T A K I N G S
WINTER ACTIVITY	PLACING A BET	MONEY MADE

1. _ _ _ _ _ _ _ REGAL SEATS / _ _ _ _ _ _ _ GIANT WASPS / _ _ _ _ _ _ _ TRIM DOWN
2. _ _ _ _ _ _ _ TIGHT GARMENTS / _ _ _ _ _ _ _ MILITARY AREAS / _ _ _ _ _ _ _ BODYGUARDS
3. _ _ _ _ _ _ _ MOUNTAIN RETREATS / _ _ _ _ _ _ _ LEATHER BAG / _ _ _ _ _ _ _ SLIDING LOCKS
4. _ _ _ _ _ _ _ NEARBY (5, 2) / _ _ _ _ _ _ _ SPOTTED CATS / _ _ _ _ _ _ _ LEAST WARM
5. _ _ _ _ _ _ _ PATIO / _ _ _ _ _ _ _ FOOD PREPARER / _ _ _ _ _ _ _ GO BACK OVER
6. _ _ _ _ _ _ LION WORKERS / _ _ _ _ _ _ ORIGINAL DOCUMENT / _ _ _ _ _ _ TROUT'S HOME
7. _ _ _ _ _ _ _ SUGAR / _ _ _ _ _ _ _ SOUP, SALAD, DESSERT / _ _ _ _ _ _ _ ANCIENT MONEY BAGS
8. _ _ _ _ _ _ _ CONS / _ _ _ _ _ _ _ MOST ABUNDANT / _ _ _ _ _ _ _ DETECTIVES
9. _ _ _ _ _ _ _ HIGH END / _ _ _ _ _ _ _ MEDICINE CONTAINER / _ _ _ _ _ _ _ SHOES, NOT SLIP-ONS
10. _ _ _ _ _ _ _ NEWS SUPPLEMENT / _ _ _ _ _ _ _ BLOW-UP MATTRESSES / _ _ _ _ _ _ _ GULL OR PUFFIN

89.

BEFORE AND AFTER

The words in each group have one thing in common: they all frequently appear either immediately before or immediately after the solution word. For example, if the group includes CHRISTMAS, APPLE, TRUNK, HOUSE, and FAMILY, the solution might be TREE (CHRISTMAS TREE, APPLE TREE, TREE TRUNK, TREE HOUSE, FAMILY TREE). When you've figured out all the solutions, read the first letter of each to discover the puzzle's secret theme.

1. ASTRONAUTS BROUGHT CLAMBER COME LOADED SAILORS SHIP STEPPED WELCOME _ _ _ _ _ _

2. BEANS BLAZER BLUE CANADIAN CAPTAIN OLD SHIPS UNIFORM YARD _ _ _ _

3. BAY CARRIER HOLD HUMAN PANTS PLANE PRECIOUS SHIPS SHORTS _ _ _ _ _

4. DEAR ELECTIONS FAST FIRM GRAB HANDS MEETINGS TIGHT TRUE _ _ _ _

5. DIVING FELL GOING JUMPED MAN SWEPT THROWN TOSSED WASHED _ _ _ _ _ _ _ _ _

6. BASIN WATER JORDAN DELTA YELLOW FLOWS SALMON BANK RUNS _ _ _ _ _

90.

WORDS × FIVE

This puzzle is similar to a crossword, but the five-letter answer to each clue is written twice—both across and down. So, if the solution to clue 1 is FLAME, you would write FLAME into the grid twice, from left to right and from top to bottom.

1. Cold Jack's surname
2. Long gun
3. Frequently
4. Hit the hay
5. Outdoor shelters

91.

WORDS × FIVE

This puzzle is similar to a crossword, but the five-letter answer to each clue is written twice—both across and down. So, if the solution to clue 1 is FLAME, you would write FLAME into the grid twice, from left to right and from top to bottom.

1	2	3	4	5
2				
3				
4				
5				

1. Middle Earth race
2. Peruvian pack animal
3. Servant
4. Nail board
5. Goat man

92.

WORD JIGSAW

The words in these quotes and quips have been sliced up into pieces, so you can no longer see where one word begins and another ends. The order of the letters inside each piece is unchanged. Can you reassemble the word pieces and figure out the original phrase?

1. ____ ______ _____ ________
__ ____ ____ __ ____ ____. —
_______ _____

AHISS DUC EWIS HARDL HINKHAN KCAL LRIC MOSTTE OMES ORTOF UKK XANST

2. ___ _______ ________ ___
_____ __ ____ _______. __
_____ __ ______. ___ _____
_____ __ _______. —______
______

ASKAN ATHERI ATRIAN EDOF EDTOAL ERMUD GLEG OTTIR OWSAN RIGHT SINGS SMIS TACLA TEVENW THEB TMOV USI WARMWE

3. ____ __ ______ __ ________
_____ __ ____ ___ _ _______
_______. —____ ___________

CHOFS DSWOR DYGOL EVE IALQUA LIT NINWIN NISOLA NOWHA SASPEC TEDPAT TERA THY YAN

4. _ _ _ _   _ _ _   _ _ _ _ _ _ _ _ _ _ _   _ _ _
_ _ _   _ _ _ _   _ _ _ _ _ _ _ _   _ _ _ _
_ _ _ _ _ _ _ _ _   _ _   _ _ _   _ _ _ _ _ _
_ _ _ _   _ _ _ _   _ _ _ _ _ _. — _ _ _ _
_ _ _ _ _ _

ARETH BLEMST DISAP DOLE EON GENOU GHEAR HAT HEMLON LWIL LYPRO NORET OUIG PEARIFY SCENCE SNO SON WANDA

5. _ _   _'_ _   _ _ _ _ _ _ _   _ _ _ _ _ _ _
_ _ _ _ _ _ _ _ _ _   _ _   _ _ _   _ _ _ _ _ _ _
_   _ _ _ _ _ _   _ _ _'_   _ _ _ _   _ _ _ _ _
_ _ _ _ _ _   _ _   _ _   _ _   _ _ _ _ _ _ _ _ _. —
_ _ _ _ _   _ _   _   _ _ _ _ _   _ _ _

ARINGS BECA EALLYD EDSAN ESTAR FAWIM IARYO ING MEINM ONTNE PANT PYKID SOIV STOBED TASEE TEDWE USEIR WEARD WEAT YUNDER

6. _ _ _ _   _ _   _ _ _ _ _,   _ _ _   _ _ _ _   _ _ _
_ _ _ _ _ _ _: _ _ _ _ _ _   _ _   _ _ _ _
_ _ _ _   _ _ _ _ _ _.

CESSH ESNO GELS HOI MAK NITS NOWSY OUHA OVELOR VET WHE WOC WAN

93.

CANDY CANE CROSSWORD

In this crossword, the ends of words are marked by thick lines rather than by black squares.

ACROSS

1. ". . . and ___ a good night!" (5)
5. British singer Rita (3)
7. Throne's platform (4)
9. They may be filled with candies (9)
10. Reveal, to a poet (3)
11. No longer working: Abbr. (3)
13. Mag. staffer (2)
15. Seasonal sound (2)
16. Term of endearment (3)
18. Flit (about) (3)
19. Guffawing noise (3)
20. Compass reading (3)
21. Chemical symbol for neon (2)
22. Football lineman, maybe (2)
24. What completes an *i* (3)
26. "Dear" person (3)
27. Dined (3)
29. Spot for ashes or coffee (3)
30. Jar part (3)
31. Bottom notes (3)

DOWN

1. Figurative device (5)
2. ___ infinitum
3. Villain's place (4)
4. Ancestry (7)
5. Ear: prefix (3)
6. Talented pilot (3)
8. Military rk. (3)
9. Flock watchers (9)
12. Write a program (4)
14. University VIP (4)
15. Chinese dynasty (3)
17. Family diagram (4)
23. French pronoun (3)
25. Fashions (6)
27. "___ Lang Syne" (4)
28. Peter, Paul, and Mary, e.g. (4)

1 2 3 4
5 6 7 8
9
10 11 12
13 14 15
16 17 18
19 20
21
22 23
24 25
26
27 28
29
30
31

94.

WORDPLAY: MISSING LETTERS

Each of the words in the following list is missing a pair of letters, which appear next to each other in the alphabet (for example, EF, or MN). Each of the letters of the alphabet appears once in the words, and none are repeated.

1. S ___ PER ___ ISE
2. BET ___ I ___ T
3. RE ___ IND ___ E
4. P ___ TRI ___ Y
5. EX ___ CER ___ ATE
6. A ___ BIA ___ CE
7. N ___ N ___ A
8. CATAL ___ ___ ES
9. DES ___ ER ___ S
10. LEN ___ T ___ EN
11. HOR ___ SCO ___ E
12. BLO ___ KA ___ E
13. IN ___ UI ___ Y

CHRISTMAS TREES

The approximate number of fresh-cut Christmas trees exported from Canada to the United States is

A. 500,000
B. 1.5 million
C. 2 million
D. 2.5 million

[Answer: B. 1.5 million]

95.

CATCH A WORD: WORLD CAPITALS

In this type of puzzle, the answer appears in its correct order but may begin in the middle of a word and be interrupted by spaces and punctuation. For example: The Canadians were victorious in hockey once again. Can you find the names of ten world capitals hidden in the sentences below?

1. Michaelangelo fell on Donatello during ninja practice.
2. The brunch included ricotta waffles and blueberry pancakes.
3. Noam would dub linguistics talks for foreign language students.
4. We'll have the company exec air our grievances on live TV.
5. Watch the *Friends* reunion to see Rachel sink into a vat of molasses.
6. The gardener sprayed on every rosebud a pesticide concoction.
7. The hamster damaged its wheel by excessive gnawing.
8. No one was sure what brought the Vikings to Newfoundland.
9. They found the forum ad-riddled if they didn't use a spam blocker.
10. First the comtessa, then several of her handmaids, entered the chamber.

96.

SUDOKU: EASY

A sudoku puzzle is a type of logic puzzle. Although it uses numbers, no mathematics is involved. The grid below is divided into nine large squares, each of which is divided into nine smaller squares. Each large square contains all the digits from 1 to 9, with each digit appearing exactly once. Each horizontal row of the puzzle also contains each digit exactly once, and so does each vertical row. By carefully observing which numbers are missing from each row, column, or square, see if you can figure out which numbers go where. There's only one possible solution to each puzzle.

				2		9		8
			9	8	3			4
			6				3	
	1				2			
3	8	5				1	2	7
			8				4	
	7				8			
9			2	7	1			
5		1		6				

97.

SUDOKU: EASY

A sudoku puzzle is a type of logic puzzle. Although it uses numbers, no mathematics is involved. The grid below is divided into nine large squares, each of which is divided into nine smaller squares. Each large square contains all the digits from 1 to 9, with each digit appearing exactly once. Each horizontal row of the puzzle also contains each digit exactly once, and so does each vertical row. By carefully observing which numbers are missing from each row, column, or square, see if you can figure out which numbers go where. There's only one possible solution to each puzzle.

	4		8	5		1	3	
						7	4	6
	1				9			
		8	7					
	9	4	1		2	6	7	
					8	2		
			5				6	
8	2	3						
	5	1		2	7		8	

98.

SYLLABLANK

The solution to each of the following puzzles is a single ten-letter word. We've chopped each word up into the smaller words listed below. Place the smaller words into the right positions on the blanks to discover the original words.

A ABLE AGE ALLY ALTO AM AND BE BUT CAP CULL DEMO EH FOR GET HER HIGH HOLE I ICE ION IS IT LENT LESS LIST LIT MEN MU NIT NOT ON PASS PORT RE SEA SON TON WAY WAY

1. IN TOTAL _ _ _ _ _ _ _ _ _ _
2. AT A CERTAIN TIME OF YEAR _ _ _ _ _ _ _ _ _ _
3. BUILDING DESTRUCTION _ _ _ _ _ _ _ _ _ _
4. BULLETS AND SHELLS _ _ _ _ _ _ _ _ _ _
5. BUSINESSMAN _ _ _ _ _ _ _ _ _ _
6. CARNATION LOCATION _ _ _ _ _ _ _ _ _ _
7. CASTLE GATE _ _ _ _ _ _ _ _ _ _
8. COACH ROBBERS _ _ _ _ _ _ _ _ _ _
9. CORRIDOR _ _ _ _ _ _ _ _ _ _
10. DOGGED _ _ _ _ _ _ _ _ _ _
11. DRAWING ATTENTION _ _ _ _ _ _ _ _ _ _
12. EARLIER _ _ _ _ _ _ _ _ _ _

99.

MAPLE LEAF

The goal of this puzzle is to form as many words as you can, using the letters contained in the leaf. Each letter can be used only once, so you can create a word with two Ts only if there are two Ts in the leaf. Each word must be three or more letters long, and all words must contain the large central letter of the leaf, along with any mix of the letters around the outside. For the ultimate challenge, see if you can find the one 10-letter word that contains ALL the letters in the leaf.

100.

NORTH POLE ANIMALS

All the words in the list below are hidden somewhere in the grid of letters. See if you can find them! Words may run in any direction, including diagonally, and spaces are ignored. When you've crossed off all the words, read the leftover letters in the grid (running left to right, from top to bottom) to reveal a hidden quote related to the puzzle's theme.

BOWHEAD
CARIBOU
ERMINE
GREENLAND SHARK
GROUND SQUIRREL
GUILLEMOTS
LEMMING
LYNX
MOOSE
MUSK OX
NARWHAL
ORCA
OTTER
POLAR BEAR
PUFFIN
RAVEN
SEAL
SKUA
SNOW GOOSE
SNOWSHOE HARE
SNOWY OWL
TERN
TUNDRA SWAN
WALRUS
WOLF
WOLVERINE

NOVICE 1

DOUBLE-DOUBLE TAKE

Spot the difference: can you find the 8 changes?

TOYS

1. According to the Rotman School of Management, this city has the highest number of candy stores *and* toy stores, per capita, in Canada:

A. Kamloops, British Columbia
B. London, Ontario
C. Sherbrooke, Quebec
D. Saskatoon, Saskatchewan
E. Brandon, Manitoba

2. Match the gift to the year in which it was the number one Christmas present.

A. Barbie	1. 1980
B. Barney Talking Doll	2. 1999
C. Beanie Babies	3. 1996
D. Trivial Pursuit	4. 1952
E. Monopoly	5. 2010
F. Mr. Potato Head	6. 1975
G. Apple iPad	7. 1983
H. Rubik's Cube	8. 1959
I. Teenage Mutant Ninja Turtles Action Figure	9. 1995
J. The Pet Rock	10. 1936
K. Tickle Me Elmo	11. 1992
L. Game Boy	12. 1990

SOLUTION NOVICE 1

Answers:
1. D. Saskatoon, Saskatchewan;
2. A. = 8; B. = 11; C. = 9; D. = 7; E. = 10; F. = 4; G. = 5; H. = 1; I. = 12; J. = 6; K. = 3; L. = 2

101.

THE ARMY

All the words in the list below are hidden somewhere in the grid of letters. See if you can find them! Words may run in any direction, including diagonally, and spaces are ignored. When you've crossed off all the words, read the leftover letters in the grid (running left to right, from top to bottom) to reveal a hidden quote related to the puzzle's theme.

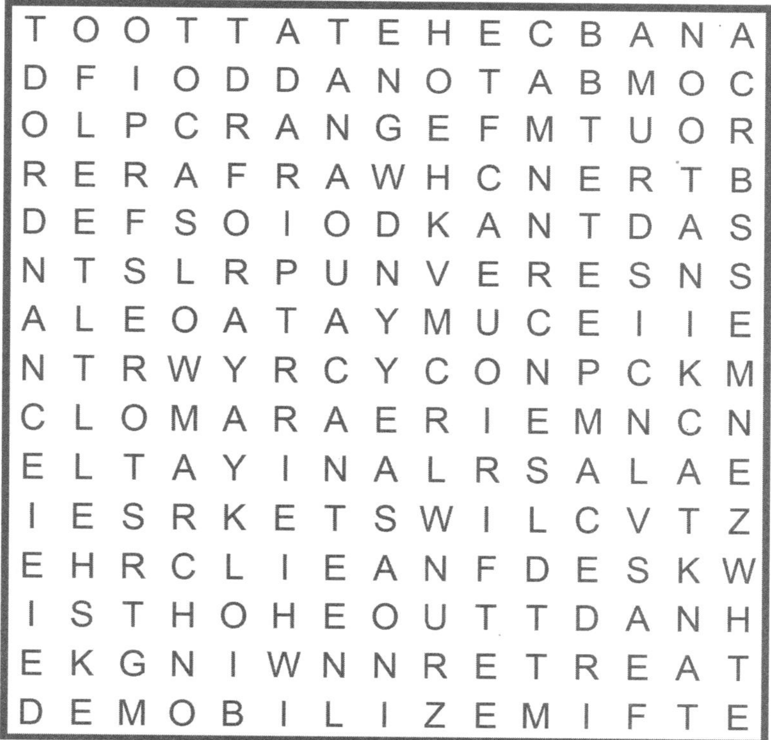

T	O	O	T	T	A	T	E	H	E	C	B	A	N	A
D	F	I	O	D	D	A	N	O	T	A	B	M	O	C
O	L	P	C	R	A	N	G	E	F	M	T	U	O	R
R	E	R	A	F	R	A	W	H	C	N	E	R	T	B
D	E	F	S	O	I	O	D	K	A	N	T	D	A	S
N	T	S	L	R	P	U	N	V	E	R	E	S	N	S
A	L	E	O	A	T	A	Y	M	U	C	E	I	I	E
N	T	R	W	Y	R	C	Y	C	O	N	P	C	K	M
C	L	O	M	A	R	A	E	R	I	E	M	N	C	N
E	L	T	A	Y	I	N	A	L	R	S	A	L	A	E
I	E	S	R	K	E	T	S	W	I	L	C	V	T	Z
E	H	R	C	L	I	E	A	N	F	D	E	S	K	W
I	S	T	H	O	H	E	O	U	T	T	D	A	N	H
E	K	G	N	I	W	N	N	R	E	T	R	E	A	T
D	E	M	O	B	I	L	I	Z	E	M	I	F	T	E

ADC
ARM
AWOL
BASE
BOMB
CANTEEN
COMBAT
DECAMP
DECORATION
DEMOB
DEPOT
DRAFT
DUTY
ENEMY
FLANK
FLEET
FOE
FORAY
LINES
MESS
MOBILIZE
NAVY
ORDNANCE
POW
RANGE
RANK
RECCE
RETREAT
ROUT
SHELL
SLOW MARCH
SNIPER
STORES
TANK
TATTOO
TRENCH WARFARE
TRUCE
VAN
WING

102.

CRYPTOGRAM

Each of the quotes below has been encrypted, with each letter of the alphabet substituted for a different letter. The substitutions are different for each puzzle. Use your code-breaking skills to discover the original quotation! (Hints: Start with short words—a one-letter word is usually A or I. Count the number of each letter—the commonest letter in English is E, followed by T, A, O, I, and N, while the most common three-letter word is THE.)

1. T HTMD LO T EKTJZ UPTU GLKK
KZMVI ICS BCMZI, LA ICS JTM EWCFZ
UPTU ICS VCM'U MZZV LU.—HCH PCEZ

2. D ZDSODTI TE EMGBCPTIO HMF
AMI'C IBBA DC D RSTQB HMF QDI'C
SBETEC.

3. K SFJ PJ K LZMPDIZ YMKY EFQJ
YRPDZ KJ BKJY RMZQ OAF KEZ
KBYZE PY KJ RMZQ OAF KEZ PQ PY.

4. T NSIZEVII FCTF GTXVI EKFCZEY NSF GKEVW ZI T LKKB NSIZEVII.—CVEBW MKBQ

5. S VSHMXGMTKRO XA S VSIISNR KXQZ S VTMMRNR RBHVSQXTE.—CSOL QKSXE

6. Q FEP LMQHIMA Q TEB RXFMOXLB, JMZAMCMZQKHM, QKF LE LYZK QZEYKF LIZMM LXVMA TMREZM OBXKP FEUK.—ZETMZL TMKHIOMB

BIRTHDAY QUIZ

How many people do you need to have in a room in order for it to be *more likely than not* that two of them share the same birthday?

[Answer: 23. In a room of just 23 people, there's a fifty-fifty chance of two people having the same birthday.]

103.

PYRAMID POWER

The pyramid is made up of a series of words, each one containing the letters used in the word directly above it (the order of the letters may be changed) plus one new letter. Solve the clues to fill in the pyramid!

1. First vowel in "vowel" ___
2. Activated ___ ___
3. Heavy weight ___ ___ ___
4. Bill ___ ___ ___ ___
5. Office consumable ___ ___ ___ ___ ___
6. Small horn ___ ___ ___ ___ ___ ___
7. Car brand ___ ___ ___ ___ ___ ___ ___
8. Belief ___ ___ ___ ___ ___ ___ ___ ___
9. Blacking out ___ ___ ___ ___ ___ ___ ___ ___ ___
10. Work in sync ___ ___ ___ ___ ___ ___ ___ ___ ___ ___
11. Items that brighten a room ___ ___ ___ ___ ___ ___ ___ ___ ___ ___ ___

BRAIN TEASER

Three days ago, yesterday was the day before Sunday. What day will it be tomorrow?

[Answer: Today is Wednesday, so tomorrow is Thursday.]

104.

PYRAMID POWER

The pyramid is made up of a series of words, each one containing the letters used in the word directly above it (the order of the letters may be changed) plus one new letter. Solve the clues to fill in the pyramid!

1. Oxygen symbol
2. Bond's bad doctor
3. Start of count
4. A bad Caesar
5. The sound of sleep
6. Singers
7. Betrayal
8. Rich sounding
9. Tree hangings

PICK A NUMBER

If you were to write out the numbers from one to twenty in words—in chronological order—and then put them in alphabetical order, which number would stay where it was?

[Answer: five]

105.

ONE STEP AT A TIME

Change the word at the top to the word at the bottom by altering one letter at a time. Each change should produce a new word. We've provided clues to help you on your way.

T H R E E

_ _ _ _ _ PROPELLED THROUGH THE AIR

_ _ _ _ _ SMALL, LONG-NOSED ANIMAL

_ _ _ _ _ TEAR UP

_ _ _ _ _ SHRANK (AWAY FROM)

_ _ _ _ _ COCONUT TOSSING STANDS

S H I P S

L I V E

_ _ _ _ MARRY A WOMAN

_ _ _ _ DECEPTION

_ _ _ _ LEGAL DOCUMENT

W E L L

BLUEBERRIES

1. The blueberry capital of Canada is
   - **A.** Sudbury, Ontario
   - **B.** Parry Sound, Ontario
   - **C.** Sussex, New Brunswick
   - **D.** Oxford, Nova Scotia
   - **E.** Mistassini, Quebec

2. Blueberries are Canada's second most valuable fruit crop. What is the first?

[Answers: 1. = D. Oxford, Nova Scotia; 2. apples]

106.

LETTER DROP

The quotation by Mordecai Richler below has been written into a grid. Words run left to right, and each line wraps around to the line below. Sadly, the letters have all dropped out of the puzzle. All the letters are in the correct columns, but their order may have changed. Can you restore the letters to their proper places and discover the quote? Punctuation is still in its original position, and spaces between words are marked by black boxes. Remember, words don't end at the end of a line unless there's a black box there.

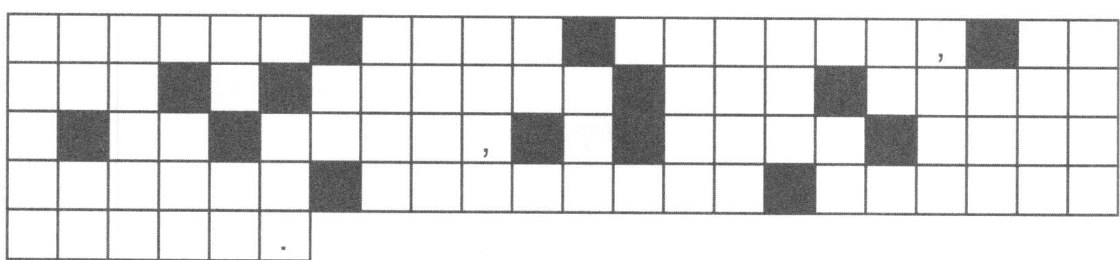

C		A																			
C	C	A	B	A			F	A					A	A						B	E
H	I	A	I	L	E		L	I	O	A	I		A	A	A	C	A	E	D	E	E
I	N	G	L	N	G	E	P	L	R	E	N	C	H	N	D	D	J	E	M	I	N
T	O	M	S	S	W	W	R	R	T	M	R	O	I	N	V	E	R	I	W	P	S

107.

LITTLE HELPERS CROSSWORD

ACROSS

1. Desert pit stop
6. Decorative pillowcase
10. Big bunch
14. Meat
15. Vehicle in a Joni Mitchell song
16. Shield border, in heraldry
17. Plant used as an alternative to cumin
19. Mother of Castor and Pollux
20. Certain lane
21. Chatter
22. Viking, for one
24. Zero
25. Tailor
26. The world has seven
27. Animal familiar in "The Golden Compass"
29. Where bats live
30. Abbr. for someone with only two names
31. Barack's German counterpart
33. Former Israeli president Weizman
34. Words before happens or were
36. Gold (prefix)
37. Words between strong and ox
38. "Sunday morning creeping like ___ . . ."
39. Retriever's reward
41. German classical music label
42. Band with the song "Kids"
44. City known as "the Venice of the North"
48. In touch with one's feelings
50. Fork over
51. Org. in "The Six Million Dollar Man"
52. When you're outside after being on the inside
53. Negative prefix
54. Bon words
55. Spot's breakfast
56. Play written for the end of Christmas
59. Symbol before a signature?
60. James of Blues
61. Parisian pathway
62. Those, in Tijuana
63. Girl from Edinburgh
64. It's human, in a phrase

DOWN

1. Cause insult
2. Inability to read
3. Doddery
4. ___ it a shame
5. Word before "life"
6. Type of weasel
7. Skateboarder Tony
8. Gimli's tool
9. Place of reflection
10. Sturdy
11. Wooden cupboard
12. Antiquated term for councillors
13. Letter opener?
18. Not on the level
23. Whichever
25. Baskerville, e.g.
26. Benefit
28. Principle pipe
29. Yell out
32. Instructions on a cookie
33. "Mi casa ___ casa"
34. World's highest cascade
35. Edible pod
37. Give it ___
38. Box in a newspaper
40. Make embarrassed
42. Bad in France
43. Crumb-dropping girl
45. Search on the Web
46. Book commemorated by Purim
47. Dawn, to Buffy
49. Barks
50. Flatbreads
53. Blue-and-white pieces of pottery
54. Venus de ___
57. Williams sisters' org.
58. Old King Cole?

1	2	3	4	5	■	6	7	8	9	■	10	11	12	13
14					■	15				■	16			
17				elf	18					■	19			
20				■	21			■	22	23				
24			■	25			■	26						
27			28			■	29	elf			■	30		
■	■	■	31			32			■	■	33			
■	34	35			■	36			■	37				■
38				■	■	39			40			■	■	■
41			■	42	43			■	44			45	46	47
48	elf		49				■	50			■	51		
52						■	53			■	54			
55				■	56	57	elf			58				
59				■	60				■	61				
62				■	63				■	64				

108.

WORDS × FIVE

This puzzle is similar to a crossword, but the five-letter answer to each clue is written twice—both across and down. So, if the solution to clue 1 is FLAME, you would write FLAME into the grid twice, from left to right and from top to bottom.

1	2	3	4	5
2				
3				
4				
5				

1. Accompanies lyrics
2. U in UHF
3. Beef cut
4. Angry
5. Bakery produce

109.

WORDS × FIVE

This puzzle is similar to a crossword, but the five-letter answer to each clue is written twice—both across and down. So, if the solution to clue 1 is FLAME, you would write FLAME into the grid twice, from left to right and from top to bottom.

1	2	3	4	5
2				
3				
4				
5				

1. Snow colour
2. Many-headed beast
3. Thoughts
4. Residue
5. Moves gently

TONGUE TWISTERS

Say each phrase quickly, three times.

1. Three twigs twined tightly.
2. Pre-shrunk silk shirts
3. Are our oars oak?
4. Red leather, yellow leather
5. Betty had better butter Brad's bread.
6. He threw three free throws.
7. Three grey geese in green fields grazing
8. Freshly fried flying fish
9. Good blood, bad blood
10. Fred fed Ted bread, and Ted fed Fred bread.

110.

STINKETY PINKETY

In this game, you are given the clues to a two-word rhyming phrase, along with some version of the words STINKETY PINKETY, which tells you how many syllables are in the answer.

Example: Giant hog (Stink Pink)
Answer: Big pig

1. Incredible caterpillar (Stinky Pinky)
2. Linen soup (Stink Pink)
3. Heavy-footed RV walker (Stinky Pinky)
4. Postal course chart (Stinky Pinky)
5. Cheese grater (Stinky Pinky)
6. Cup for ants (Stink Pink)
7. Disgusting choice (Stink Pink)
8. Bizarre facial hair (Stink Pink)
9. Farm machinery portrayer (Stinky Pinky)
10. Hot sauce disaster (Stinkety Pinkety)

QUIZ

In what province is the community of Ecum Secum?

A. Alberta
B. Manitoba
C. Nova Scotia
D. Ontario
E. Prince Edward Island

[Answer: C. Nova Scotia]

111.

WORDPLAY: HEADS OR TAILS

In each pair of words, the letters at the beginning of the word have been switched with the letters at the end to form a new word. See if you can uncover the missing words.

Example

P R O **M** **I** S E — S E **M** **I** P R O

VOW — PART-TIME PLAYER

1. _ E _ _ _ _ _ — _ _ _ _ _ E _
   TAKE ANOTHER LOOK — BOARD GAME PIECE
2. _ E _ _ _ _ — _ _ _ _ E _
   PLAN — ENDORSED
3. _ _ I G N _ — _ I G N _ _
   PUTS IN A ROW — LIGHT OR HORN
4. _ _ _ _ E _ — _ E _ _ _ _
   TV AUDIENCE MEMBER — CRITIQUE
5. _ _ _ _ E _ — _ E _ _ _ _
   FOOT PARTS — EXPLORE
6. _ _ _ _ _ E _ — _ E _ _ _ _ _
   CONTRARY — TELL A TALE
7. _ A _ _ _ _ — _ _ _ _ A _
   BEMOAN — IN THE HEAD
8. _ E _ _ _ _ _ — _ _ _ _ _ E _
   PLEASURE — ABLAZE
9. _ E _ _ _ _ _ — _ _ _ _ _ E _
   BOUNCE BACK — BRITISH RASCAL
10. _ E _ _ _ _ _ — _ _ _ _ _ E _
    LOOTED — RUINED

112.

ANTLERGRAM

The goal of antlergrams is to form as many words as you can using the letters in the moose's nose and antlers. Each letter can be used only once, which means you can form a word with two Ts only if there are two Ts in the puzzle. Each word must be three or more letters long and must contain the letter in the nose, along with any combination of the letters from the antlers. For the ultimate challenge, see if you can find the one 9-letter word that contains ALL the letters in the puzzle.

113.

CATCH A WORD: COFFEE STORE OFFERINGS

In this type of puzzle, the answer appears in its correct order but may begin in the middle of a word and be interrupted by spaces and punctuation. For example: The Canadi<u>ans wer</u>e victorious in hockey once again. Can you find the names of ten coffee store offerings—some drinks, some flavour shots—hidden in the sentences below?

1. Mark could sleep in, as he has school at ten tomorrow morning.
2. Teddy really liked Big Bird, but Vera found the Elmo character more enjoyable.
3. While Debbie put on her mascara, Melissa applied her eyeliner.
4. Rocky and Apollo have announced a rematch at noon tomorrow.
5. The first baseman told the revved-up ump: "Kindly give our guy the home run he clearly ran!"
6. If right off the bat you do the cha-cha, it eases the stress of competitive dancing.
7. If you get the moving van, I'll arrange a box pickup next week.
8. The samurai observed the ninja vanish before his very eyes.
9. The main character of *Apocalypse Now* is a merc in 'Nam on leave, given a secret mission.
10. Where does that ghost get off, eerily haunting the abandoned castle?

114.

SKILLATHON

The goal is to find as many words as possible made up of the letters in the word or phrase below. Words must be made of four or more letters. No plurals allowed. Only one tense or form of a verb is permitted (if you find WALK, you can't also have WALKS, WALKED, WALKING, etc.). The exception is when two forms have different meanings—e.g., BORE and BORED.

MARITIMES

Try to beat our experts. They found 89 words.

115.

FAIRY TALES

All the words in the list below are hidden somewhere in the grid of letters. See if you can find them! Words may run in any direction, including diagonally, and spaces are ignored. When you've crossed off all the words, read the leftover letters in the grid (running left to right, from top to bottom) to reveal a hidden quote related to the puzzle's theme.

S S O R C E R E R Q U E E N O
C P M W I C K E D W I T C H N
D A E A I A M U L E T I M N C
O R S L G Z D W A R F T A L E
H W A T L I A M A I D E N A U
A Y S G L G C R K N I G H T P
L O I G O E N G D T O K T E O
F D E K I N G K I S S S O P N
L E W B R A V E S F A W W I A
I M T I G L N E E N O O E Q T
N O G O T A C T L F E R R U I
G N R S O N R A F I H D E E M
F F A A I D I R X Y T E A S E
L E E R A L L I A N C E R T T
B E P N D I P N S T E E D O G

ALLIANCE
AMULET
BEAST
BRAVE
CASTLE
DEMON
DRAGON
DWARF
ELF
FOREST
FROG
GIANT
HALFLING
HERO
KING
KISS
KNIGHT
LAND
MAGIC
MAIDEN
ONCE UPON A TIME
PIXIE
PRINCESS
QUEEN
QUEST
SORCERER
SPELL
STEED
SWORD
TOWER
WICKED WITCH
WIZARD

116.

REBUS

In these puzzles, the arrangement of the letters and symbols suggests a common word or expression. For example, this combination

COVER
GOING

is "going undercover" (the word GOING is under the word COVER—literally). See how many you can figure out.

1. C O **BABY** L D

2. snow ⟶ SNOW

3. S ki

4. ⬇
NOEL NOEL NOEL NOEL NOEL

5. 

117.

SUDOKU: EASY

A sudoku puzzle is a type of logic puzzle. Although it uses numbers, no mathematics is involved. The grid below is divided into nine large squares, each of which is divided into nine smaller squares. Each large square contains all the digits from 1 to 9, with each digit appearing exactly once. Each horizontal row of the puzzle also contains each digit exactly once, and so does each vertical row. By carefully observing which numbers are missing from each row, column, or square, see if you can figure out which numbers go where. There's only one possible solution to each puzzle.

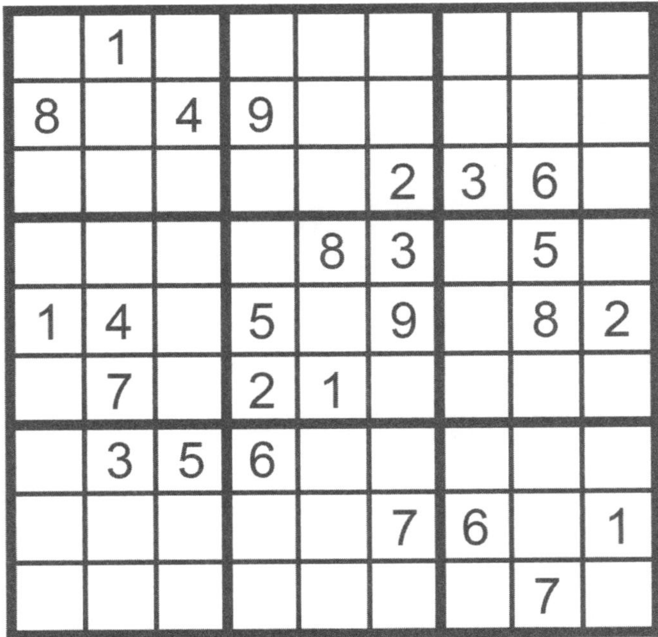

	1							
8		4	9					
					2	3	6	
				8	3		5	
1	4		5		9		8	2
	7		2	1				
	3	5	6					
					7	6		1
							7	

118.

SUDOKU: EASY

A sudoku puzzle is a type of logic puzzle. Although it uses numbers, no mathematics is involved. The grid below is divided into nine large squares, each of which is divided into nine smaller squares. Each large square contains all the digits from 1 to 9, with each digit appearing exactly once. Each horizontal row of the puzzle also contains each digit exactly once, and so does each vertical row. By carefully observing which numbers are missing from each row, column, or square, see if you can figure out which numbers go where. There's only one possible solution to each puzzle.

<table>
<tr><td></td><td></td><td></td><td>4</td><td></td><td>7</td><td></td><td>6</td><td></td></tr>
<tr><td></td><td>3</td><td></td><td></td><td>9</td><td></td><td>5</td><td>1</td><td></td></tr>
<tr><td></td><td></td><td></td><td></td><td>1</td><td></td><td>4</td><td>7</td><td></td></tr>
<tr><td></td><td></td><td>9</td><td>6</td><td></td><td></td><td></td><td>8</td><td></td></tr>
<tr><td></td><td>4</td><td></td><td></td><td></td><td></td><td></td><td>5</td><td></td></tr>
<tr><td></td><td>8</td><td></td><td></td><td></td><td>1</td><td>3</td><td></td><td></td></tr>
<tr><td></td><td>6</td><td>8</td><td></td><td>7</td><td></td><td></td><td></td><td></td></tr>
<tr><td></td><td>1</td><td>3</td><td></td><td>6</td><td></td><td></td><td>9</td><td></td></tr>
<tr><td></td><td>2</td><td></td><td>8</td><td></td><td>9</td><td></td><td></td><td></td></tr>
</table>

119.

ANAGRAMS

The following items are all anagrams of the titles of Christmas movies, from various decades. See how many you can solve.

1. STAR IS TOY'S CHARM

   _ _________ _____

2. INFURIATED FELLOWS

   __'_ _ _________ ____

3. SOFTER, HOMELY, ARTHRITIC NUTTER

   _______ __ ______-______
   ______

4. RASH SLOPE EXPERT

   ___ _____ _______

5. SOB IF WITH SHEEP

   ___ ______'_ ____

6. HE'D RAID

   ___ ____

7. THE HERO SCOWLS SCATHING MIRTH

   ___ ___ ______ _____
   ____

8. AS ODDNESS DRAWS RICH

   ______ ____________

120.

SYLLABLANK

The solution to each of the following puzzles is a single eight-letter word. We've chopped each word up into the smaller words listed below. Place the smaller words into the right positions on the blanks to discover the original words.

A AT BAR CAP CITY CUR DO DON ELL FAN GOLD HO HO I I I I IN IN LESS LOG MAR ME ON ON ORB PEN PUN RAM RE RED SHED TAG TONE TRY VIE WED

1. CHECKED WORK — __ __   __ __ __   __ __ __
2. BECAME LIABLE — __ __   __ __ __   __ __ __
3. DEEP VOICE — __ __ __   __   __ __ __ __
4. FIVE-SIDED SHAPE — __ __ __   __ __ __   __ __
5. YELLOW FLOWER — __ __ __   __   __ __ __ __
6. WITH NOWHERE TO LIVE — __ __   __ __   __ __ __ __
7. VOLUME — __ __ __   __   __ __ __ __
8. FOOT SOLDIERS — __ __   __ __ __   __ __ __
9. CHARITABLE GIFT — __ __ __   __ __   __   __ __
10. GIVEN JUST DESSERTS — __ __ __   __   __ __ __ __
11. 3-D IMAGE — __ __   __ __ __   __ __ __
12. SOUND OF A VISITOR — __ __   __ __ __   __ __ __

ANIMAL TRIVIA

1. How many stomachs does a moose have?
2. How many eyelids does a camel have on each eye?

[Answers: 1. Four—during the fall a moose can eat more than 50 kilograms a day. 2. Three—the third lid is very thin and acts as a kind of windshield wiper to help protect a camel's eye from sand.]

121.

WORD JIGSAW

The words in these quotes and quips have been sliced up into pieces, so you can no longer see where one word begins and another ends. The order of the letters inside each piece is unchanged. Can you reassemble the word pieces and figure out the original phrase?

1. _ _ _ _   _ _ _   _ _ _   _ _ _ _ _ _   _ _ _   _ _ _ -
_ _ _ _   _ _ _ _   _ _ _   _ _ _ _ _ _ _   _ _ _ _
_ _ _   _ _ _ _ _ _   _ _ _ _ _ . — _ _ _ _ _ _
_ _ _ _ _

ALCHE ARTHEF COTT DEE EACHA EFORF ERWAL EST EWBOR GEHAS ITTES MEDTHEN NYE TERS TTIM

2. _ _   _ _ _ _ _ _   _ _ _ _ _ _ _   _ _ _ _ _ _ _ :
_ _ _   _ _ _ _ _ _   _ _ _ _ _ _ _   _   _ _ _ _ _ _
_ _ _ _ _ _ _ _ _ ,   _ _ _   _ _ _ _   _ _ _ _ _
_ _ _ _ _ . — _ _ _ _ _ _ _ _   _ _   _ _ _ _ _ _ _

ALITT ANNO ESBUTT ETIM HEYNE INSST LESOM NDREDO QUI REAKMAR RETCH SEDE SVIGN TDES TROYKI URCHA VERB WEC

3. _ _   _   _ _ _ _ _ _   _ _ _ _ _   _ _ _   _ _ _ _ _ _
_ _ _   _ _ _ _ _ _   _ _ _   _ _ _   _ _ _   _ _ _ _ ,
_ _ _   _ _ _ _   _ _ _ _   _ _ _   _ _ _   _ _ _
_ _ _ _ _ _ . — _ .   _ _ _ _ _ _ _ _   _ _ _ _ _ _ _

ART ATAD DEAT DTAL HOUL INNERP ISEL KWELLB MERSE NOTTO OWELLAN TMA TTOOW UGHAM UTNO WISEL YBUT YONES YWSO

4. _ _ _   _ _ _   _ _   _ _ _ _ _ _ _   _ _ _   _ _ _
_ _ _ _.   _ _ _ _   _ _   _ _ _ _ _ _   _ _ _ _
_ _ _ _   _ _ _ _ _   _ _ _ _.¯ _ _ _ _ _ _
_ _ _ _ _   _ _ _ _ _

ANDNO ARFUL ARILKE ELCO ENRAIN ERBE ERMARI EWYE HATHA HINGST LOFT METHEN VENEV WWEW

5. _ _ _ _ _ _ _ _,   _ _ _ _ _ _: _ _   _ _ _   _ _
_   _ _ _ _ _ _ _   _ _ _   _ _ _   _ _ _ _ _ _ _.¯
_ _'_   _   _ _ _ _ _ _ _ _ _   _ _ _ _

BERGE END EWHO FULL HASFRI IFE ILUR ISAFA NOMAN ONDER ORGE REMEM SITSAW

6. _   _ _ _ _ _   _ _ _ _ _ _ _   _ _   _ _ _   _ _ _ _
_   _ _ _   _ _ _ _ _ _   _ _ _ _.   _ _'_   _ _ _
_ _ _   _ _   _ _ _,   _ _ _ _ _ _.   _ _ _ _ _   _ _
_ _ _ _   _ _ _ _ _   _   _ _ _ _ _ _   _ _ _ _.¯ _
_ _ _ _ _ _ _   _ _ _ _ _   _ _ _ _ _ _ _ _ _

ACHAR ADLITT ALLYMA CHAB DATA EDSAL EITS HRIS INE ITTLEL ITWA LETRE LIEB LLRE NOTBA OUGHT OVE ROWNC SSU TMAS USTNE VERTH YBEITJ

122.

SONG FROM THE HEART CROSSWORD

ACROSS

1. Hawaiian island
5. ___ the line
8. Starchy plant
12. Manipulates
13. Make a living
14. Humpback animal
15. Beginning of holiday verse hidden in puzzle
17. "Star" spice
18. It's illegal to park in front of them
19. "Anyone for ___?"
20. Type of ball
21. Wound
22. The verse, part 2
27. Mirage, perhaps
28. Victor's assistant
29. Thing to lend someone
32. Mix sugar into coffee, e.g.
33. Act of goodwill, to an American
35. Fiona married one
36. '80s Europop group
37. Build (up)
38. Benefit
39. December 31 to January 1, from one perspective
42. Turns down
44. Quebec law
45. Overwrought
46. End of the verse
51. Part of a whale
52. Point at which rays of light converge
53. Not poetic
54. CPA's recs.
55. Loungewear
56. Swedish syrup
57. Mother of Minos, in myth
58. Chemical suffixes

DOWN

1. Pained expression
2. Blanched
3. Listen to
4. Bygone U.N.member
5. Make tighter
6. Table scraps
7. Naval rnk.
8. Substance that makes wine dry
9. Type of acid
10. Pine product
11. Matador cries
13. The doldrums
14. Friend of Antony
16. Politenesses
19. Andrea Bocelli, e.g.
21. Apple's apple, for one
22. Donald Duck cartoonist Don
23. Sworn words
24. British prog-rock supergroup
25. Good man
26. One with a gift
29. Antiquated exclamation
30. 24 Down album
31. Depend (on)
33. Devilish one
34. "Woe is me!"
35. Eggs
37. Fool's mineral
38. Forever, for short
39. Month named for an emperor
40. Wooly beast
41. Certain seasonal songs
42. Opposite of sub
43. Vodka's is around 80
45. Recipe amts.
46. International economic grp.
47. ___ Few Dollars More
48. Skype picture
49. Bumpkin
50. Some headings
52. Indian actress Aishwarya

1	2	3	4	■	■	5	6	7	■	■	8	9	10	11
12				■	13				■	14				
15				16					■	17				
18								■	19					
■	■	■	■	20			■	21						■
22	23	24	25				26					■	■	■
27					■	■	28				■	29	30	31
32				■	33	34				■	35			
36			■	37				■	■	38				
■	■	■	39					40	41					
■	42	43					■	44			■	■	■	■
45						■	46				47	48	49	50
51					■	52								
53					■	54				■	55			
56				■	■	57			■	■	58			

123.

TRIPLE MEANINGS

Many English words have multiple meanings. Here, we've given three different definitions that each describe the same word. Can you figure out the words?

1.	THROW	HIDE	MOVE FAST	______
2.	REDDEN	CARD HAND	WASH OUT	______
3.	PREDICAMENT	SQUEEZE	CONSERVE	______
4.	WORRY	ORNAMENT	RIDGE	______
5.	STEEP BANK	DECEIVE OPPONENT	CHEERFULLY CRASS	______
6.	WEIGHT	STERLING	CRUSH	______
7.	ILL NO MORE	SPECULATOR	SUPERIOR	______
8.	BUMP	VESSEL	CLASH	______
9.	NOT ATTEND	YOUNG LADY	FAIL	______

T.V. QUIZ

In October 2012, *Degrassi* surpassed this series as the longest-running Canadian-produced English-language drama in the country's history:

A. *The Beachcombers*
B. *Street Legal*
C. *Danger Bay*
D. *E.N.G.*
E. *Cold Squad*

[Answer: A. *The Beachcombers*]

124.

MAPLE LEAF

The goal of this puzzle is to form as many words as you can, using the letters contained in the leaf. Each letter can be used only once, so you can create a word with two Ts only if there are two Ts in the leaf. Each word must be three or more letters long, and all words must contain the large central letter of the leaf, along with any mix of the letters around the outside. For the ultimate challenge, see if you can find the one 10-letter word that contains ALL the letters in the leaf.

125.

HOLIDAY MOVIES

All the words in the list below are hidden somewhere in the grid of letters. See if you can find them! Words may run in any direction, including diagonally, and spaces are ignored. When you've crossed off all the words, read the leftover letters in the grid (running left to right, from top to bottom) to reveal a hidden quote related to the puzzle's theme.

A C N O B O D Y S F O O L H R
F I S A M E R I C A N T A I L
I B L T M E A A S B C A R O L
R A I E N I S R S U A C G H A
S T F I T O N O T L P B R R O
T M D I T H D B O H F S E T T
B A O N C R A I R Y U Y M H O
L N E U C E A L E U N R L I T
O R L O U S H E W H G I I N T
O E T U P L E A O E A E N M H
D T C R A S H N R A A R S A E
R U B R A Z I L D V M P D N R
B R I D G E T J O N E S O A E
L N P R O M E T H E U S T N F
I S H O M E A L O N E N T G O

AMERICAN TAIL
ARTHUR
BABE
BATMAN RETURNS
BRAZIL
BRIDGET JONES
CRASH
DIE HARD
DINER
FIRST BLOOD
GO
GREMLINS
HOME ALONE
ICE HARVEST
IN BRUGES
LETHAL WEAPON
NOBODYS FOOL
PROMETHEUS
RENT
THE REF
THIN MAN

126.

LETTER DROP

The quotation by John Cleese below has been written into a grid. Words run left to right, and each line wraps around to the line below. Sadly, the letters have all dropped out of the puzzle. All the letters are in the correct columns, but their order may have changed. Can you restore the letters to their proper places and discover the quote? Punctuation is still in its original position, and spaces between words are marked by black boxes. Remember, words don't end at the end of a line unless there's a black box there.

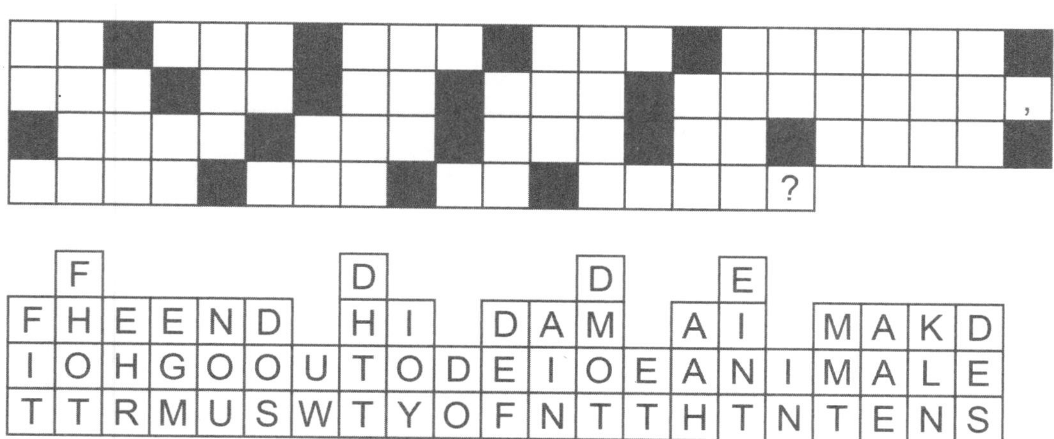

127.

WORDS × SIX

This puzzle is similar to a crossword, but the six-letter answer to each clue is written twice—both across and down. So, if the solution to clue 1 is GOBLIN you would write GOBLIN in the grid two times, from left to right and from top to bottom.

1	2	3	4	5	6
2					
3					
4					
5					
6					

1. Name names
2. Selected
3. Element in blue paint
4. In working order
5. Buyer's counterpart
6. Goes in

NOVICE 2

DOUBLE-DOUBLE TAKE

Spot the difference: can you find the 8 changes?

HOLIDAY FOOD

1. According to Turkey Farmers of Canada, in 2015 Canadians purchased 3.3 million whole turkeys at Christmas—equal to this amount of all whole turkeys sold over the year:

A. 26 percent
B. 33 percent
C. 47 percent
D. 52 percent
E. 58 percent

2. True or false?

A. Turkeys can't see in colour.
B. Turkeys have great hearing, a poor sense of smell, and an excellent sense of taste.

3. Every December 23, the people of Oaxaca, Mexico, celebrate a particular vegetable, carving it to create scenes that compete for prizes. That vegetable is an oversized:

A. Potato
B. Onion
C. Radish
D. Turnip
E. Cucumber

4. In Quebec, eggnog is sold under a French name that is translated as:

A. Golden milk
B. Creamy milk
C. Hen's milk
D. Christmas milk
E. Holiday milk

SOLUTION NOVICE 2

Answers:
1. C. 47 percent;
2. A. False B. True;
3. C. Radish (The celebration is called the Night of the Radishes);
4. C. Hen's milk

128.

WORDS × SIX

This puzzle is similar to a crossword, but the six-letter answer to each clue is written twice—both across and down. So, if the solution to clue 1 is GOBLIN you would write GOBLIN in the grid two times, from left to right and from top to bottom.

1	2	3	4	5	6
2					
3					
4					
5					
6					

1. Dance clubs
2. Contaminated
3. Sandwich topping
4. Lining up music tracks
5. Citrus fruit
6. Rough grasses

129.

ONE STEP AT A TIME

Change the word at the top to the word at the bottom by altering one letter at a time. Each change should produce a new word. We've provided clues to help you on your way.

P E A C E

_ _ _ _ _ ORANGEY SHADE

_ _ _ _ _ SANDY SHORE

_ _ _ _ _ TO DRY WOOD

_ _ _ _ _ BUNK ON A SHIP

_ _ _ _ _ STARTING POINT

_ _ _ _ _ WIDTH

_ _ _ _ _ COUNTRY MUSICIAN BROOKS

E A R T H

P I P E R

_ _ _ _ _ WRITING MATERIAL

_ _ _ _ _ FRUIT-PEELING DEVICE

_ _ _ _ _ ONE WHO READS CAREFULLY

_ _ _ _ _ SKIN VENTS

_ _ _ _ _ TYPES OF MEAT

_ _ _ _ _ NERDS

_ _ _ _ _ UNIVERSITY ACCOMMODATIONS

_ _ _ _ _ AFRICAN PALM TREES

D R U M S

130.

ANTLERGRAM

The goal of antlergrams is to form as many words as you can using the letters in the moose's nose and antlers. Each letter can be used only once, which means you can form a word with two Ts only if there are two Ts in the puzzle. Each word must be three or more letters long and must contain the letter in the nose, along with any combination of the letters from the antlers. For the ultimate challenge, see if you can find the one 9-letter word that contains ALL the letters in the puzzle.

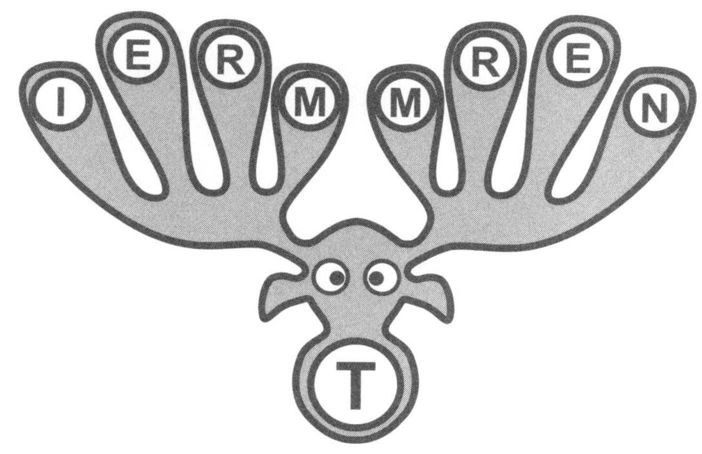

131.

CRYPTOGRAM

Each of the quotes below has been encrypted, with each letter of the alphabet substituted for a different letter. The substitutions are different for each puzzle. Use your code-breaking skills to discover the original quotation! (Hints: Start with short words—a one-letter word is usually A or I. Count the number of each letter—the most common letter in English is E, followed by T, A, O, I, and N, while the most common three-letter word is THE.)

1. V O ' N L N T V B U O V W V T W L T O O S L O
__ __ ' __

X Q P H K Q F X G V E E U Q O L K N Q H K
__ __

T S Q E B N O B H Q E V W X Q P O L I B V O W H Q J
__ __

L U Q O S B H M B H N Q U ' N M E L O B . —F L A B
__ __ __ __ __ __ __ __ __ __ __ __ __ __ ' __ __ __ __ __ __ __ . —__ __ __ __

K L H H X
__ __ __ __ __

2. P T R A J N S N S K N J , I F Y N M I T ' J N I D N J
__ __ __ __ __ __ __ __ __ __ __ __ , __ __ __ __ __ __ __ ' __ __ __ __ __ __

A X N X C O O , M I T K N U C F A I E C Y B T E
__ __ __ __ __ __ __ , __ __ __ __ __ __ __ __ __ __ __ __ __ __ __ __ __

R E N N G . —Y X W J O N R R Y X T O L
__ __ __ __ __ . —__ __ __ __ __ __ __ __ __ __ __ __ __ __

3. KLVVDXJII? ZKLZ'I XTZKDXO HTBJ

ZKLX KJLFZK LXN L VTTB HJHTBR.—

LFWJBZ IGKAJDZPJB

4. HXRRUN TBN XI JMNC T CTYYSJ

JTXIP TCR T WYSTR HXCR WNBXC

PS EMTCBN GUTENI.—TVPMSY VCFCSJC

5. EPD QMPA EPD'LU NUBBFMN PTS

AOUM ITT BOU MIWUC FM EPDL

JTIKQ JPPQ OIRU W.S. IHBUL

BOUW.—ILMPTS ZITWUL

6. OHTJE YRRB LGE EHG C ZDJMME IHHP

PHI, LGM RM YHT'M LGE MWJ YCI

HN WRF MCRB.—WJTDE YWJJBJD FWCY

132.

SUDOKU: MEDIUM

A sudoku puzzle is a type of logic puzzle. Although it uses numbers, no mathematics is involved. The grid below is divided into nine large squares, each of which is divided into nine smaller squares. Each large square contains all the digits from 1 to 9, with each digit appearing exactly once. Each horizontal row of the puzzle also contains each digit exactly once, and so does each vertical row. By carefully observing which numbers are missing from each row, column, or square, see if you can figure out which numbers go where. There's only one possible solution to each puzzle.

		4		6	9			
	3					8		
2			8		1			
	4	2	3			9	8	
	7						3	
	9	3			8	7	2	
			5		3			2
		6					7	
			4	7		3		

133.

SUDOKU: MEDIUM

A sudoku puzzle is a type of logic puzzle. Although it uses numbers, no mathematics is involved. The grid below is divided into nine large squares, each of which is divided into nine smaller squares. Each large square contains all the digits from 1 to 9, with each digit appearing exactly once. Each horizontal row of the puzzle also contains each digit exactly once, and so does each vertical row. By carefully observing which numbers are missing from each row, column, or square, see if you can figure out which numbers go where. There's only one possible solution to each puzzle.

		9	8	3			6	2
8					2		5	
		7			1	4		
5	2					3		
		1					2	5
		4	9			2		
	6		1					4
9	1			4	7	8		

CHRISTMAS MUSIC

1. The song "Christmas Time" was recorded and co-written by

   A. Bryan Adams
   B. Anne Murray
   C. Shania Twain
   D. Jann Arden

2. Who wrote the song "White Christmas"?

   A. Cole Porter
   B. Irving Berlin
   C. Percy Faith
   D. Randy Brooks

3. In the song "The Twelve Days of Christmas," my true love brought to me seven

   A. golden rings
   B. geese a-laying
   C. calling birds
   D. lords a-leaping
   E. swans a-swimming

[Answers: 1. = A. Bryan Adams; 2. = B. Irving Berlin; 3. = E. swans a-swimming]

134.

CATCH A WORD: COLOURS

In this type of puzzle, the answer appears in its correct order but may begin in the middle of a word and be interrupted by spaces and punctuation. For example: The Canadians were victorious in hockey once again. Can you find the names of ten colours hidden in the sentences below?

1. The vibe I get from that guy isn't good.
2. The house was positively drab, lacking in decoration.
3. Although the bean casserole was delicious, it wasn't worth the wind I got.
4. Hamlet couldn't tell whether the ghost of his father was demonic or angelic.
5. When he heard Thomas yell, Owen looked back and saw that they were being chased by a bear.
6. When Winslow hit Emma, he was sent to detention.
7. After having eaten no fewer than seven cannoli, Vera was stuffed.
8. Diane put the hair clip in Kate's locker, where she had taken it from.
9. The portions they're giving you are so meagre, you'll never get enough vitamin B.
10. His boot's new golden spur pleased the grizzled old cowboy.

135.

FIFTY WORDS FOR SNOW

All the words in the list below are hidden somewhere in the grid of letters. See if you can find them! Words may run in any direction, including diagonally, and spaces are ignored. When you've crossed off all the words, read the leftover letters in the grid (running left to right, from top to bottom) to reveal a hidden quote related to the puzzle's theme. getting an inch of snow is like winning ten cents in the lottery - bill watterson

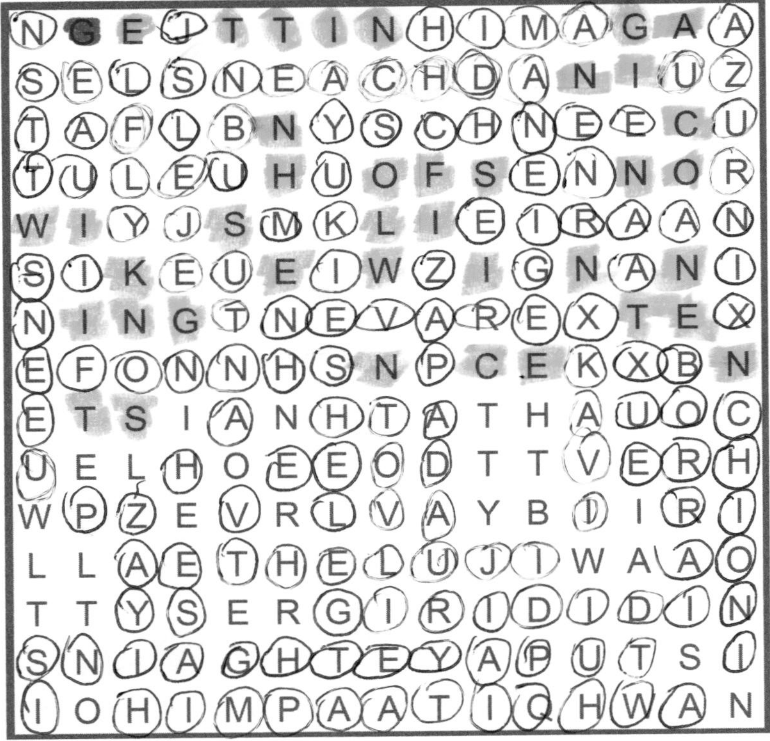

APUT
AZU
BORRA
CHIONI
EIRA
FONN
HIMA
HIMPAAT
INYEVE
IQHWA
IRI DIDI
KAVI
LUMI
NEF
NEIGE
NEU
NEVAR
NIX
NIYEBE
SALJU
SCHNEE
SNEEG
SNEACHDA
SNEEUW
SNIAGHTEY
TALJ
THELUJI
TOVET
TUYET
UPAS
XAAR
XUE
YUKI
ZAPADA
ZHAH

136.

THREE-WAY ANAGRAMS

These sets of three common words or phrases are all anagrams of each other. We've given you the definitions. Can you figure out the words?

Example

S K A T I N G	S T A K I N G	T A K I N G S
WINTER ACTIVITY	PLACING A BET	MONEY MADE

1. _ _ _ _ _ AIRCRAFT; _ _ _ _ _ MUESLI BRAND; _ _ _ _ _ BETWEEN INDIA AND CHINA
2. _ _ _ _ _ _ _ _ _ FLIRT; _ _ _ _ _ _ _ _ _ MAKES SMALLER; _ _ _ _ _ _ _ _ _ HEROICALLY FREED
3. _ _ _ _ _ _ _ MORE BRIGHT; _ _ _ _ _ _ _ SHRIVEL; _ _ _ _ _ _ _ TWIST IN PAIN
4. _ _ _ _ _ _ _ BRIEF PROMO; _ _ _ _ _ _ _ SPRING HOLIDAY; _ _ _ _ _ _ _ RETURN TO CHAIR
5. _ _ _ _ _ WALK SLOWLY; _ _ _ _ _ DAME NELLIE; _ _ _ _ _ POINT THE FINGER
6. _ _ _ _ _ STANDARD CAR; _ _ _ _ _ MOUNTAIN RANGE; _ _ _ _ _ HAMLET'S PEOPLE
7. _ _ _ _ _ _ _ SUSPEND TEASINGLY; _ _ _ _ _ _ _ BENT; _ _ _ _ _ _ _ BRITISH ACTRESS JACKSON
8. _ _ _ _ _ UNDERSTAND; _ _ _ _ _ GABRIEL, FOR ONE; _ _ _ _ _ JOINED LINES
9. _ _ _ _ _ _ _ BIRTHED SHEEP; _ _ _ _ _ _ _ CHAOS; _ _ _ _ _ _ _ ACCUSED
10. _ _ _ _ _ _ _ GLITTER; _ _ _ _ _ _ _ OUTCOME; _ _ _ _ _ _ _ LEAF SOUND

137.

PYRAMID POWER

The pyramid is made up of a series of words, each one containing the letters used in the word directly above it (the order of the letters may be changed) plus one new letter. Solve the clues to fill in the pyramid!

1. Iodine symbol — I
2. Circular number — P I
3. Very top — T I P
4. Saliva — S P I T
5. Assume — _ _ _ _ _
6. Sticky note — P O S T I T
7. Quiet stance — _ _ _ _ _ _ _
8. Accelerate (3 wds) — S T E P O N I T
9. Signed documents — _ _ _ _ _ _ _ _ _
10. Festive plant — P O I N S E T T I A

FILM QUIZ

Which of these movies was not filmed (or partly filmed) in Canada?

- **A.** *Interstellar*
- **B.** *Titanic*
- **C.** *The Fly*
- **D.** *My Big Fat Greek Wedding*
- **E.** *Jurassic World*

[Answer: E. *Jurassic World*]

138.

PYRAMID POWER

The pyramid is made up of a series of words, each one containing the letters used in the word directly above it (the order of the letters may be changed) plus one new letter. Solve the clues to fill in the pyramid!

1. Most common letter ___
2. Parisian "the" ___ ___
3. Language learning ___ ___ ___
4. Untruths ___ ___ ___ ___
5. Tiny land ___ ___ ___ ___ ___
6. Book names ___ ___ ___ ___ ___ ___
7. WCs ___ ___ ___ ___ ___ ___ ___
8. Places for TV shows ___ ___ ___ ___ ___ ___ ___ ___
9. Holiday hanging ___ ___ ___ ___ ___ ___ ___ ___ ___

TRUE OR FALSE?

1. The Chinese New Year is celebrated on the second new moon following the winter solstice.
2. In Italy, some people wear red underwear on New Year's Day so they'll have good luck all year.
3. The name of the traditional New Year's song "Auld Lang Syne" means "time heals everything."

[Answers: 1. true; 2. true; 3. false—it means "times gone by."]

139.

WORDPLAY: WORD TRANSFORMATIONS

These pairs of words each contain the same letters in the same order, except for one letter, which is the only one shown. Can you figure out the word pairs?

Example

S T O P — S T E P

HALT — STAIR

Answer: stop, step

1. _ _ _ _ _ _ E — _ _ _ _ _ _ T
   SMOCK — SCIENTIST

2. _ _ _ _ _ _ _ N — _ _ _ _ _ _ _ S
   SKIN PROTEIN — ARTWORKS

3. _ _ C _ _ _ _ _ _ — _ _ T _ _ _ _ _ _
   INSPIRE — FOLLOWERS

4. _ _ _ _ _ _ S — _ _ _ _ _ _ T
   UGLY — RETREAT

5. W I N D E D — W I N K E D
   BREATHLESS — CLOSED EYE

6. _ _ _ _ _ E — _ _ _ _ _ S
   FIGHTING SPORT — GOLD MEASURE

7. _ _ _ _ _ _ G — _ _ _ _ _ _ E
   DEFEATING UTTERLY — UNVARYING

8. _ _ _ H _ _ — _ _ _ T _ _
   CLEANS — SQUANDERS

9. _ _ _ _ _ _ A _ — _ _ _ _ _ _ E _
   PARTYING — FAIRGROUND RIDE

10. _ _ _ _ _ G _ — _ _ _ _ _ U _
    RETURN INJURY — INCOME

140.

SYLLABLANK

The solution to each of the following puzzles is a single six-letter word. We've chopped each word up into the smaller words listed below. Place the smaller words into the right positions on the blanks to discover the original words.

A A A A A ALE AN BE CON EGO FIN FOR GIN HE I IS LED MAD MAR ME POT RE RE SAT SUES TART TEE THE TIN TO

1. POLITICAL COMEDY ___ ___ ___ ___ ___ ___
2. PRECEDE ___ ___ ___ ___ ___ ___
3. CONCERNS ___ ___ ___ ___ ___ ___
4. PLAID ___ ___ ___ ___ ___ ___
5. BACK OF THE EYE ___ ___ ___ ___ ___ ___
6. SHINING LIGHT ___ ___ ___ ___ ___ ___
7. RECOVERED ___ ___ ___ ___ ___ ___
8. FEEL GUM PAIN ___ ___ ___ ___ ___ ___
9. FRENCH LADY ___ ___ ___ ___ ___ ___
10. PAGE EDGE ___ ___ ___ ___ ___ ___
11. LAST PERFORMANCE ___ ___ ___ ___ ___ ___
12. POPULAR TUBER ___ ___ ___ ___ ___ ___

SHAKESPEAREAN MOUNTAINS

Three of these mountains are found in Canada. Which one is not an actual mountain?

A. Mount Romeo
B. Mount Juliet
C. Mount Macbeth
D. Mount Falstaff

[Answer: D. Mount Falstaff]

141:

TOUCH OF FROST CROSSWORD

ACROSS

1. U.S. agriculture agcy.
4. Tells a tale
11. It's for the course
14. Noises of awe
15. Not on the ball
16. Word before Maria
17. Theatre finery
19. Tell a white one
20. Type of tape
21. Varieties
22. Shade of black
23. Fellow whose outfit is scattered throughout this puzzle
26. Stand on a soapbox
27. Medium string
28. Alternative to 60 Across
30. Wail
31. Petri dish substance
32. Little one
33. Ancient knowledge
36. Fruity chemical
38. A whole lot
39. Basic material
40. Magritte prop
41. Letter after pi
43. Bach track
45. Fowl houses
47. Mr. T's unit
48. It's set in stone
51. Killers album "Sam's ___"
52. Kirk opponent
55. Mideast ruler
56. One of the Gershwins
57. The fireside
60. Well contents
61. Asmara's country
62. Lead-in to a name
63. Denials
64. Place for plants
65. Abbv. before a date

DOWN

1. Some Explorers
2. Canadian musical poet
3. Science fiction giant
4. Regret
5. Some dashes
6. Woman from Mexico, e.g.
7. Off the map
8. Do poorly
9. "You are" in Spain
10. Girl band considered the first K-Pop group
11. Novel by James Franco
12. Industry that's up in the air
13. Gives a second term
18. Not at all
22. Boo-hoo
24. "Old MacDonald" refrain, repeated
25. Even though
26. Three-time Hart Trophy winner
28. Go grey
29. Queen Anne's lace is a wild one
31. Chowed down
33. Important real estate factor
34. Choral-orchestral work
35. Some library transactions
37. Healing spring
38. Opera topper
40. Spray-on product
42. Ad ___
44. Darken, in a way
45. Air Canada ___
46. Nina of blues
49. What you dress to
50. It goes with meet
52. Japanese kick
53. Hippie musical
54. Partner of sciences
57. 45 Across resident
58. What's-___-name
59. Approximately

1	2	3	■	4	5	6	7	8	9	10	■	11 P	12 A	13 R
14			■	15							■	16		E
17			18								■	19		E
20				■	■	21				■	22			L
23				24	25		■	■	■	26				E
■	■	27					■	28	29					C
■	■	■	30			■	31				■	32		T
33	34	35		■	36	37				■	38			S
39			■	40				■	41	42		■	■	■
43			44				■	45				46	■	■
47					■	■	■	48					49	50
51				■	52	53	54		■	■	55			
56			■	57					58	59				
60			■	61							■	62		
63			■	64							■	65		

142.

WORD JIGSAW

The words in these quotes and quips have been sliced up into pieces, so you can no longer see where one word begins and another ends. The order of the letters inside each piece is unchanged. Can you reassemble the word pieces and figure out the original phrase?

1. _ _ _ _   _ _   _ _ _   _ _ _ _   _ _ _   _ _ _ _
_ _   _ _ _ _ _ _ _   _ _ _ _ _   _ _ _ _ _
_ _ _ _ _ _ _   _ _ _ _   _   _ _ _ _ _ _ _?
_ _ _ _ _   _ _ _ _ _-_ _ _ _ _ _ _ _ _.

AROF DINGDOW GET HILESLI HOBIA NACHIM NEYSAN STROP TACLAU TDOYO THEFE TINGS TUCKW UCALL WHA

2. _ _ _   _ _   _ _ _ _ _ _ _ _   _ _ _
_ _ _ _ _ _ _ _ _   _ _ _ _ _ _ _ _   _ _ _ _ _
_ _ _ _?   _ _ _ _   _ _ _   _ _   _ _ _ _-
_ _ _ _'_ _   _ _ _ _ _   _ _ _ _ _   _ _ _ _ _
_ _ _   _ _ _   _ _ _ _ _ _.

ARTHE DTH ECK ETCHRIS EYLLS FESG OGIRAF OGOO RAN SOUTFO SPRESEN THEIRN TICK TMA TSE VERYYE WHYD YARES YONE

3. _   _ _ _ _ _ _   _ _   _ _ _ _ _ _ _   _ _ _ _
_ _ _ _-_ _ _ _   _ _ _   _ _ _ _ _ _ _ _ _.   _
_ _ _ _   _ _   _ _   _ _ _   _ _ _ _-_ _ _ _
_ _ _ _ _ _ _ _ _ _   _ _ _   _ _ _ _   _ _ _ _
_ _   _ _ _ _   _ _,   _ _ _   _ _   _
_ _ _ _ _ _ _ _ _   _ _ _ _ _   _ _   _ _   _ _ _ _ _
_ _ _ _   _ _ _ _   _ _   _ _ _ _
_ _ _ _ _ _ _ _ _ _. —_ _ _ _ _ _ _   _ _ _ _ _ _

APPIN BUTINAD DEPAR DKN EMTOW ENTPR ERSO EWOUL FORCH GPHYL IBO IFFER ILLER INTSOH LISD MASIT MEGIF OLDTH OOKITTO OWWHEN PUNWR RAPIT RIST ROTH TANDT THEGIF TMEN TMYB TOSTO TWRAP TWRAP UGH

4. _ _   _ _   _   _ _ _ _,   _ _ _ _-_ _ _ _ _ _,
_ _ _ _ _   _ _ _ _ _ _ _ _ _ _   _ _   _ _ _ _ _ _,
_ _ _ _   _ _ _ _ _   _ _ _ _ _   _ _
_ _ _ _ _ _ _ _ _   _ _   _ _ _ _ _ _ _   _ _ _
_ _ _ _ _ _,   _ _ _ _ _   _ _   _ _ _ _ _ _ _   _ _
_ _ _   _ _ _ _ _   _ _   _ _ _ _ _ _ _ _ _ _ _ _
_ _ _ _ _ _ _ _ _ _   _ _   _ _ _ _ _ _ _ _   _ _ _
_ _ _ _   _ _ _ _ _ _. _ _ _ _ _ _ _ _   _ _ _ _ _ _ _

ANDSOR ASE BLEAD CONTA DEDNO DHUMO DSOIR ENHAN ERE FECTI GIOU GOO HATWHI HERE HEWORL HINGST INGINT IREV ISE ISIN ISNOTH ITI JUST KENS LESDIC LETH MENTOFT ONIND RESI ROWT SAFA SASLA STIBLY TERAND UGH URCHAR

5. _ _ _ _ _   _ _   _ _ _ _   _ _ _   _ _ _ _   _ _ _
_ _ _ _ _ _   _ _ _   _ _ _ _ _
_ _ _ _ _ _ _ _ _ _ _   _ _   _   _ _ _ _ _
_ _ _ _ _   _ _ _ _ _ _ _ _ _. _ _ _ _   _ _ _ _ _ _ _

ACKEN ANDLO ASICING ENTSO FATRUL GIFT IME LYTHEB PEGBR REDI RYCHRI SOFT STMAS URE VEARES YMER

6. _ _ _ _ _ _ _ _ _   _ _   _ _ _ _   _   _ _ _   _ _
_ _ _   _ _ _ _ _ _ _ _ _ _   _ _   _ _ _   _ _ _
_ _ _ _,   _ _ _   _ _ _   _ _ _   _ _ _   _ _   _ _ _
_ _ _ _   _ _ _ _   _ _ _   _ _ _   _ _ _ _ _ _.

AYATT CHRI ESU EWOR FICEY GUYI HEFAT HEOF ITGE KANDT KEAD LTH NTH OUDOAL REDIT SISLI STMA THEC TSALL

143.

SKILLATHON

The goal is to find as many words as possible made up of the letters in the word or phrase below. Words must be made of four or more letters. No plurals allowed. Only one tense or form of a verb is permitted (if you find WALK, you can't also have WALKS, WALKED, WALKING, etc.). The exception is when two forms have different meanings—e.g., BORE and BORED.

APRICOT

Try to beat our experts. They found 40 words.

144.

REBUS

In these puzzles, the arrangement of the letters and symbols suggests a common word or expression. For example, this combination

COVER
GOING

is "going undercover" (the word GOING is under the word COVER—literally). See how many you can figure out.

1.  ICE

2.  WINTER

3.  FROST

4.  OUT

5.  CHRISTMAS

145.

WORDS × FIVE

This puzzle is similar to a crossword, but the five-letter answer to each clue is written twice—both across and down. So, if the solution to clue 1 is FLAME, you would write FLAME into the grid twice, from left to right and from top to bottom.

1	2	3	4	5
2				
3				
4				
5				

1. Monopoly and Clue
2. Help
3. Tropical fruit
4. Number of reindeer (without Rudolph)
5. A deadly sin

146.

WORDS × FIVE

This puzzle is similar to a crossword, but the five-letter answer to each clue is written twice—both across and down. So, if the solution to clue 1 is FLAME, you would write FLAME into the grid twice, from left to right and from top to bottom.

1. Shout with approval
2. Word of greeting
3. Comes before grease and room
4. Run off together
5. Paddled

147.

SUDOKU: MEDIUM

A sudoku puzzle is a type of logic puzzle. Although it uses numbers, no mathematics is involved. The grid below is divided into nine large squares, each of which is divided into nine smaller squares. Each large square contains all the digits from 1 to 9, with each digit appearing exactly once. Each horizontal row of the puzzle also contains each digit exactly once, and so does each vertical row. By carefully observing which numbers are missing from each row, column, or square, see if you can figure out which numbers go where. There's only one possible solution to each puzzle.

					3			4
	8	3				9		5
1			8	7			3	
8		1	9		6			
			3		5	2		9
	3			9	4			1
4		6				3	9	
9			2					

148.

SUDOKU: MEDIUM

A sudoku puzzle is a type of logic puzzle. Although it uses numbers, no mathematics is involved. The grid below is divided into nine large squares, each of which is divided into nine smaller squares. Each large square contains all the digits from 1 to 9, with each digit appearing exactly once. Each horizontal row of the puzzle also contains each digit exactly once, and so does each vertical row. By carefully observing which numbers are missing from each row, column, or square, see if you can figure out which numbers go where. There's only one possible solution to each puzzle.

3					7	6		
			1		3			7
	7		9	4		1		
8	9					3		
		7					1	4
		4		5	1		8	
5			6		9			
		6	2					3

149.

CRYPTOGRAM

Each of the quotes below has been encrypted, with each letter of the alphabet substituted for a different letter. The substitutions are different for each puzzle. Use your code-breaking skills to discover the original quotation! (Hints: Start with short words—a one-letter word is usually A or I. Count the number of each letter—the most common letter in English is E, followed by T, A, O, I, and N, while the most common three-letter word is THE.)

1. J F H H S W M E Z , B D H S M ' E F I S K M Y Z M E F C , J S X K S Q F B O F T F E I F F H S M L Z Z J F S R F E L ? — I Z F R J F O K S Y N F E Z

2. F N U S G L G F K T I K J U P K G C K L P U K F G Z Q U Z F G V Z Y U I K X C U G F K T T V H C X C F V P U J G Z G C I U . . . G Z C F K Z F T R . — S U J U F P G J K P F G Z

3. S M W V P O G Z L V Q V G G V W J Z Q P L V P L O X Y V W Q X V W Q H S A Z X X L E O U Q L V A Z R L S U Q G Z W V U P Z G W V P S A Z U N , P L Z G Z H E O U Q W Z A Z G Y Z F E G Z P L V W P L G Z Z S W V M V F S U N . — U V O G Z W R Z L E O X F V W

4. EVFQ WIE WLJVXT YHB JVSJVJWB,
WLB RVJCBHTB YVK LRNYV TWROJKJWQ.
YVK J'N VEW TRHB YPERW WLB
SEHNBH.—YFPBHW BJVTWBJV

5. R QCLP XE R DRGF GCTTZG FXEL
SDRS DILPZH QORHZGE ESGXPZ BDZV
SDZH LRV'S DXS IVZ RVISDZG.—
NXUUH LRVVIV

6. S YNOV QC IFSNOK NSDXV VXALEHOK
KAYYHFE IAF TYHEVSG ELFDNFC.
OAR S KAO'V ZOAR RXHV XN YAAZE
YSZN.—NQA TXSYSTE

150.

WINTER SPORTS

All the words in the list below are hidden somewhere in the grid of letters. See if you can find them! Words may run in any direction, including diagonally, and spaces are ignored. When you've crossed off all the words, read the leftover letters in the grid (running left to right, from top to bottom) to reveal a hidden quote related to the puzzle's theme.

C	S	D	A	E	R	I	A	L	Y	K	D	I	B	I
R	N	O	G	I	S	T	H	E	E	R	O	N	I	S
O	M	G	N	N	L	Y	K	S	A	P	O	G	A	K
S	O	S	O	O	R	C	T	O	W	T	N	S	T	I
S	G	L	R	H	O	E	B	R	E	I	E	N	H	J
C	U	E	D	H	Y	W	O	L	T	U	D	O	L	O
O	L	D	I	S	O	P	E	A	E	E	N	W	O	R
U	D	R	C	N	A	K	K	N	L	A	R	S	N	I
N	M	A	S	A	S	S	G	S	N	U	D	H	A	N
T	L	C	E	G	E	N	B	T	O	B	G	O	B	G
R	R	E	E	R	I	O	A	K	A	N	A	E	A	R
Y	M	A	U	L	B	N	D	A	L	E	G	A	N	N
O	N	G	R	F	R	E	E	S	T	Y	L	E	D	Y
M	I	U	S	K	I	B	A	L	L	E	T	O	Y	U
F	C	S	S	P	E	E	D	S	K	A	T	I	N	G

AERIAL
BANDY
BIATHLON
BOBSLED
CROSS COUNTRY
CURLING
DOGSLED RACE
FIGURE SKATING
FREESTYLE
HOCKEY
LUGE
MOGUL
NORDIC
SKELETON
SKI BALLET
SKIJORING
SNOWBOARD
SNOWSHOE
SPEED SKATING

151.

BEFORE AND AFTER

The words in each group have one thing in common: they all frequently appear either immediately before or immediately after the solution word. For example, if the group includes CHRISTMAS, APPLE, TRUNK, HOUSE, and FAMILY, the solution might be TREE (CHRISTMAS TREE, APPLE TREE, TREE TRUNK, TREE HOUSE, FAMILY TREE). When you've figured out all the solutions, read the first letter of each to discover the puzzle's secret theme.

1. FLED MURDER POLICE POTENTIAL PRIMARY PRIME PRINCIPAL SCIENTISTS STRONGLY _ _ _ _ _ _ _

2. BAFFLING CIPHER CODE COMPLETE GERMAN GREAT MACHINE UNRESOLVED WRAPPED _ _ _ _ _ _ _

3. ATTENTION BEHIND CONTACT FRIEND GETTING PROXIMITY RELATIONSHIPS TIES TOGETHER _ _ _ _ _

4. ANCIENT DAILY DANCE MATING MORNING OBJECTS PRACTICE SACRIFICE SATANIC _ _ _ _ _ _

5. BROWN CONTAINING MANILA PADDED PLEASE RETURN SEALED STAMPED WHITE _ _ _ _ _ _ _ _

6. DOLLAR FLOOR HAT LAYER PRIORITY PRIORITY SPEED TANK TEN _ _ _

152.

TREE CROSSWORD

ACROSS

2. Taxonomic suffix
4. Milky white gems
6. Town that is home to the National Air Force Museum of Canada
7. Calgary to Edmonton heading
8. "PS, I Love You" author Cecelia
10. Trace maker
12. Collections of files
14. Ornaments, e.g.
15. What comes before Wed.
16. Naval letters

DOWN

1. Seasonal song suggested by this puzzle's shape
2. Type of furnace
3. Argues (with)
4. And/___
5. "___ there!"
8. Prefix meaning "one quintillionth"
9. "___ Dominus" (Vivaldi piece)
10. What Santa carries in Paris
11. Summer sign
12. German domain name
13. Atomic symbol for tin

CHRISTMAS MOUNTAINS

In what province will you find North Pole Mountain, Mount St. Nicholas, and mountains named after the eight reindeer in the poem "A Visit from St. Nicholas"?

A. British Columbia
B. Alberta
C. Ontario
D. Nova Scotia
E. New Brunswick

[Answer: E. New Brunswick (There is no Mount Rudolph—the name was considered too commercial.)]

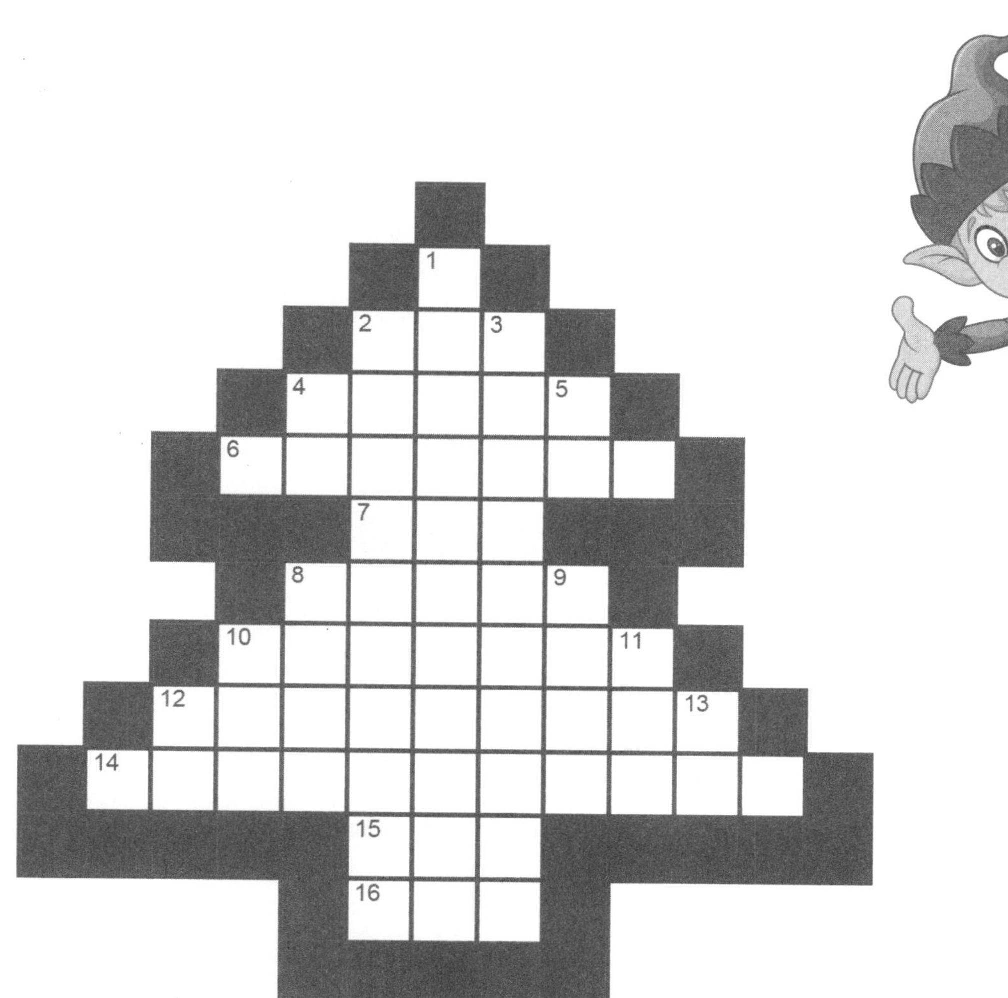
1
2
3
4
5
6
7
8
9
10
11
12
13
14
15
16

153.

MAPLE LEAF

The goal of this puzzle is to form as many words as you can, using the letters contained in the leaf. Each letter can be used only once, so you can create a word with two Ts only if there are two Ts in the leaf. Each word must be three or more letters long, and all words must contain the large central letter of the leaf, along with any mix of the letters around the outside. For the ultimate challenge, see if you can find the one 10-letter word that contains ALL the letters in the leaf.

NOVICE 3

DOUBLE-DOUBLE TAKE

Spot the difference: can you find the 8 changes?

NEW YEAR, NEW YOU

1. According to a 2015 poll, only 3 in 10 Canadians will make a New Year's resolution. Of that number, 73 percent eventually break them. Name the two resolutions among the following that are *not* among the top five for Canadians:

   A. Live a healthier lifestyle
   B. Spend less and save more money
   C. Spend more time with family and friends
   D. Read more
   E. Learn something new

2. The Jewish New Year is called:

   A. Hanukkah
   B. Passover
   C. Festivus
   D. Rosh Hashanah
   E. Sukkot

Answers:
1. B. Spend less and save more money and D. Read more;
2. D. Rosh Hashanah

ACTS OF KINDNESS

Since its publication in 1853, Charles Dickens' *A Christmas Carol* has inspired people to do good deeds—not just at Christmas time. Here are some acts of kindness to consider doing in the coming year:

1. Say something special to everyone you meet during the next 12 hours.
2. Send someone a small gift anonymously.
3. A little appreciation goes a long way—provide vitamin E for "encouragement."
4. Treat a friend to the movies . . . for no reason.
5. Call a lonely person.
6. Donate your gently used clothes or books to an organization.
7. Don't underestimate the power of a hug. Hug a friend!
8. Invite someone who lives alone to dinner.
9. Thank your brother or sister or cousin for a past kindness.
10. Paint a picture for someone.
11. Teach someone a new skill.
12. Call, email, or write a note to a long-lost friend or relative.
13. Send a personal thank-you note to someone who once helped you out.
14. Share a memory with a friend or relative.
15. Visit a shut-in friend.
16. Compliment someone on their clothing, their hair, or their smile.
17. Let a former teacher know how important he or she has been to you.
18. Make a point of welcoming someone to your school or neighbourhood.
19. Send an old photograph to a friend and explain what it means to you.
20. Share your smile. You'll discover that smiling is contagious.

SOLUTION NOVICE 3

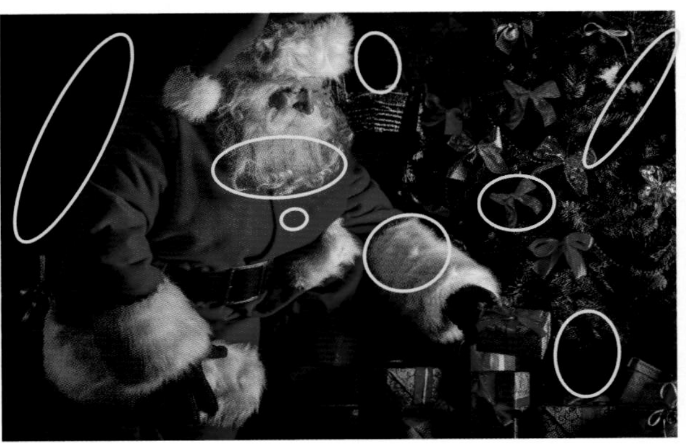

154.

ONE STEP AT A TIME

Change the word at the top to the word at the bottom by altering one letter at a time. Each change should produce a new word. We've provided clues to help you on your way.

P U R E

_ _ _ _ CONVINCED

_ _ _ _ IN PAIN

_ _ _ _ ARRANGE

_ _ _ _ CARBON PARTICLES

_ _ _ _ AMMUNITION

_ _ _ _ DISPLAY

S N O W

G O O D

_ _ _ _ ATTITUDE

_ _ _ _ AMERICAN FUNGUS

_ _ _ _ NOT STRONG

_ _ _ _ UNTAMED

W I L L

WHERE AM I?

Name a place in the world whose name is made up of three words or names, each with six letters.

[Answer: Prince Edward Island]

155.

CATCH A WORD: COUNTRIES 1

In this type of puzzle, the answer appears in its correct order but may begin in the middle of a word and be interrupted by spaces and punctuation. For example: The Canadians were victorious in hockey once again. Can you find the names of 10 countries hidden in the sentences below?

1. Queen Elizabeth I never was wed, entirely of her own volition.
2. The detective pursued a muscular gent in an unmarked white van.
3. How kind of you to offer us Siamese cats.
4. The wolf ran celebratory laps around its felled prey.
5. The Soviet naming system relies heavily on patronymics.
6. Not drinking enough water can worsen glandular problems.
7. Professor X scratched his chin and furrowed his brow.
8. This man can dance the can-can; can a dancer do that?
9. Spassky knew a lesser opponent would have taken his pawn.
10. Heidi Klum, ex-icon of *Sports Illustrated*, hosts many television shows.

156.

ANTLERGRAM

The goal of antlergrams is to form as many words as you can using the letters in the moose's nose and antlers. Each letter can be used only once, which means you can form a word with two Ts only if there are two Ts in the puzzle. Each word must be three or more letters long and must contain the letter in the nose, along with any combination of the letters from the antlers. For the ultimate challenge, see if you can find the one 9-letter word that contains ALL the letters in the puzzle.

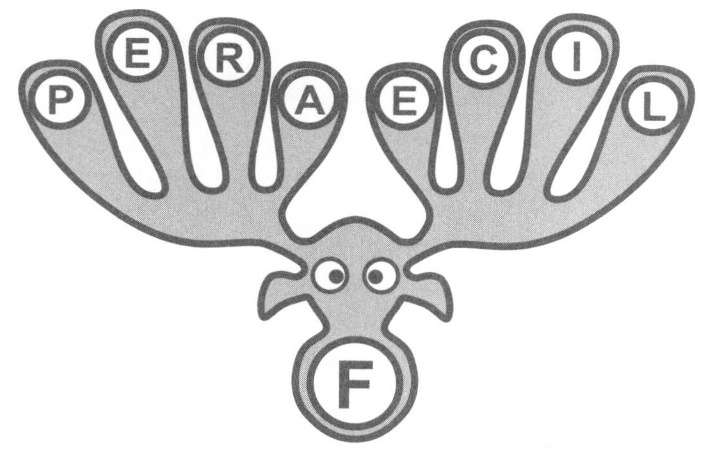

157.

PYRAMID POWER

The pyramid is made up of a series of words, each one containing the letters used in the word directly above it (the order of the letters may be changed) plus one new letter. Solve the clues to fill in the pyramid!

1. Letter number five ___
2. Sound of hesitation ___ ___
3. Germany's continent ___ ___ ___
4. South American country ___ ___ ___ ___
5. Burst forth ___ ___ ___ ___ ___
6. Fictional bear ___ ___ ___ ___ ___ ___
7. Delight ___ ___ ___ ___ ___ ___ ___
8. Camera hole ___ ___ ___ ___ ___ ___ ___ ___
9. Too early ___ ___ ___ ___ ___ ___ ___ ___ ___
10. Hearing aid (2 wds) ___ ___ ___ ___ ___ ___ ___ ___ ___ ___
11. Coldness or warmth ___ ___ ___ ___ ___ ___ ___ ___ ___ ___ ___

BOOK TRIVIA

Who wrote *Sunshine Sketches of a Little Town*? (Bonus points for naming the town in which the story is set and the real town it is based on.)

[Answer: Stephen Leacock. The book is set in the fictitious town of Mariposa, which is based on Orillia, Ontario.]

158.

PYRAMID POWER

The pyramid is made up of a series of words, each one containing the letters used in the word directly above it (the order of the letters may be changed) plus one new letter. Solve the clues to fill in the pyramid!

1. MC^2 ___
2. Disgusted sound ___ ___
3. Fresh ___ ___ ___
4. Made with needlework ___ ___ ___ ___
5. Burgundies ___ ___ ___ ___ ___
6. Body cords ___ ___ ___ ___ ___ ___
7. Bystander ___ ___ ___ ___ ___ ___ ___
8. Most blizzardy ___ ___ ___ ___ ___ ___ ___ ___
9. For cars in winter (2 wds) ___ ___ ___ ___ ___ ___ ___ ___ ___

SPOT THE LINK

What do these five things have in common?

A. funny goaltenders
B. unkind villagers
C. quirky relatives
D. old parliamentarians
E. silly toques

[Answer: In each pair of words, the first word begins with one letter of the alphabet and the second word begins with the following letter.]

159.

WORDS × SIX

This puzzle is similar to a crossword, but the six-letter answer to each clue is written twice—both across and down. So, if the solution to clue 1 is GOBLIN you would write GOBLIN in the grid two times, from left to right and from top to bottom.

1	2	3	4	5	6
2					
3					
4					
5					
6					

1. Ocean bottom
2. Make unreadable
3. Clear of guilt
4. Return like a ball
5. Proclamations
6. Loathe

160.

WORDS × SIX

This puzzle is similar to a crossword, but the six-letter answer to each clue is written twice—both across and down. So, if the solution to clue 1 is GOBLIN you would write GOBLIN in the grid two times, from left to right and from top to bottom.

1	2	3	4	5	6
2					
3					
4					
5					
6					

1. Have charisma
2. French dog
3. Cops
4. Newsroom boss
5. Cozy corner
6. Ogled

161.

HIDDEN TREE TOPPERS CROSSWORD

ACROSS

1. Chill
4. Turn on a point
9. Place for dogs
13. French cheese colour
15. "West Side Story" role
16. To me, en Paris
17. Thickening agent in the kitchen
19. Joyful shouts
20. Meshes with the group
21. Pavlovic of tennis
23. "___ got mail"
25. Villainous
28. Playwright David and others
30. Sid Meier series, for short
31. Bar beverage
32. Egyptian god of the horizon
33. Iberian river
36. Comedy starring Emma Stone
38. Right at sea
41. One who goes back and forth
44. When Hamlet meets his father's ghost
45. 559, to a Roman
49. Shiba ___
50. Pub. employees?
52. Tropical getaway
54. San Jose's country
58. Animal scents
59. "___ tale. Told by an idiot, full of sound and fury . . ."
60. Sudden
62. Click of the fingers
63. Sprinter's mistake
67. Spanish other
68. Type of bulb
69. Black-and-white cookie
70. Left hand keys
71. Makes jazzy noises
72. Young'un

DOWN

1. Law & Order's network
2. Nobel Prize–winning U.N. grp.
3. Eau de toilette, e.g.
4. Touches affectionately, as a puppy
5. Grant-___ (government funding)
6. Actress Lisi
7. Not prescrip.
8. Polynesian island
9. Person on the bill
10. Actresses Seyfried and Plummer
11. How one may screw up
12. Sue Grafton's "___ for Killer"
14. Steven's surname, in a children's cartoon
18. Proofreader's "ignore edit"
22. Delirious person
23. Peruvian singer Sumac
24. Sturdy tree
26. Skedaddle
27. Formal vote
29. Where Spongebob's pineapple is
34. "Godfather" enforcer
35. Banking inits.
37. Has as a sum
39. Subordinate of a pres.
40. Make public, as a grievance
41. Polaroid
42. Sprinkles with oil
43. Pastry filling
46. What Indy is searching for
47. Bother
48. Early IBMs
51. First passes
53. Outback birds
55. ___ the tongue
56. Kind of lily
57. ___ omen (Latin "God forbid")
61. Gym counts
62. "___ man walks into a bar . . ."
64. Arctic bird
65. Hiking gear company
66. Copper's friend, in a movie

1	2	3	■	■	4	5	6	7	8	■	9	10	11	12
13			14	■	15					■	16			
17				18						■	19			
■	■	20						■	21	22				■
23	24				■	25		26						27
28					29	■	■	30			■	31		
32				■	33	34	35		■	36	37			
■	■	■	38	39					40			■	■	■
41	42	43			■	44				■	45	46	47	48
49			■	50	51		■	■	52	53				
54			55				56	57	■	58				
■	59					■	60		61				■	■
62				■	63	64							65	66
67				■	68					■	69			
70				■	71					■	■	72		

CATS AND DOGS

1. Approximately how many pets are there in Canada?
   - A. 13 million
   - B. 26 million
   - C. 39 million

2. On average, cats sleep about how many hours a day?
   - A. 8 hours
   - B. 10 hours
   - C. 12 hours
   - D. 16 hours

3. How many teeth do normal adult dogs have?
   - A. 24 teeth
   - B. 36 teeth
   - C. 42 teeth
   - D. 48 teeth

4. Do cats have fewer or more teeth than dogs?

5. What is a dog's most highly developed sense?
   - A. taste
   - B. smell
   - C. hearing
   - D. sight

[Answers: 1. = B. 26 million; 2. = D. 16 hours; 3. = C. 42 teeth; 4. fewer—cats have only 30 teeth; 5. = smell]

162.

CATCH A WORD: COUNTRIES 2

In this type of puzzle, the answer appears in its correct order but may begin in the middle of a word and be interrupted by spaces and punctuation. For example: The Canadians were victorious in hockey once again. Can you find the names of 10 countries hidden in the sentences below?

1. Her genial, geriatric father was staying for tea.
2. The raja panders to all of his court.
3. Their World Cup defeat was painful to admit.
4. Sensationalism was a strategy P. T. Barnam employed in promoting his circus.
5. The dog misbehaved, having not been trained in the vital years.
6. De-emphasizing road safety could endanger many lives.
7. Gold, satin, diamonds, and all manner of treasures were presented to the visiting princess.
8. The waiter and his wife whisper under the table.
9. Through Bogota I wander, looking for souvenirs.
10. The teams would, for sport, tug a line of rope back and forth between them.

163.

NEW YEAR'S EVE

All the words in the list below are hidden somewhere in the grid of letters. See if you can find them! Words may run in any direction, including diagonally, and spaces are ignored. When you've crossed off all the words, read the leftover letters in the grid (running left to right, from top to bottom) to reveal a hidden quote related to the puzzle's theme.

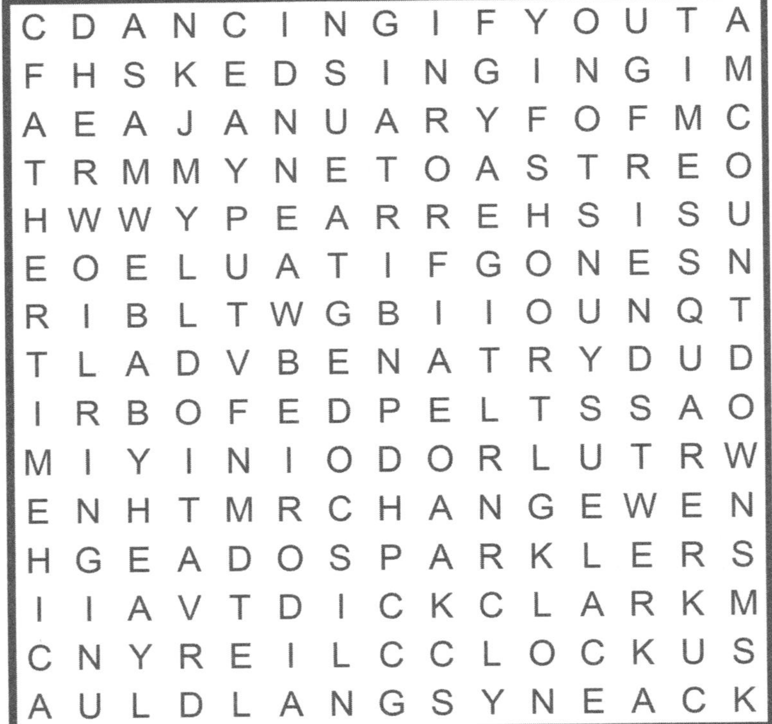

C	D	A	N	C	I	N	G	I	F	Y	O	U	T	A
F	H	S	K	E	D	S	I	N	G	I	N	G	I	M
A	E	A	J	A	N	U	A	R	Y	F	O	F	M	C
T	R	M	M	Y	N	E	T	O	A	S	T	R	E	O
H	W	W	Y	P	E	A	R	R	E	H	S	I	S	U
E	O	E	L	U	A	T	I	F	G	O	N	E	S	N
R	I	B	L	T	W	G	B	I	I	O	U	N	Q	T
T	L	A	D	V	B	E	N	A	T	R	Y	D	U	D
I	R	B	O	F	E	D	P	E	L	T	S	S	A	O
M	I	Y	I	N	I	O	D	O	R	L	U	T	R	W
E	N	H	T	M	R	C	H	A	N	G	E	W	E	N
H	G	E	A	D	O	S	P	A	R	K	L	E	R	S
I	I	A	V	T	D	I	C	K	C	L	A	R	K	M
C	N	Y	R	E	I	L	C	C	L	O	C	K	U	S
A	U	L	D	L	A	N	G	S	Y	N	E	A	C	K

AULD LANG SYNE
BABY
BALL
CHAMPAGNE
CHANGE
CLOCK
COUNTDOWN
DANCING
DICK CLARK
DROP
EVE
FATHER TIME
FIRST
FRIENDS
HAT
JANUARY
MIDNIGHT
PARTY
RING IN
SINGING
SPARKLERS
TIMES SQUARE
TOAST
TWELVE

164.

REBUS

In these puzzles, the arrangement of the letters and symbols suggests a common word or expression. For example, this combination

COVER
GOING

is "going undercover" (the word GOING is under the word COVER—literally). See how many you can figure out.

1. HAND
HAND
HAND = work
HAND
HAND

2. 

3. 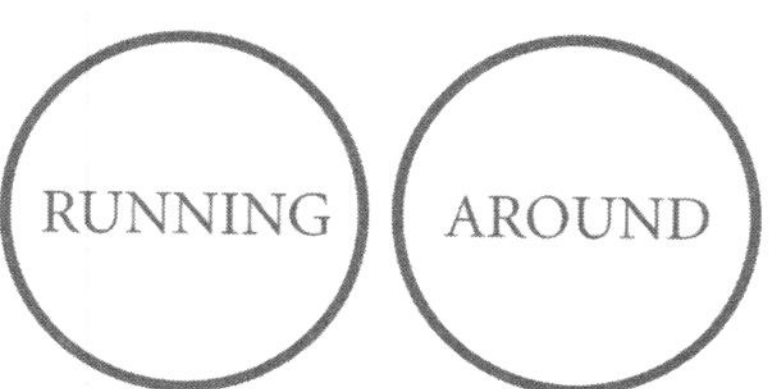

4. SOUP

5. ER
DD
LA

165.

LETTER DROP

The quotation by J. B. S. Haldane below has been written into a grid. Words run left to right, and each line wraps around to the line below. Sadly, the letters have all dropped out of the puzzle. All the letters are in the correct columns, but their order may have changed. Can you restore the letters to their proper places and discover the quote? Punctuation is still in its original position, and spaces between words are marked by black boxes. Remember, words don't end at the end of a line unless there's a black box there.

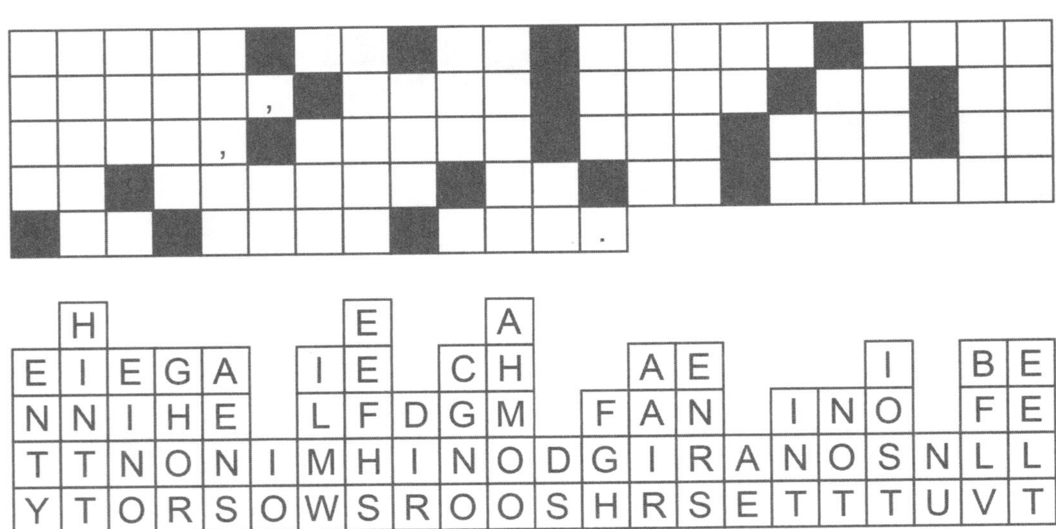

166.

SKILLATHON

The goal is to find as many words as possible made up of the letters in the word or phrase below. Words must be made of four or more letters. No plurals allowed. Only one tense or form of a verb is permitted (if you find WALK, you can't also have WALKS, WALKED, WALKING, etc.). The exception is when two forms have different meanings—e.g., BORE and BORED.

WILDERNESS

Try to beat our experts. They found 182 words.

167.

FESTIVE COLOURS CROSSWORD

ACROSS

1. Lawyer: Abbr.
4. Matthew 26 question
9. Whitish
13. Paired together
15. "___ Ghost" (Ondaatje novel)
17. Year-round, as a plant
18. Compare (to)
19. Dates
20. Gives the cold shoulder
22. The self
23. Texting pronoun
24. Spanish "the best"
26. Mideast ruler
27. Where "Cheers" is set
29. Abate
30. Loaf (about)
31. Stick on, as a wall
32. BB-gun model that Ralphie wants
34. Golfer Tony
36. Some breads
37. One of five in a song
41. Sci-fi guns
45. Fertilizer chemical
46. So, to a Scot
47. Nova Scotia university
48. Footnote word
49. Goethe play scored by Beethoven
51. Pelvic X-ray, for short
52. Rent
53. Neil Diamond's "I Am ___"
54. Stairwell unit
55. Vacations
57. First Disney girl
60. Four-door
61. Turning kitchen gadget
62. Sideswipe result
63. Ad ___ per aspera
64. Dealer's merch.

DOWN

1. Jungle-themed costume
2. Greek cafe
3. Maple syrup, before being refined
4. Ravel's "Piano Concerto ___ Major"
5. To be, in Barcelona
6. "___ my case!"
7. Even wee-er
8. Digits on a personnel card
9. Best buds
10. Singer DiFranco
11. At a frantic pace
12. Lament, poetically
14. ___-80 (old computer model)
16. Raucous sleeping person
21. Folk singer with wild hair
24. Slang for a western film
25. They shouldn't be broken
26. Milano of movies
28. Crone (var.)
33. Show a response
35. Flour moth genus
37. Pressures (into)
38. In sequence
39. Current that follows the wind
40. Most June babies
42. In the process of revision
43. Glued to one's seat
44. Combat engineers
50. Toothed (suffix)
53. Fails to be
54. "Thar ___ blows!"
56. Guy with goat legs
58. "___ the Memory of Childhood" (Georges Perec novel)
59. New Deal agcy.

1	2	3	■	4	5	6	7	8	■	9	10	11	12	■
13			14						■	15				16
17									■	18				
19				■	■	20			21		■	22		
23			■	24	25					■	26			
27			28			■	29			■	30			
31						■	32			33				
■	■	■	34			35	■	36				■	■	■
37	38	39					40	■	41			42	43	44
45				■	46			■	47					
48				■	49			50			■	51		
52			■	53					■	■	54			
55			56		■	57			58	59				
60					■	61								
■	62				■	63					■	64		

168.

SUDOKU: MEDIUM

A sudoku puzzle is a type of logic puzzle. Although it uses numbers, no mathematics is involved. The grid below is divided into nine large squares, each of which is divided into nine smaller squares. Each large square contains all the digits from 1 to 9, with each digit appearing exactly once. Each horizontal row of the puzzle also contains each digit exactly once, and so does each vertical row. By carefully observing which numbers are missing from each row, column, or square, see if you can figure out which numbers go where. There's only one possible solution to each puzzle.

			5	3				8
				4	8			6
		9				3		
1		3		6			8	
		2				9		
	6			5		2		1
		8				7		
2			3	8				
3				1	6			

169.

SUDOKU: MEDIUM

A sudoku puzzle is a type of logic puzzle. Although it uses numbers, no mathematics is involved. The grid below is divided into nine large squares, each of which is divided into nine smaller squares. Each large square contains all the digits from 1 to 9, with each digit appearing exactly once. Each horizontal row of the puzzle also contains each digit exactly once, and so does each vertical row. By carefully observing which numbers are missing from each row, column, or square, see if you can figure out which numbers go where. There's only one possible solution to each puzzle.

4	3				8		1	
							3	
1	6	9	4			8		
					1			3
7			6	8	2			9
8			5					
		1			4	6	9	2
	8							
	9		3				7	8

170.

BEFORE AND AFTER

The words in each group have one thing in common: they all frequently appear either immediately before or immediately after the solution word. For example, if the group includes CHRISTMAS, APPLE, TRUNK, HOUSE, and FAMILY, the solution might be TREE (CHRISTMAS TREE, APPLE TREE, TREE TRUNK, TREE HOUSE, FAMILY TREE). When you've figured out all the solutions, read the first letter of each to discover the puzzle's secret theme.

1.	BELT	BLAZING	DIRECT	_ _ _
	HAT	HOT	RISE	
	SET	SHONE	TROPICAL	
2.	CHEMICAL	GROWTH	MANAGER	_ _ _ _ _
	NATIVE	POWER	PROCESSING	
	SPECIES	TREATMENT	TREES	
3.	ACID	CHECK	CLOUDS	_ _ _ _
	COLD	DRIVING	FALL	
	FOREST	FREEZING	HEAVY	
4.	BENEFICIAL	BITING	BUZZING	_ _ _ _ _ _ _
	DEAD	PESKY	REPEL	
	STINGING	SWARMING	WINGED	
5.	HUMAN	LOVERS	MOTHER	_ _ _ _ _ _
	PHOTOGRAPHY	RESERVE	SECOND	
	SENSITIVE	TRAIL	TRUE	
6.	ACCUSTOMED	CROPS	HAIR	_ _ _ _
	LARGER	LOUDER	OLD	
	PLANTS	QUICKLY	WORSE	

171.

THE NUTCRACKER

All the words in the list below are hidden somewhere in the grid of letters. See if you can find them! Words may run in any direction, including diagonally, and spaces are ignored. When you've crossed off all the words, read the leftover letters in the grid (running left to right, from top to bottom) to reveal a hidden quote related to the puzzle's theme.

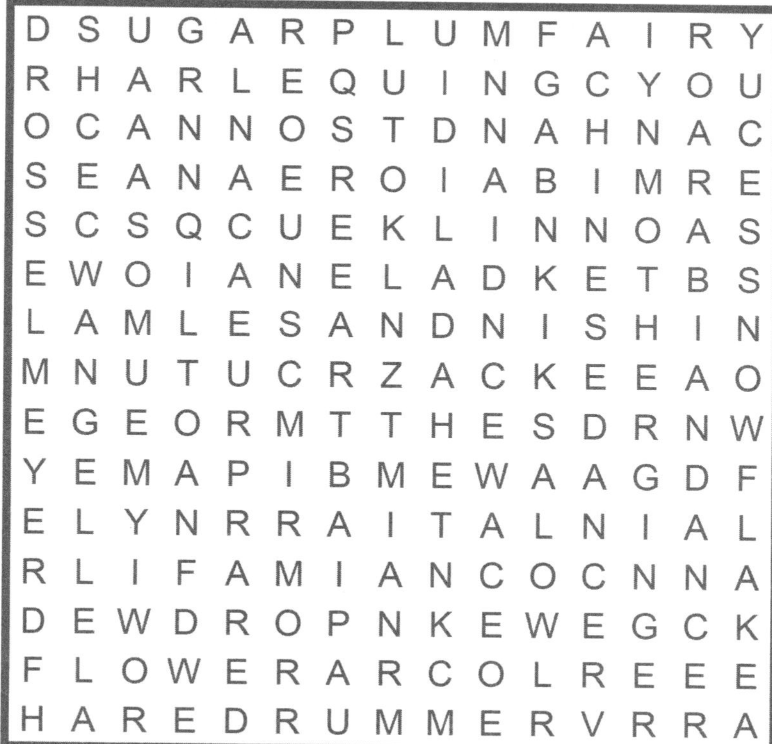

D	S	U	G	A	R	P	L	U	M	F	A	I	R	Y
R	H	A	R	L	E	Q	U	I	N	G	C	Y	O	U
O	C	A	N	N	O	S	T	D	N	A	H	N	A	C
S	E	A	N	A	E	R	O	I	A	B	I	M	R	E
S	C	S	Q	C	U	E	K	L	I	N	N	O	A	S
E	W	O	I	A	N	E	L	A	D	K	E	T	B	S
L	A	M	L	E	S	A	N	D	N	I	S	H	I	N
M	N	U	T	U	C	R	Z	A	C	K	E	E	A	O
E	G	E	O	R	M	T	T	H	E	S	D	R	N	W
Y	E	M	A	P	I	B	M	E	W	A	A	G	D	F
E	L	Y	N	R	R	A	I	T	A	L	N	I	A	L
R	L	I	F	A	M	I	A	N	C	O	C	N	N	A
D	E	W	D	R	O	P	N	K	E	W	E	G	C	K
F	L	O	W	E	R	A	R	C	O	L	R	E	E	E
H	A	R	E	D	R	U	M	M	E	R	V	R	R	A

ANGEL
ARABIAN DANCER
CHINESE DANCER
CLARA
COLUMBINE
DEWDROP
DROSSELMEYER
FLOWER
FRITZ
HARE DRUMMER
HARLEQUIN
MICE
MOTHER GINGER
MOUSE KING
OWL
PRINCE
SNOWFLAKE
SOLDIER
SUGARPLUM FAIRY

172.

WORDS × FIVE

This puzzle is similar to a crossword, but the five-letter answer to each clue is written twice—both across and down. So, if the solution to clue 1 is FLAME, you would write FLAME into the grid twice, from left to right and from top to bottom.

1	2	3	4	5
2				
3				
4				
5				

1. Loaf
2. Bounce back
3. VIPs
4. Where a marriage starts
5. Colouring experts

173.

WORDS × FIVE

This puzzle is similar to a crossword, but the five-letter answer to each clue is written twice—both across and down. So, if the solution to clue 1 is FLAME, you would write FLAME into the grid twice, from left to right and from top to bottom.

1	2	3	4	5
2				
3				
4				
5				

1. Schoolyard ball game
2. Portion out
3. Shout before defib
4. Awwstralian awwnimal
5. Scarecrow innards

174.

MAPLE LEAF

The goal of this puzzle is to form as many words as you can, using the letters contained in the leaf. Each letter can be used only once, so you can create a word with two Ts only if there are two Ts in the leaf. Each word must be three or more letters long, and all words must contain the large central letter of the leaf, along with any mix of the letters around the outside. For the ultimate challenge, see if you can find the one 10-letter word that contains ALL the letters in the leaf.

175.

SYLLABLANK

The solution to each of the following puzzles is a single seven-letter word. We've chopped each word up into the smaller words listed below. Place the smaller words into the right positions on the blanks to discover the original words.

A A A A A ABLE AM ANT BAN BE CAB DAM DON EM GINS GO HE I I I I I
ME NET NOW ON OR OR OVER PENS PER RE RILL RING WART WE

1. FRIENDLY __ __   __   __ __ __ __
2. BEGINNINGS __ __   __   __ __ __ __
3. PM'S INNER CIRCLE __ __ __   __   __ __ __
4. RETIREE PAYMENT __ __ __ __   __   __ __
5. STEEL BALL __ __   __   __ __ __ __
6. NON-EXISTENT PLACE __ __ __   __ __   __ __
7. GIANT APE __ __   __ __ __ __   __
8. IMPRESS __ __ __ __   __   __ __
9. WHEN BATTLES OCCUR __ __ __ __   __   __ __
10. GIVE UP __   __ __ __   __ __ __
11. ABOVE A KING __ __   __ __ __   __ __
12. FIRM __   __ __ __   __ __ __

CHRISTMAS MOVIES

Name the Canadian actor featured in each of the following Christmas-themed movies:

1. *All I Want for Christmas*
2. *Dr. Seuss' How the Grinch Stole Christmas*
3. *Home Alone*

[Answers: 1. Leslie Nielsen; 2. Jim Carrey; 3. John Candy]

176.

CRYPTOGRAM

Each of the quotes below has been encrypted, with each letter of the alphabet substituted for a different letter. The substitutions are different for each puzzle. Use your code-breaking skills to discover the original quotation! (Hints: Start with short words—a one-letter word is usually A or I. Count the number of each letter—the commonest letter in English is E, followed by T, A, O, I, and N, while the most common three-letter word is THE.)

1. B XNQBX HESWCT XBOYZK BD QNOE GNMWK FZWC DZWQ'EW CND KN YNNT, BCT KQIUBDZSVWK FSDZ QNOE UENPXWIK FZWC DZWQ'EW CND KN PBT. —BECNXT Z. YXBKYNF

2. M QIGHIRD LXWWIG VMZ YL CPIJ DPI LXJ YL LPYJYJT, DPI UGIIAI YL UKSCYJT, DPI UYGVL MGI LYJTYJT, MJV DPI KMCJ WSCIG YL UGSNIJ. —OMWIL VIJD

3. E ZSXXLKLXR XSSX RMS ALBBLTPWRO LC SJSDO YZZYDRPCLRO; EC YZRLKLXR XSSX RMS YZZYDRPCLRO LC SJSDO ALBBLTPWRO.—ILCXRYC TMPDTMLWW

4. D UMFJQM VDN LT NTER. OTE, DN WVM FTTI, ZENW YUJLC NTER WT WVM UMFJQM.—WVTZDN IMRRMU

5. CAGCLU TNVYJOQ LNKV QZQFJQU; ZNXRJZY CZZNLU XRQF UN FKPR.—NUPCV GJASQ

COUNT ME IN

What unusual quality do the following words share?

A. height
B. flour
C. tern
D. thirsty
E. once

[Answer: Remove one letter from each word and they all spell a numeral.]

177.

SANTA'S ADDRESS CROSSWORD

ACROSS

1. One of the fairies in "Sleeping Beauty"
6. Blood typing system
9. Length from fingertip to elbow
14. Glove type
15. "Wicked!"
16. Past, archaically
17. Spanish friend
18. Where Santa lives, according to the Danes
20. Newfoundland island whose name means "codfish"
22. Visit
23. Chop (off)
24. Gets dark
25. Casablanca's location, briefly
28. "Love Will Keep Us ___"
32. In, in a sense
34. Web address
35. Italian dough
36. "Funeral Blues" poet
37. Go crazy
39. Type of belief
42. Adjust the strings
43. "M*A*S*H" setting
45. Ontario region
47. Race unit
48. Extract
50. Save for later
52. Formal support
53. Domesticate
55. Engine speed letters
56. Beige shade
57. Greenery
61. It's 90 degrees N, 0 degrees W
65. Forever, to a poet
66. How some plays are performed
67. Hockey target
68. Audacity
69. Second years
70. Word after yellow, red, or black
71. It really blows

DOWN

1. Extra weight
2. Holy man
3. Relating to the ear
4. Amuse (someone)
5. Mexican salamander
6. Member of a Toronto team
7. Keep from doing something
8. Ukrainian port
9. Game related to rummy
10. Like some ducklings
11. Constrictor
12. B&B
13. "The Mary Tyler Moore Show" newsreader
19. Italian peak
21. Ladybug's food
24. Stroll (about)
25. Parameters, in math
26. Ill-___ (unlucky)
27. Go back on a deal
28. Homeland of the real St. Nicholas
29. Baltimore bird
30. Steinem or Estefan
31. ". . . ___ I saw Elba"
33. Shack
38. Gumshoe, for short
40. Get
41. Public transit nickname
44. A cockney drops them
46. Where Santa lives, according to the Finns
49. Rain covering
51. Cheery person
54. Subatomic particles
56. Scratch into stone
57. Greek salad topping
58. How plans may go
59. Fell in
60. Observer
61. Domine dirige ___
62. Lennon's love
63. Grave letters?
64. Stan of Spider-Man

1	2	3	4	5	■	6	7	8	■	9	10	11	12	13
14					■	15			■	16				
17					■	18			19					
20					21		■	22				■	■	■
■	■	■	23			■	24				■	25	26	27
28	29	30				31		■	32		33			
34			■	35				■	■	36				
37			38	■	39			40	41	■	42			
43				44	■	■	45			46	■	47		
48					49	■	50				51			
52			■	53		54		■	55			■	■	■
■	■	■	56				■	57				58	59	60
61	62	63					64		■	65				
66					■	67			■	68				
69					■	70			■	71				

178.

TREE DECORATIONS

All the words in the list below are hidden somewhere in the grid of letters. See if you can find them! Words may run in any direction, including diagonally, and spaces are ignored. When you've crossed off all the words, read the leftover letters in the grid (running left to right, from top to bottom) to reveal a hidden quote related to the puzzle's theme.

ANGEL
BELLS
BOW
CANDLES
CANDY CANE
GARLAND
ICICLE
IVY
LAWN FIGURES
LIGHTS
MISTLETOE
ORNAMENT
PINECONE
POINSETTIA
SLEIGH
SNOWFLAKE
SNOWMEN
STAR
STOCKING
TINSEL
TREE
WREATH

179.

ONE STEP AT A TIME

Change the word at the top to the word at the bottom by altering one letter at a time. Each change should produce a new word. We've provided clues to help you on your way.

S A N T A

_ _ _ _ _ LARGE, FLAT FISH

_ _ _ _ _ JAPANESE COMIC

_ _ _ _ _ FISHING BOAT

_ _ _ _ _ SPASMS OF PAIN

_ _ _ _ _ SHEETS OF GLASS

_ _ _ _ _ COVERS IN CONCRETE

_ _ _ _ _ ROOF EDGES

E L V E S

S A C K

_ _ _ _ UNWELL

_ _ _ _ CAPSIZE

_ _ _ _ BAD BEHAVIOURS

_ _ _ _ AIRTIGHT CONTAINERS

_ _ _ _ LOTS

T O Y S

"MY TRUE LOVE"

According to the traditional song "The Twelve Days of Christmas," how many presents did my true love send to me *in total*?

[Answer: 364 presents]

180.

ANTLERGRAM

The goal of antlergrams is to form as many words as you can using the letters in the moose's nose and antlers. Each letter can be used only once, which means you can form a word with two Ts only if there are two Ts in the puzzle. Each word must be three or more letters long and must contain the letter in the nose, along with any combination of the letters from the antlers. For the ultimate challenge, see if you can find the one 9-letter word that contains ALL the letters in the puzzle.

NOVICE 4

DOUBLE-DOUBLE TAKE

Spot the difference: can you find the 8 changes?

HOLIDAY TUNES

1. This was the first Christmas album by a male artist to debut at number one:

A. Frank Sinatra's *A Jolly Christmas*
B. Bruce Cockburn's *Christmas*
C. Justin Bieber's *Under the Mistletoe*
D. Michael Bublé's *Christmas*
E. Johnny Mathis' *Christmas Album*

2. Who are the two reindeer from the song "Rudolph the Red-Nosed Reindeer" named after weather phenomena?

3. In 2008, Anne Murray released her seventh Christmas album. It was the Canadian singer's last release before retiring:

A. *The Season Will Never Grow Old*
B. *Anne Murray's Christmas Album*
C. *What a Wonderful Christmas*
D. *Best of the Season*
E. *Christmas Wishes*

4. Name the Christmas songs with these initials:

A. IBTLALLC
B. AIWFCIMTFT
C. HYAMLC
D. SCICTT
E. FTS

5. Name the Christmas songs that these lines are from:

A. I brought some corn for popping
B. If only in my dreams
C. So hurry down the chimney tonight
D. Faithful friends who are dear to us
E. Pretend that he is Parson Brown

Answers:
1. C. Justin Bieber's *Under the Mistletoe*
2. Donner and Blitzen. In German, their names mean "thunder" and "lightning".
3. B. *Anne Murray's Christmas Album*
4. A. "It's Beginning to Look a Lot Like Christmas"
B. "All I Want for Christmas Is My Two Front Teeth"
C. "Have Yourself a Merry Little Christmas"
D. "Santa Claus Is Coming to Town"
E. "Frosty the Snowman"
5. A. "Let It Snow"
B. "I'll Be Home for Christmas"
C. "Santa Baby"
D. "Have Yourself a Merry Little Christmas"
E. "Winter Wonderland"

SOLUTION NOVICE 4

181.

REBUS

In these puzzles, the arrangement of the letters and symbols suggests a common word or expression. For example, this combination

COVER
GOING

is "going undercover" (the word GOING is under the word COVER—literally). See how many you can figure out.

1. COLD

2. NEW ◎ YEAR

3. SNOW

4. THE
   ———
   MISTLETOE

5. kings kings kings

6. C
   H
   I
   M
   N
   E
   Y

182.

SUDKOKU: MEDIUM

A sudoku puzzle is a type of logic puzzle. Although it uses numbers, no mathematics is involved. The grid below is divided into nine large squares, each of which is divided into nine smaller squares. Each large square contains all the digits from 1 to 9, with each digit appearing exactly once. Each horizontal row of the puzzle also contains each digit exactly once, and so does each vertical row. By carefully observing which numbers are missing from each row, column, or square, see if you can figure out which numbers go where. There's only one possible solution to each puzzle.

	8			7		4		6
		5	9				2	
6							1	
		1						4
9	3		5		7		6	2
2						9		
	1							3
	4				2	6		
3		9		4			8	

183.

SUDOKU: MEDIUM

A sudoku puzzle is a type of logic puzzle. Although it uses numbers, no mathematics is involved. The grid below is divided into nine large squares, each of which is divided into nine smaller squares. Each large square contains all the digits from 1 to 9, with each digit appearing exactly once. Each horizontal row of the puzzle also contains each digit exactly once, and so does each vertical row. By carefully observing which numbers are missing from each row, column, or square, see if you can figure out which numbers go where. There's only one possible solution to each puzzle.

	8		2		9	5		
2		1				3		4
								8
9		6		2				
			8		7			
				9		2		1
6								
1		5				9		3
		2	1		8		4	

184.

PYRAMID POWER

The pyramid is made up of a series of words, each one containing the letters used in the word directly above it (the order of the letters may be changed) plus one new letter. Solve the clues to fill in the pyramid!

1. Gravity force — G
2. Silver symbol — A G
3. Playground game — T A G
4. Biting fly — G N A T
5. Star handler — _ _ _ _ _
6. Gem — G A R N E T
7. Make larger — _ _ _ _ _ _ _
8. Create power — _ _ _ _ _ _ _ _
9. Youths — _ _ _ _ _ _ _ _ _
10. Accords — _ _ _ _ _ _ _ _ _ _

BRAIN TEASER

Brad and Noelle both have some oranges. If Brad gives Noelle an orange, they will both have the same number of oranges. If Noelle gives Brad an orange, Brad will have twice as many as Noelle. How many oranges do they each have?

[Answer: Brad has seven oranges and Noelle has five oranges.]

185.

PYRAMID POWER

The pyramid is made up of a series of words, each one containing the letters used in the word directly above it (the order of the letters may be changed) plus one new letter. Solve the clues to fill in the pyramid!

1. Toy chain backward letter ___
2. Sun god ___ ___
3. Listener ___ ___ ___
4. Scorch ___ ___ ___ ___
5. Horses ___ ___ ___ ___ ___
6. Gets more weapons ___ ___ ___ ___ ___ ___
7. Food growers ___ ___ ___ ___ ___ ___ ___
8. Below elbows ___ ___ ___ ___ ___ ___ ___ ___
9. Readies disk again ___ ___ ___ ___ ___ ___ ___ ___ ___
10. Yukon ground ___ ___ ___ ___ ___ ___ ___ ___ ___ ___

GEOGRAPHY QUIZ

Which of these cities is closest to St. John's, Newfoundland and Labrador?

A. Dublin, Ireland
B. Miami, Florida
C. Thunder Bay, Ontario

[Answer: A. Dublin, Ireland]

186.

SKILLATHON

The goal is to find as many words as possible made up of the letters in the word or phrase below. Words must be made of four or more letters. No plurals allowed. Only one tense or form of a verb is permitted (if you find WALK, you can't also have WALKS, WALKED, WALKING, etc.). The exception is when two forms have different meanings—e.g., BORE and BORED.

DOUBLE-DOUBLE

Try to beat our experts. They found 51 words.

187.

MAPLE LEAF

The goal of this puzzle is to form as many words as you can, using the letters contained in the leaf. Each letter can be used only once, so you can create a word with two Ts only if there are two Ts in the leaf. Each word must be three or more letters long, and all words must contain the large central letter of the leaf, along with any mix of the letters around the outside. For the ultimate challenge, see if you can find the one 10-letter word that contains ALL the letters in the leaf.

188.

BRR . . . CROSSWORD

ACROSS

1. They're equal to 0.3 metres
5. Word before 1, 29, 48, and 68 Across and 4, 9, 53, and 57 Down
9. Go downhill
13. Hokkaido people
14. In progress
16. Bear
17. Verb type (abbr.)
18. Having rolled "r"s
19. Range in the home
20. Garlic relatives
22. Esmerelda claimed it
24. Zellweger of "Bridget Jones's Diary"
26. Vacation, for short
27. Repeated affirmation
29. Experienced
33. Bee beginning
34. "Great" pope
36. Deathly prefix
38. Actress Davis
40. Swedish "said"
42. Bring down
43. Tezuka Boy
45. Jolly laughs
47. Alternative to St.
48. Put at ease
50. German songs
52. Steering device
53. Gunfire
54. Hand-held woodworking tool
59. Strait between Egypt and Saudi Arabia
62. "___ the Garden Wall" (children's TV series)
63. Shirley and others
65. South Pacific island
66. Thalia was one of comedy
67. Serpent deities
68. Partner of response
69. Biblical prophet
70. Noggin
71. Word after book or split

DOWN

1. Tank
2. "___ kleine Nachtmusik"
3. Agrees to (a contract)
4. Foolish person
5. Yellow car
6. Handy
7. ___ del Rio (Spanish town)
8. Worf's portrayer
9. Take on, as a burden
10. Mountain flower
11. Continuously
12. Refuse
15. First name in astronomy
21. Retro console
23. Like the titular Roger
25. Baseball amts.
27. Baba ___
28. Religious dem.
29. Brought forth
30. Reluctant
31. Quito resident
32. Gosling thriller
35. Lion of Oz
37. Unique situation
39. Fancy wardrobes
41. ". . . mi, fa, ___ ti . . ."
44. End ___ era
46. Residue
49. The skin is the largest
51. Show, showily
53. Sit and worry
54. Robin Cook novel
55. Haploid cell
56. Mexican money
57. Pic
58. Ancient Indian kingdom
60. "___ Lang Syne"
61. Guitarist Cline
64. Dir. from Toronto to D.C.

1	2	3	4	■	5	6	7	8	■	■	9	10	11	12
13				■	14				15	■	16			
17				■	18					■	19			
20				21	■	22				23				
■	■	24			25		■	■	26			■	■	■
27	28					■	29	30				31	32	■
33			■	34		35			■	36				37
38			39	■	40				41	■	42			
43				44	■	45				46	■	47		
■	48				49			■	50		51			
■	■	■	52			■	■	53					■	■
54	55	56				57	58		■	59			60	61
62				■	63				64	■	65			
66				■	67					■	68			
69				■	■	70				■	71			

189.

LETTER DROP

The quotation by Agatha Christie below has been written into a grid. Words run left to right, and each line wraps around to the line below. Sadly, the letters have all dropped out of the puzzle. All the letters are in the correct columns, but their order may have changed. Can you restore the letters to their proper places and discover the quote? Punctuation is still in its original position, and spaces between words are marked by black boxes. Remember, words don't end at the end of a line unless there's a black box there.

RING IN THE NEW!

1. What is New Year's Eve called in Scotland?

2. Which city hosts the first major New Year's Eve celebration each year?

3. Which one of the following is *not* among the top ten New Year's resolutions?

   A. get more organized
   B. stop smoking
   C. exercise more
   D. stop making resolutions
   E. save money

4. About how many pounds of confetti do organizers drop on the New Year's Eve crowd in New York City's Times Square?

   A. 1,000 pounds
   B. 1,500 pounds
   C. 2,000 pounds
   D. 5,000 pounds

[Answers: 1. Hogmanay; 2. Sydney, Australia; 3. = D. stop making resolutions; 4. = C. 2,000 pounds]

190.

WORD JIGSAW

The words in these quotes and quips have been sliced up into pieces, so you can no longer see where one word begins and another ends. The order of the letters inside each piece is unchanged. Can you reassemble the word pieces and figure out the original phrase?

1.

ABUM ALO ANGOU ASHO ATSA CKE DBUM ETSNE GNTH ICKER ITSLI KEALIT KEBUM MIN ONTLI OPLED PERS PERST PERSTI RIMAR RSTOME RTCUT SIDONT TDEMET TICKERIS TIN TLESI TOFPE VERH YSHEYL

2.

ANPRO ELVESI ETHEH FIRELET ISON MOURS OUSE SINC TALI USWAR VERB

3.

DFEE DROBER EANDO EARES ECRE EGRAV EMATE ETOTH LSAFE LTAK NGCR RHAVI TBRAULT THER THERSI TSIWIL

4. _ _ _ _ _ _ _   _ _ _ _   _ _   _ _ _ _ _   _ _ _
_ _ _ _   _ _ _ _ _   _ _ _ _ _ _ _   _ _ _ _ _ _
_ _ _   _ _ _   _ _ _ _ _ _ _ _ _ _.   _ _ _ _ _,
_ _   _ _ _ _ _ _,   _ _ _   _ _ _ _   _ _ _ _ _
_ _ _ _ _ _ _.

AREO DFIGU DOCT EIGH ELLUST EOFC HEREA HOAREO LIONPE NLYR OPLEW ORST OUN OURSE REO RES TTHES VENMIL VERSE VERW

5. _   _ _ _ _   _ _ _ _   _ _ _ _   _ _ _ _ _ _
_ _ _ _ _ _   _ _   _ _,   _ _ _   _   _ _ _ _
_ _ _   _ _ _ _ _   _ _   _ _ _ _   _ _ _ _ _ _
_ _ _ _ _ _ _   _   _ _ _ _   _ _   _ _ _   _ _ _
_ _ _ _   "_ _ _ _ _ _ _ _ _." — _ _ _ _ _ _ _
_ _ _ _ _ _

AITTW ARTIN BUTIW DTHIN ECAU ETRIM EWHE GSHAP HTDEM ILIK KETOU KSTO NGOO ORDFO OWEE PENTOME RTNIG SEILI SETHEW TELLAN YONEB

6. _ _ _ _ _ _ _ _   _ _ _   _ _ _ _ _
_ _ _   _ _ _ _   _ _ _ _ _ _ _ _ _
_ _   _ _ _ _ _ _ _ _ _ _ _   _ _ _
_ _ _ _ _ _ _ _ _ _.   _   _ _ _ _ _ _
_ _ _ _ _ _   _ _   _ _ _ _ _,   _ _ _ _ _
_ _ _ _ _   _ _   _ _ _ _   _ _ _ _ _ _ _ _
_ _   _ _   _ _   _ _ _ _ _ _ _ _ _. — _ _ _ _
_ _ _ _ _ _ _ _

ANDTE ARSAR DKUR DOAFT EBOTH ELFPRE ERWAR FERTOLA FRUS GUPTO HAUSTIO HEREIS HTER INCET LAUG LEANIN LESSC NANDEX NEGUT NIMYS NSESTO RESPO TRATIO TVON UGHS

191.

BEFORE AND AFTER

The words in each group have one thing in common: they all frequently appear either immediately before or immediately after the solution word. For example, if the group includes CHRISTMAS, APPLE, TRUNK, HOUSE, and FAMILY, the solution might be TREE (CHRISTMAS TREE, APPLE TREE, TREE TRUNK, TREE HOUSE, FAMILY TREE). When you've figured out all the solutions, read the first letter of each to discover the puzzle's secret theme.

1. APPLIED CLEAR DRIES FINAL GLOSS NAIL OLD PICTURE REMOVER _ _ _ _ _ _ _

2. BLUNT DIGITAL MAKER MUSICAL PANEL SCIENTIFIC STRINGED SURVEY USEFUL _ _ _ _ _ _ _ _ _ _

3. AGE BOY FASHIONED FOLKS FRIEND GUARD PLAIN TESTAMENT YEARS _ _ _

4. CLASSROOM DANCE IMPORTANT LEARNED LIFE MUSIC PIANO PRIVATE VALUABLE _ _ _ _ _ _ _

5. BREAD COOKING FASHION LANGUAGE OPERA RENAISSANCE RESTAURANT SAUSAGE WINE _ _ _ _ _ _ _

6. BRACE CREW MASSAGE PAIN SCRAWNY SLENDER STIFF SURGERY TURTLE _ _ _ _

192.

SANTA'S WORKSHOP

All the words in the list below are hidden somewhere in the grid of letters. See if you can find them! Words may run in any direction, including diagonally, and spaces are ignored. When you've crossed off all the words, read the leftover letters in the grid (running left to right, from top to bottom) to reveal a hidden quote related to the puzzle's theme.

Y	H	O	U	B	B	N	O	R	T	H	P	O	L	E
E	E	M	T	S	T	E	E	N	S	T	N	I	C	K
R	L	I	L	N	O	T	A	C	I	R	Y	Y	O	U
B	P	L	E	T	T	E	M	R	S	C	L	A	U	S
R	E	K	G	I	V	I	N	G	D	N	E	O	T	P
B	R	N	A	U	G	H	T	Y	O	U	P	T	I	M
S	S	T	E	L	L	E	I	N	G	A	Y	Y	O	S
T	U	B	B	E	L	T	B	U	C	K	L	E	E	C
O	T	O	E	B	W	H	H	T	Y	L	S	I	A	H
C	O	O	A	L	G	N	H	T	O	A	K	S	C	I
K	Y	T	L	I	V	G	D	J	A	O	U	A	L	M
I	S	S	E	S	I	E	I	S	O	C	O	C	I	N
N	M	L	I	N	R	N	S	C	G	T	O	K	S	E
G	S	T	O	P	R	E	S	E	N	T	W	N	T	Y
F	A	T	H	E	R	C	H	R	I	S	T	M	A	S

BEARD
BELLS
BELT BUCKLE
BOOTS
CHIMNEY
COOKIES
ELVES
FATHER CHRISTMAS
GIVING

HELPERS
JOLLY
LIST
MILK
MRS CLAUS
NAUGHTY
NICE
NIGHTCAP
NORTH POLE

PRESENT
RED
SACK
SLEIGH
ST NICK
STABLE
STOCKING
TOYS

193.

CATCH A WORD: ANIMALS

In this type of puzzle, the answer appears in its correct order but may begin in the middle of a word and be interrupted by spaces and punctuation. For example: The Canadi<u>ans were</u> victorious in hockey once again. Can you find the names of ten animals hidden in the sentences below?

1. As she sprinted from the predator, she began to pant. Her legs were tired.
2. If you want respect, you gotta be a real man!
3. You may want to add salt to taste.
4. The heist is on. We'll go at midnight.
5. The professional boxer punched Muhammad Ali on the nose.
6. The potluck was a success. Corn on the cob rated highly with the visitors.
7. The concerned citizens watched the fireman drill into the collapsed building.
8. He placed a decoy *Otello* record by the speaker so no one would know he was partaking of Verdi's *Rigoletto* instead.
9. Despite his skills as a magician, prestige remained out of reach.
10. The blaze branded him with a nasty sickle-shaped scar.

194.

ONE STEP AT A TIME

Change the word at the top to the word at the bottom by altering one letter at a time. Each change should produce a new word. We've provided clues to help you on your way.

Y U L E

__ __ __ __ STUBBORN ANIMAL

__ __ __ __ FACIAL DOT

__ __ __ __ ATOMIC AMOUNTS

__ __ __ __ ONLINE LAUGHS

L O G S

D E C K

__ __ __ __ WATERFOWL

__ __ __ __ FAMOUS FINN

__ __ __ __ BOAT BODY

H A L L

HAPPY HANUKKAH

1. What Hanukkah game is based on an old German gambling game?
   - **A.** mah-jong
   - **B.** canasta
   - **C.** pinochle
   - **D.** cribbage
   - **E.** dreidel

2. According to the *Canadian Oxford Dictionary*, which are the two accepted spellings of Hanukkah?
   - **A.** Hanukkah and Chanukah
   - **B.** Hanukkah and Chanukkah
   - **C.** Hanukkah and Hanukah
   - **D.** Hanukkah and Hannukkah

[Answers: 1. = E. dreidel; 2. = A. Hanukkah and Chanukah]

195.

TRIPLE MEANINGS

Many English words have multiple meanings. Here, we've given three different definitions that each describe the same word. Can you figure out the words?

1.	INJURED SKIN	EAT SHRUBS	BRUSH LIGHTLY	________
2.	LOWER HEAD	BIRD	IMMERSE	________
3.	HOGWASH	POPE'S DECREE	ACT VIOLENTLY	________
4.	DELICATE	DISMOUNT	KINDLE	________
5.	FISH	DEEP	BAND INSTRUMENT	________
6.	SHUT UP	TRESS	CANAL SECTION	________
7.	PAPER LAYER	TRAVEL	WORK AT	________
8.	COOK	FISH	CHIP	________
9.	PUSH	MEDIA	BESEECH	________

TRUE OR FALSE?

1. Canada has the world's longest coastline.
2. Montreal is the world's second largest (by population) French-speaking city.
3. Abraham Lincoln was president of the United States when Canada became a country.
4. The United States purchased Alaska from Russia the year British Columbia entered Confederation.

[Answers: 1. true; 2. true; 3. false; 4. false—The United States purchased Alaska in 1867. British Columbia entered Confederation in 1871.]

196.

TRIPLE MEANINGS

Many English words have multiple meanings. Here, we've given three different definitions that each describe the same word. Can you figure out the words?

1.	BILL	TEST	TICK	________
2.	ABLE	TIN	TOILET	________
3.	SMALL FLAG	LIFTING DEVICE	ASIAN FRUIT	________
4.	ESCAPE	INSECT	TRAVEL HIGH	________
5.	STONE	AIRCRAFT	SPRAY	________
6.	LETTERING	BASIN	SPRING	________
7.	SKIN SPOT	BURROWER	CHEMICAL QUANTITY	________
8.	LAME	CONTEST	HUNTED ANIMALS	________
9.	CONNECT	METAL LOOP	TORCH	________

RIDDLES

1. What gets wet when drying?
2. Throw away the outside and cook the inside. Then eat the outside and throw away the inside. What is it?
3. What word becomes shorter when you add two letters to it?

[Answers: 1. a towel; 2. corn on the cob; 3. the word *short*]

197.

SUDOKU: HARD

A sudoku puzzle is a type of logic puzzle. Although it uses numbers, no mathematics is involved. The grid below is divided into nine large squares, each of which is divided into nine smaller squares. Each large square contains all the digits from 1 to 9, with each digit appearing exactly once. Each horizontal row of the puzzle also contains each digit exactly once, and so does each vertical row. By carefully observing which numbers are missing from each row, column, or square, see if you can figure out which numbers go where. There's only one possible solution to each puzzle.

		5		6	4	1	3	
4							2	
3					1			
	8					6		
6			7		2			3
		9					8	
			9					4
	3							7
	6	4	3	1		5		

198.

SUDOKU: HARD

A sudoku puzzle is a type of logic puzzle. Although it uses numbers, no mathematics is involved. The grid below is divided into nine large squares, each of which is divided into nine smaller squares. Each large square contains all the digits from 1 to 9, with each digit appearing exactly once. Each horizontal row of the puzzle also contains each digit exactly once, and so does each vertical row. By carefully observing which numbers are missing from each row, column, or square, see if you can figure out which numbers go where. There's only one possible solution to each puzzle.

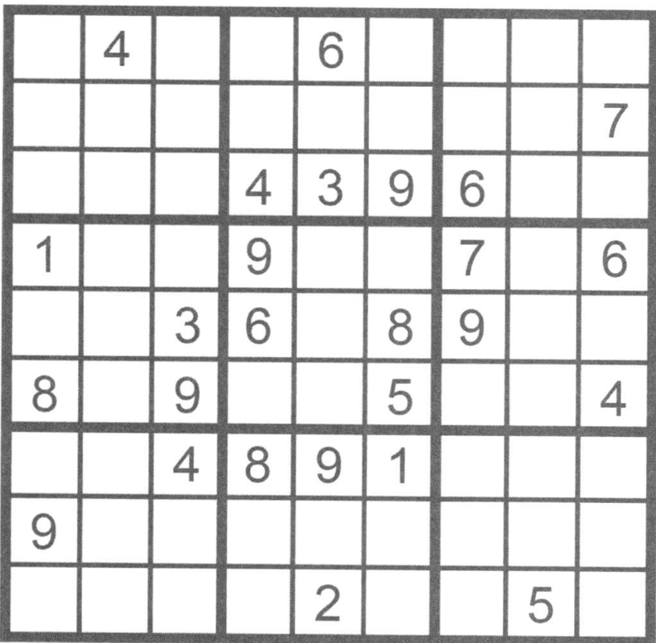

	4			6				
								7
			4	3	9	6		
1			9			7		6
		3	6		8	9		
8		9			5			4
		4	8	9	1			
9								
				2			5	

199.

“COLD OUTSIDE” CROSSWORD

ACROSS

1. Earth
5. Bad state of mind
11. Boxing org.
14. Winged, as an insect
15. Suspects
16. Eye, to a poet
17. Venti, at Starbucks
18. Negative attitude
19. Never in Germany
20. With 42 Across, Simon & Garfunkel song
22. Opposite of dis
23. Web traffic inits.
24. Passover celebrations
26. Sault ___ Marie
29. Pascal is one
32. Three basic subjects, for short
33. With 42 Across, Doors song
35. Tristan’s love
38. Squeaks by, with “out”
39. Bolt in athletics
41. Type of file
42. Word that completes the songs in this puzzle
44. Search for leftovers
46. Beloved (Northern English)
47. Salinger heroine
48. Military decoration letters
49. Lathered
52. Make a typo, say
54. Part of a play
55. What Obi-Wan sensed in the Force
62. The golden ratio
63. Curly pasta
64. Word after aloe
65. Not anti
66. Pertaining to Norse mythology
67. Cupid counterpart
68. Coin in Kyoto
69. Laurel genus
70. Neck part

DOWN

1. Name of Queen Victoria’s dog
2. Pelvic bones
3. Heckle
4. Comedians Anthony and Parker
5. Bring shame to
6. “Como ___ usted?”
7. Former Domino’s Pizza mascot
8. “Picnic” author William
9. Surround sound name
10. Comfortable shoes
11. With 42 Across, song popularly covered by the Eurythmics
12. Rose of “Sleeping Beauty”
13. Helps, in a way
21. Alone in France
25. Go on monotonously
26. Seethe
27. Polynesian carving
28. Change, as to a document
30. Medical tubes
31. Make fun of
34. Bar, in legalese
35. With 42 Across, Gil Scott-Heron song
36. Crib
37. Type of pwr.
40. Suffix with phon
43. Visine measure
45. Punch or kick
49. Maudlin
50. Earthy yellow
51. The D in LED
53. One of the Teen Titans
56. Wake
57. Stackable soups
58. Combined, to a Montrealer
59. Tiber tributary
60. Cut out
61. Comfort

1	2	3	4	■	5	6	7	8	9	10	■	11	12	13
14				■	15						■	16		
17				■	18						■	19		
20				21							■	22		
■	■	■	23			■	■	■	24		25			
26	27	28	■	29		30	31	■	■	32			■	■
33			34					■	35				36	37
38				■	39			40		■	41			
42				43		■	44			45				
■	■	46			■	■	47				■	48		
49	50				51	■	■	■	52		53	■	■	■
54			■	55		56	57	58				59	60	61
62			■	63						■	64			
65			■	66						■	67			
68			■	69						■	70			

200.

WORDS × SIX

This puzzle is similar to a crossword, but the six-letter answer to each clue is written twice—both across and down. So, if the solution to clue 1 is GOBLIN, you would write GOBLIN into the grid twice, from left to right and from top to bottom.

1	2	3	4	5	6
2					
3					
4					
5					
6					

1. Daily delivery
2. Set of notes
3. Wagered
4. Removing
5. Settle a score
6. Below windows

201.

WORDS × SIX

This puzzle is similar to a crossword, but the six-letter answer to each clue is written twice—both across and down. So, if the solution to clue 1 is GOBLIN, you would write GOBLIN into the grid twice, from left to right and from top to bottom.

1	2	3	4	5	6
2					
3					
4					
5					
6					

1. British potato chips
2. Holiday site
3. Maker of money
4. Origin
5. Short version
6. Anxiety

202.

TWELVE DAYS OF CHRISTMAS

All the words in the list below are hidden somewhere in the grid of letters. See if you can find them! Words may run in any direction, including diagonally, and spaces are ignored. When you've crossed off all the words, read the leftover letters in the grid (running left to right, from top to bottom) to reveal a hidden quote related to the puzzle's theme.

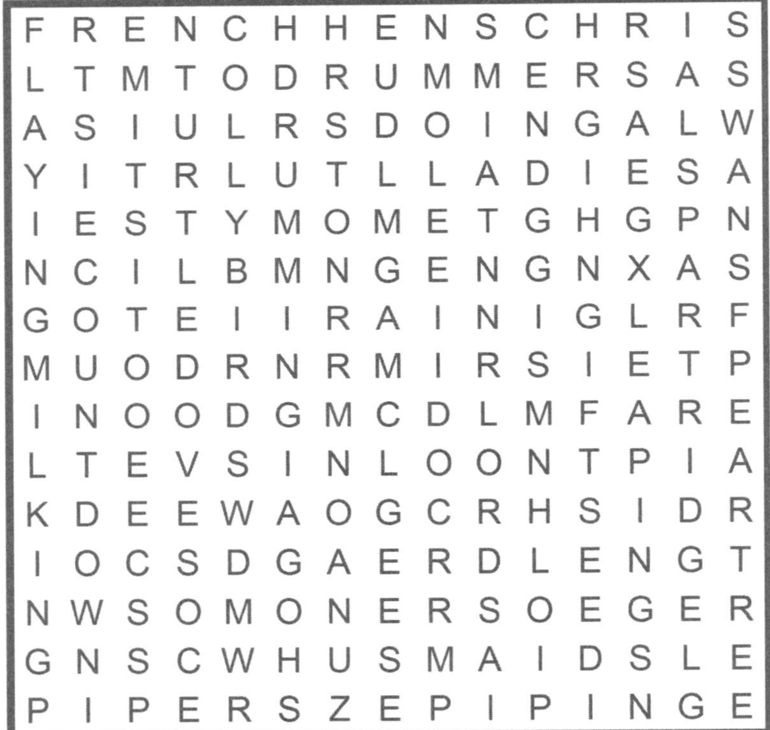

COLLY BIRDS
COUNTDOWN
COWS
DANCING
DRUMMERS
DRUMMING
FRENCH HENS
GEESE
GIFTS
GOLD RINGS
LADIES
LAYING
LEAPING
LORDS
MAIDS
MILKING
PARTRIDGE
PEAR TREE
PIPERS
PIPING
SWANS
SWIMMING
TURTLEDOVES

203.

MAPLE LEAF

The goal of this puzzle is to form as many words as you can, using the letters contained in the leaf. Each letter can be used only once, so you can create a word with two Ts only if there are two Ts in the leaf. Each word must be three or more letters long, and all words must contain the large central letter of the leaf, along with any mix of the letters around the outside. For the ultimate challenge, see if you can find the one 10-letter word that contains ALL the letters in the leaf.

204.

WORD JIGSAW

The words in these quotes and quips have been sliced up into pieces, so you can no longer see where one word begins and another ends. The order of the letters inside each piece is unchanged. Can you reassemble the word pieces and figure out the original phrase?

1. ____'_ ___ ___ ___ ___
____ _____? _ _____.

ADFO ANDB RICK RYOUR TEE THAB TSRED WHA

2. _____'_ __ ____ _____ __
___ ___ ___ _____ ______. —
_____ ________

EFAMI ESNOS EWHOL INFELD INGA LYJER ORTH RYSE SFUNF THER UCHTH

3. _ _______ _____ _____
____ _ ___. ___ ______
____, "_'__ _____ ___, ___
___'_ _____ ________."

ABLEW ABOO ALKSIN ARMAN ERVEY HING LLS OUB SAYSI STERC TANYT THEB TOABAR TSTAR UTDON

4. __ _______ ____ ___ ____
___ ____ ____ _ ______
___, ____ ___ ____ ______?

AVEYO CUPH EHEADW EHIT FFEE GED IFSO ITHACO MEON NMUG SYOUO UBEE VERTH

IN JEOPARDY

On an episode of the TV quiz show Jeopardy! *a contestant lost all his winnings after failing at Canadian geography. Below are the "answers" he missed. Do you know the questions?*

1. The swan is a symbol of this Ontario city; each year, white and black swans are released into the Avon River.
2. This Alberta resort was the first municipality to be incorporated within a Canadian national park.
3. In 1992 this city's velodrome, built for the Olympic Games, was transformed into an environmental biodome.
4. Residents of this Saskatchewan city are called Moose Javians.

[Questions: 1. What is Stratford? (The contestant guessed Edmonton); 2. What is Banff? (He picked Whistler); 3. What is Montreal? (He came up empty); 4. What is Moose Jaw? (He hit his button and guessed Winnipeg)]

205.

REBUS

In these puzzles, the arrangement of the letters and symbols suggests a common word or expression. For example, this combination

COVER
GOING

is "going undercover" (the word GOING is under the word COVER—literally). See how many you can figure out.

1. PERFORMANCE
   PERFORMANCE

2. AGE (AGE) AGE

3. YOUR LOSSE-

4. ↓
   WRITTEN

5. 1 difficulty

206.

ANTLERGRAM

The goal of antlergrams is to form as many words as you can using the letters in the moose's nose and antlers. Each letter can be used only once, which means you can form a word with two Ts only if there are two Ts in the puzzle. Each word must be three or more letters long and must contain the letter in the nose along with any combination of the letters from the antlers. For the ultimate challenge, see if you can find the one 9-letter word that contains ALL the letters in the puzzle.

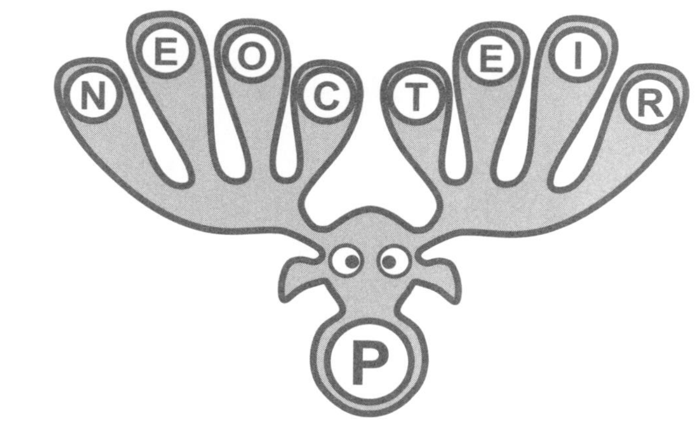

207.

PYRAMID POWER

The pyramid is made up of a series of words, each one containing the letters used in the word directly above it (the order of the letters may be changed) plus one new letter. Solve the clues to fill in the pyramid!

1. University abbrev. ___
2. Ancient city ___ ___
3. Go fast ___ ___ ___
4. Change direction ___ ___ ___ ___
5. Piano tweaker ___ ___ ___ ___ ___
6. Hills, flowers, animals ___ ___ ___ ___ ___ ___
7. Mythological creature ___ ___ ___ ___ ___ ___ ___
8. Shorten ___ ___ ___ ___ ___ ___ ___ ___
9. Wary ___ ___ ___ ___ ___ ___ ___ ___ ___

BRAIN TEASERS

A. A wheel has ten spokes. How many spaces does it have between the spokes?

B. A woman and her daughter have the same digits in their ages but in reverse. A year ago the mother was twice as old as her daughter was. How old are they now?

C. Find a number whose double exceeds its half by 99.

[Answers: A = ten; B = 73 and 37; C = 66]

EXPERT 1

DOUBLE-DOUBLE TAKE

Spot the difference: can you find the 12 changes?

HOLIDAY TRADITIONS

1. Who among these actors has not played Ebenezer Scrooge?

   A. Albert Finney
   B. George C. Scott
   C. Jim Carrey
   D. Michael Caine
   E. Ryan Gosling

2. Charles Dickens considered several other names before deciding on Tiny Tim for the character in *A Christmas Carol.* Name the three contenders:

   A. Puny Pete
   B. Cheerful Charlie
   C. Small Sam
   D. Tiny Theodore
   E. Little Larry

3. Arrange the most popular card-sending holidays in the order of number of cards sent:

   A. Valentine's Day
   B. Easter
   C. Christmas
   D. Mother's Day
   E. Father's Day

SOLUTION EXPERT 1

Answers:
1. E. Ryan Gosling;
2. A. Puny Pete,
C. Small Sam,
E. Little Larry;
3. C. Christmas (most cards sent),
A. Valentine's Day, D. Mother's Day,
E. Father's Day,
B. Easter

208.

PYRAMID POWER

The pyramid is made up of a series of words, each one containing the letters used in the word directly above it (the order of the letters may be changed) plus one new letter. Solve the clues to fill in the pyramid!

1. Entertainment TV ___
2. Canadian "huh?" ___ ___
3. Skirt bottom ___ ___ ___
4. Mosquito protector ___ ___ ___ ___
5. Embarrassment ___ ___ ___ ___ ___
6. Containers for sultanas? ___ ___ ___ ___ ___ ___
7. Military strolls ___ ___ ___ ___ ___ ___ ___
8. Soft wool ___ ___ ___ ___ ___ ___ ___ ___
9. Repeat competitions ___ ___ ___ ___ ___ ___ ___ ___ ___
10. Home of the *Guardian* ___ ___ ___ ___ ___ ___ ___ ___ ___ ___

TIPS FOR HOLIDAY DECORATING

1. Pick a theme and set a budget.
2. Recruit helpers and clean your house the day *before* you decorate.
3. Tackle the biggest job first—while you have energy.
4. Put away or dispose of packing boxes and materials as you go along.
5. Take photos of displays that you want to recreate next year.

209.

SKILLATHON

The goal is to find as many words as possible made up of the letters in the word or phrase below. Words must be made of four or more letters. No plurals allowed. Only one tense or form of a verb is permitted (if you find WALK, you can't also have WALKS, WALKED, WALKING, etc.). The exception is when two forms have different meanings—e.g., BORE and BORED.

NEWFOUNDLAND

Try to beat our experts. They found 144 words.

210.

SYLLABLANK

The solution to each of the following puzzles is a single ten-letter word. We've chopped each word up into the smaller words listed below. Place the smaller words into the right positions on the blanks to discover the original words.

AN ANT ANTS AS BE BIT CON DIAL DISC DISH DISH GENE GRAM HA HER I I I
IN MAR ON ONE OR OVER PER PRIM PRO RATE RE RE RING SHED SLUM SON
STAR STY TIES TON VAT WAS

1. FIND WHAT WAS LOST — __ __   __ __ __ __   __ __ __ __
2. FLABBERGASTED — __ __   __ __ __   __   __ __ __ __
3. FROM EARTH'S BEGINNING — __ __ __ __   __ __   __ __ __ __
4. GOING HUNGRY — __ __ __ __   __ __ __   __   __ __
5. GROW BACK — __ __   __ __ __ __   __ __ __ __
6. HAVING A NAP — __ __ __ __   __ __   __ __ __ __
7. KITCHEN APPLIANCE — __ __ __ __   __ __ __   __ __ __
8. LANDLORD'S HOUSES — __ __ __   __ __ __   __ __ __ __
9. LANGUAGE EXPERT — __ __ __ __   __ __ __   __   __ __
10. LYING WAYS — __ __ __ __   __ __ __   __ __ __
11. NOT VOWELS — __ __ __   __ __ __   __ __ __ __
12. OCCUPIER — __ __   __ __   __ __ __   __ __ __

BRAIN TEASER

Kate is twice as old as her brother and half as old as her father. In 22 years, her brother will be half as old as his father. How old is Kate now?

[Answer: Kate is now 22 years old.]

211.

SHIPPING

All the words in the list below are hidden somewhere in the grid of letters. See if you can find them! Words may run in any direction, including diagonally, and spaces are ignored. When you've crossed off all the words, read the leftover letters in the grid (running left to right, from top to bottom) to reveal a hidden quote related to the puzzle's theme.

I	K	A	F	N	A	V	A	L	E	H	W	S	P	O	M	E
T	C	B	Y	E	K	A	W	N	H	Y	H	O	I	F	N	G
I	E	E	S	R	N	S	I	A	E	D	E	G	B	N	D	T
M	D	A	B	C	R	R	Y	L	L	R	E	O	T	U	G	B
Y	O	M	H	S	A	E	H	W	I	O	L	L	P	T	O	H
E	N	O	I	M	L	T	F	A	I	F	F	S	A	A	T	Y
C	R	A	B	L	I	M	E	Y	P	O	R	T	T	N	L	R
P	G	U	A	H	C	N	I	W	H	I	S	C	U	L	L	T
I	S	G	L	O	W	H	E	O	O	L	E	P	O	R	U	F
H	I	H	E	L	M	S	L	R	I	T	L	N	U	J	H	A
S	E	I	N	F	I	T	A	I	S	S	S	D	I	S	S	R
R	E	D	N	E	T	O	W	I	T	E	D	B	N	G	E	C
A	E	T	U	B	Y	E	N	J	L	E	R	O	A	A	N	R
W	E	O	F	K	R	E	U	Q	R	A	B	D	I	I	I	E
T	I	D	N	C	S	N	G	Y	R	O	D	F	U	R	L	T
A	U	M	I	A	K	R	E	K	N	A	T	S	H	I	P	A
M	E	N	T	T	C	U	R	R	E	N	T	K	E	E	L	W

ABEAM	BUOY	FUNNEL	JIB	PFD	STOW	WAKE
ALOFT	CANOE	FURL	JUNK	PORT	SUBMARINE	WARSHIP
ANCHOR	CREW	GALLEY	KEEL	PUNT	TACK	WATERCRAFT
BAIL	CURRENT	GUNWALE	LIMEY	ROPE	TANKER	WHEEL
BARQUE	DECK	HELM	LINES	ROW	TENDER	WINCH
BOAT	DORY	HOIST	LOG	RUDDER	TIDE	YAWL
BOOM	ENGINE	HULL	NAVAL	SAIL	TUG	
BOW	FERRY	HYDROFOIL	OAR	SCULL	UMIAK	

212.

A CHARLES DICKENS CHRISTMAS

All the words in the list below are hidden somewhere in the grid of letters. See if you can find them! Words may run in any direction, including diagonally, and spaces are ignored. When you've crossed off all the words, read the leftover letters in the grid (running left to right, from top to bottom) to reveal a hidden quote related to the puzzle's theme.

BELLE
CANDLE
CHARWOMAN
CLERK
CRIPPLED
DICKENS
FEZZIWIG
FRAN
GHOST
GOOSE
HUMBUG
KINDNESS
MARLEY
MISER
PAST
PRESENT
PUDDING
SCROOGE
SPIRIT
STAVE
TINY TIM
TOMBSTONE
TURKEY
YET TO COME

213.

WINTER CONSTRUCTION CROSSWORD

ACROSS

1. Media inits.
4. Fogs
9. See-through, as fabric
14. Bro or sis
15. Dr. Seuss book "Hop ___"
16. Disentangle
17. Here, in Havana
18. Person-to-person information
20. Sugar coating
22. "___ my soul to the company store . . ."
23. Indonesian orchestra
25. A long way away
26. Waiting room material
29. Warm hues
31. Trinidad partner
33. Engines have a serpentine one
36. "Oh, woe!"
38. Ice cap descriptor
39. Common website page
41. This place, to a cockney
42. Loses it
43. Carried
44. Hindu deity (var.)
46. "Lord of the Rings" town
47. Prepares for prayers
49. Words after "ready"
51. Sounds of agreement
52. Reveal, in poetry
54. Lunchtime
58. French burro
60. Horse apple
61. With 70 Across, festive dwelling with decorations scattered throughout the puzzle
66. Ash holder
67. Towards the back
68. French aerospace agency
69. Not gross
70. Casino advantage
71. "It's The Sun Wot ___" (British headline and political catchphrase)
72. Drink with sushi

DOWN

1. Activist Kielburger
2. World-record-holding powerlifter Swanson
3. Insurance file
4. Jungle boy
5. Odysseus's rescuer
6. Hundreds and thousands
7. British foxes
8. Send-up
9. Squishy candy
10. "I'll take that as ___."
11. Sumerian sun god
12. Red spot
13. Mumbled agreement
19. What the Earth was believed to be, once
21. Green-haired Sailor Scout
24. Santa ___ (California)
26. Cheekbone-related
27. One of the Greek loves
28. Flowering shrub
30. Indian attire
32. Small chocolates
33. Sweet Ukrainian bread
34. Dark wood
35. Traditional histories
37. "Edge of ___" (song)
40. Chromosome ending
45. From ___ Z
48. Painful heel growth
50. Talented in
53. Easily injured joint
55. Intimidate
56. Acquiesce
57. "Fiddler on the Roof" role
59. Rubik's first name
61. Startled interjection
62. Japanese colour
63. Modern, in Montreal
64. "Noble" element
65. "Entourage" agent

1	2	3	■	4	5	6	7	8	■	9	10	11	12	13
14			■	15					■	16				
17			■	18					19					
20			21		■	22					■	■	■	■
23					24		■	25			■	26	27	28
■	■	■	29				30	■	31		32			
33	34	35		■	36			37	■	38				
39				40	■	41			■	42				
43					■	44			45	■	46			
47					48	■	49			50		■	■	■
51			■	52		53	■	54				55	56	57
■	■	■	■	58			59		■	60				
61	62	63	64						65		■	66		
67					■	68					■	69		
70					■	71					■	72		

214.

MAPLE LEAF

The goal of this puzzle is to form as many words as you can, using the letters contained in the leaf. Each letter can be used only once, so you can create a word with two Ts only if there are two Ts in the leaf. Each word must be three or more letters long, and all words must contain the large central letter of the leaf, along with any mix of the letters around the outside. For the ultimate challenge, see if you can find the one 10-letter word that contains ALL the letters in the leaf.

ANIMAL CRACKERS

*Many idioms include animals—*a bull in a china shop *and* ants in your pants *are two examples. In the first column, you'll find the meaning of the "animal idiom." In the second column, you'll find the animal in the idiom. Try to figure out each idiom by matching the meaning to the animal.*

A. Extremely uncommon
B. Really nervous about something stressful
C. To offer something valuable to someone who doesn't appreciate it
D. Why aren't you speaking when you should be?
E. To switch plans when you're halfway through something
F. To pretend to be upset or affected by something
G. A problem that everyone is aware of but nobody talks about
H. The biggest or best part
I. Someone who does one particular thing well but has limited skills in other areas
J. To pretend to be dead or asleep

1. Butterflies
2. Cat
3. Crocodile
4. Elephant
5. Hen
6. Horses
7. Pony
8. Swine
9. Possum
10. Lion

[Answers: A. = 5. as rare as hen's teeth; B. = 1. butterflies in your stomach; C. = 8. cast pearls before swine; D. = 2. cat got your tongue?; E. = 6. change horses in midstream; F. = 3. cry crocodile tears; G. = 4. the elephant in the room; H. = 10. the lion's share; I. = 7. a one-trick pony; J. = 9. play possum]

215.

BEFORE AND AFTER

The words in each group have one thing in common: they all frequently appear either immediately before or immediately after the solution word. For example, if the group includes CHRISTMAS, APPLE, TRUNK, HOUSE, and FAMILY, the solution might be TREE (CHRISTMAS TREE, APPLE TREE, TREE TRUNK, TREE HOUSE, FAMILY TREE). When you've figured out all the solutions, read the first letter of each to discover the puzzle's secret theme.

1. COCONUT ICE LIGHT _ _ _ _ _
   PIE PUFF SAUCE
   SHAVING SODA SOUR

2. BREATHING CURRENCY DISK _ _ _ _
   EVIDENCE FEELINGS PRESSED
   SWALLOWED TIMES WORK

3. CLIENTS DOUBTS FANTASIES _ _ _ _ _ _ _ _ _
   FRIENDS GUESTS NOTIONS
   OFFERS SERIOUSLY TROOPS

4. ACCESS CHAIR REACH _ _ _ _
   ANSWER RIDICULOUSLY PREY
   PICKINGS VICTORY BREATHE

5. BREAD CHICKEN DIAGONALLY _ _ _ _ _
   LARGER PIZZA THICK
   THIN THROUGH TOMATO

6. CLOTHES ITEM JEWELRY _ _ _ _ _ _ _ _ _
   PERFUME PROHIBITIVELY PROPOSITION
   TASTES TOO WINE

216.

ANTLERGRAM

The goal of antlergrams is to form as many words as you can using the letters in the moose's nose and antlers. Each letter can be used only once, which means you can form a word with two Ts only if there are two Ts in the puzzle. Each word must be three or more letters long and must contain the letter in the nose, along with any combination of the letters from the antlers. For the ultimate challenge, see if you can find the one 9-letter word that contains ALL the letters in the puzzle.

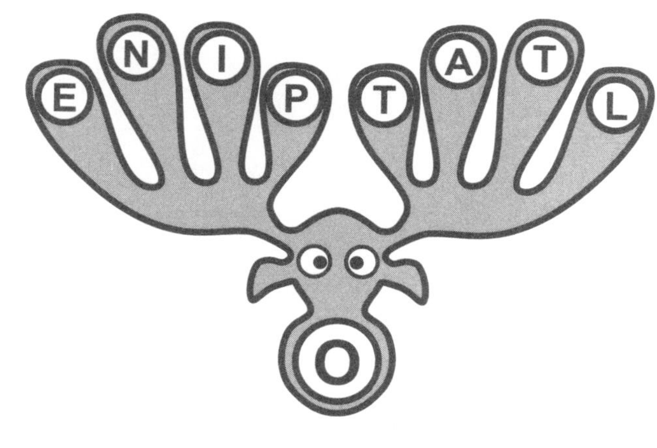

217.

CRYPTOGRAM

Each of the quotes below has been encrypted, with each letter of the alphabet substituted for a different letter. The substitutions are different for each puzzle. Use your code-breaking skills to discover the original quotation! (Hints: Start with short words—a one-letter word is usually A or I. Count the number of each letter—the commonest letter in English is E, followed by T, A, O, I, and N, while the most common three-letter word is THE.)

1. V APU P HKZUFNQXG YAVGUAKKU, HAVYA VJ DKXOA IFYPXJF VD'J APNU DK PUTXJD DK P LVJFNPIGF PUXGDAKKU. —GPNNC UPWVU

2. ITK KFZRP UYZG BFP EKI ITK LSZB, UWI ITK OKDSAG BSWOK EKIO ITK DTKKOK.

3. LMW MIVCPWZZ FD XHLLWV TZ CTVWJLAG KVFKFVLTFPIA LF LMW ZFDLPWZZ FD LMW XVWIC.

4. YK YG'J E HLQQS KMT SMCT GBMCXBGJ
EQU SMC HCG YQ SMCT GDM PLQGJ'
DMTGB, GBLQ JMWLMQL, JMWLDBLTL
YJ WEZYQX E HLQQS.—JGLRLQ DTYXBG

5. FV SOAXWIN OIW JFNLOIIWJ OQJ
ESWIYXRWQ JWVIZEHWJ, JZWNQ'D FD
VZSSZA DTOD WSWEDIFEFOQN EOQ LW
JWSFYTDWJ, RCNFEFOQN JWQZDWJ,
EZALZXN JWIOQYWJ, RZJWSN JWMZNWJ,
DIWW NCIYWZQN JWLOIHWJ, OQJ JIX
ESWOQWIN JWMIWNNWJ?

6. W YDOU UP Z NPPJCUPED ZOA ZCJDA
UGD CZSDCYPLZO YGDED UGD CDSM-
GDSQ CDIUWPO YZC. CGD CZWA WM
CGD UPSA LD WU YPHSA ADMDZU UGD
QHEQPCD.—KDPEKD IZESWO

218.

SUDOKU: HARD

A sudoku puzzle is a type of logic puzzle. Although it uses numbers, no mathematics is involved. The grid below is divided into nine large squares, each of which is divided into nine smaller squares. Each large square contains all the digits from 1 to 9, with each digit appearing exactly once. Each horizontal row of the puzzle also contains each digit exactly once, and so does each vertical row. By carefully observing which numbers are missing from each row, column, or square, see if you can figure out which numbers go where. There's only one possible solution to each puzzle.

2		8		7			1	6
3					6			5
					4	3		
				9		5		1
	9						2	
5		6		8				
		1	7					
9			1					2
4	8			5		1		7

219.

SUDOKU: HARD

A sudoku puzzle is a type of logic puzzle. Although it uses numbers, no mathematics is involved. The grid below is divided into nine large squares, each of which is divided into nine smaller squares. Each large square contains all the digits from 1 to 9, with each digit appearing exactly once. Each horizontal row of the puzzle also contains each digit exactly once, and so does each vertical row. By carefully observing which numbers are missing from each row, column, or square, see if you can figure out which numbers go where. There's only one possible solution to each puzzle.

							1	
	8			2		4	7	
		6	5		1	3		
	1		3					
7	2		9		6		4	3
					2		6	
		9	4		8	1		
	3	4		6			9	
	5							

220.

THE HOCKEY GAME

All the words in the list below are hidden somewhere in the grid of letters. See if you can find them! Words may run in any direction, including diagonally, and spaces are ignored. When you've crossed off all the words, read the leftover letters in the grid (running left to right, from top to bottom) to reveal a hidden quote related to the puzzle's theme.

T C C A P T A I N H E E G O O

D O H P L A Y E R I L E P D W

R E F E R E E H L O S C U K H

E Y G N C A M A E N R I C I I

S T H A S K O M E E N I K B S

B E S L L G I F A O T F N G T

A A M T A E E N B T F Y O K L

U W C Y P D C M G O C A N N E

C I A K S K A T E S M H E A A

E N N D H Z T C H E B E N S T

N G T G O A A A T C M E E E Y

T E O U T F N N C O R A M N N

E R T A M E I D I A S L N H L

R T H E H O M E I C E G O O D

O L D H P O C K E H Y G A M E

ARENA
BACKHAND
CAPTAIN
CENTRE
CHECKING
COACH
DEFENCE
FACEOFF
GOALIE
HELMET
HOME ICE
MATCH
NET
NHL
PENALTY
PLAYER
POINT
PUCK
REFEREE
RINK
SKATES
SLAPSHOT
WHISTLE
WINGER
ZAMBONI

221.

ONE STEP AT A TIME

Change the word at the top to the word at the bottom by altering one letter at a time. Each change should produce a new word. We've provided clues to help you on your way.

P O R T

_ _ _ _ PLANT NAME ENDING

_ _ _ _ HAD ON

_ _ _ _ METAL STRAND

W I N E

T A P E

_ _ _ _ MEMORIAL MUSIC

_ _ _ _ SPINNING TOYS

_ _ _ _ PULLS WITH A ROPE

B O W S

NORTHERN LIGHTS

The "Aurora Capital of the World," claiming to have the most spectacular natural light show *anywhere*, is

A. the northern shore of Lake Superior
B. Churchill, Manitoba
C. Elk Falls Park in British Columbia
D. the Northwest Territories
E. Nunavut

[Answer: D. the Northwest Territories]

222.

WORDS × FIVE

This puzzle is similar to a crossword, but the five-letter answer to each clue is written twice—both across and down. So, if the solution to clue 1 is FLAME, you would write FLAME into the grid twice, from left to right and from top to bottom.

1	2	3	4	5
2				
3				
4				
5				

1. Ink leaving borders
2. Basic lifting device
3. Each and ___
4. Creepy
5. Clothesline alternative

223.

WORDS × FIVE

This puzzle is similar to a crossword, but the five-letter answer to each clue is written twice—both across and down. So, if the solution to clue 1 is FLAME you would write FLAME in the grid two times, from left to right and from top to bottom.

1	2	3	4	5
2				
3				
4				
5				

1. About time
2. Just right
3. Show emotion
4. Squirrel away
5. Change

224.

COUNTDOWN CROSSWORD

ACROSS

1. Wee, to a Scot
4. Big event
8. Open public space
13. Darken
14. Dogwalker's tool
16. Styled, as a moustache
17. They come in a dozen
18. Comedian Kovacs
19. Viking drinks
20. End of an adage about saving
23. Actress who played Jupiter in a 2015 movie
24. Second word in RSVP
25. "The Old Man and the ___"
28. Strong desire
33. Rowling's protagonist
35. Eye-shaped
36. Untamed
37. December greetings, or the theme hidden in 20, 28, 48, and 57 Across
43. Skye of "Say Anything"
44. Work rvw.
45. Shrink back
48. "How ___ must one man have . . ."
53. Some dashes
54. Make a mistake
56. Debate team subj.
57. Improvises (a song), musically
62. Part of a shadow
65. Wise person
66. Whiz kid
67. Gold measure
68. Dip or dance
69. Addr. in the countryside
70. With an ___ (keeping in mind)
71. Memory unit
72. Abbreviation in the kitchen

DOWN

1. Descriptor for a romance novel
2. Shiny-object lover
3. '80s Olympian Bailey
4. Vale
5. Ethereal
6. Highway division
7. Large section of the map
8. Citrus fruit with a thick skin
9. Schumann song
10. ___ carte
11. Last letter
12. What they write at Sterling Cooper
15. Word on a bath towel
21. "___ whal"
22. Light bite
25. Begin to wake up
26. Fish served barbecued in sushi
27. Dull suffix?
29. Trio after M
30. Little lambs eat it
31. Familiar term for grandmother
32. P&G toothpaste
34. Erstwhile American airline
37. Part of a steering wheel
38. Licorice liqueur
39. Pig place
40. State about 800 km south of ON
41. TV chef who "can cook"
42. Tarzan actor Ron
43. Diamonds, to thieves
46. Italian dessert
47. Baseball stat
49. Suffix with trick
50. "If I only had ___"
51. Responds to
52. Kramer's portrayer
55. Some loaves
57. Comedic fall
58. Hunk of rock
59. Without purpose
60. Exam
61. Scottish hillside
62. Four-stringed instrument,
63. Month after the cruelest month
64. Theology deg.

1	2	3	■	4	5	6	7	■	■	8	9	10	11	12
13			■	14				15	■	16				
17			■	18					■	19				
20			21						22			■	■	■
23				■	■	■	■	24			■	25	26	27
28				29	30	31	32	■	33		34			
■	■	■	■	35				■	■	■	36			
■	37	38	39					40	41	42				■
43				■	■	■	44				■	■	■	■
45				46	47	■	48				49	50	51	52
53			■	54		55	■	■	■	■	56			
■	■	■	57				58	59	60	61				
62	63	64			■	65					■	66		
67					■	68					■	69		
70					■	■	71				■	72		

225.

PYRAMID POWER

The pyramid is made up of a series of words, each one containing the letters used in the word directly above it (the order of the letters may be changed) plus one new letter. Solve the clues to fill in the pyramid!

1. Vitamin in carrots ___
2. Thanks ___ ___
3. Consumed ___ ___ ___
4. Flesh ___ ___ ___ ___
5. Hot water ___ ___ ___ ___ ___
6. British river ___ ___ ___ ___ ___ ___
7. Nonbelief ___ ___ ___ ___ ___ ___ ___
8. Deck hand ___ ___ ___ ___ ___ ___ ___ ___
9. Old vessel ___ ___ ___ ___ ___ ___ ___ ___ ___
10. Condolences ___ ___ ___ ___ ___ ___ ___ ___ ___ ___
11. Philosophy ___ ___ ___ ___ ___ ___ ___ ___ ___ ___ ___

226.

PYRAMID POWER

The pyramid is made up of a series of words, each one containing the letters used in the word directly above it (the order of the letters may be changed) plus one new letter. Solve the clues to fill in the pyramid!

1. Ninth letter ___
2. After do and re ___ ___
3. Glowing weakly ___ ___ ___
4. Object ___ ___ ___ ___
5. Those in charge ___ ___ ___ ___ ___
6. Area controlled ___ ___ ___ ___ ___ ___
7. Jewel ___ ___ ___ ___ ___ ___ ___

MANE LAND

This island is home to over 400 free-roaming horses protected by law from human interference:

A. Michipicoten Island, Ontario
B. Sable Island, Nova Scotia
C. Fogo Island, Newfoundland and Labrador
D. Baffin Island, Nunavut
E. Île d'Orléans, Quebec

[Answer: B. Sable Island, Nova Scotia]

227.

BEFORE AND AFTER

The words in each group have one thing in common: they all frequently appear either immediately before or immediately after the solution word. For example, if the group includes CHRISTMAS, APPLE, TRUNK, HOUSE, and FAMILY, the solution might be TREE (CHRISTMAS TREE, APPLE TREE, TREE TRUNK, TREE HOUSE, FAMILY TREE). When you've figured out all the solutions, read the first letter of each to discover the puzzle's secret theme.

1. ACQUIRED BITTER BUDS EXQUISITE GOOD IMPECCABLE POOR SOUR TEST _ _ _ _ _

2. ARMS CANADIAN DOOR EYES MOUTH SPACE SWUNG WIDE WINDOW _ _ _ _

3. AMERICAN HABITAT LAND LANGUAGE PEOPLES PLANTS SOIL SON BORN _ _ _ _ _ _

4. GIFT ME ORDER REEL REFLEX RULE RUNNING SIGHT WRITER _ _ _

5. ARREST ATTACK CONSTRUCTION CONTROL FIRE PLACED PRESSURE SIEGE WAY _ _ _ _ _

6. BENEFITS COVERAGE CREDIT DOWNWARDS FOREVER FULLY OURSELVES ROOTS SYMPATHY _ _ _ _ _ _

228.

REBUS

In these puzzles, the arrangement of the letters and symbols suggests a common word or expression. For example, this combination

COVER
GOING

is "going undercover" (the word GOING is under the word COVER—literally). See how many you can figure out.

1. 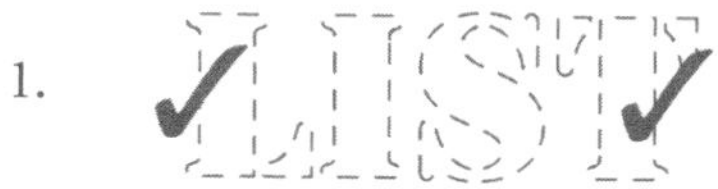

2. BLACK

3. 

4. DEC. 25 DEC. 25 DEC. 25 DEC. 25
DEC. 25 DEC. 25 DEC. 25 DEC. 25
DEC. 25 DEC. 25 DEC. 25 DEC. 25

5. MANawayGER

229.

CATCH A WORD: FABRICS

In this type of puzzle, the answer appears in its correct order but may begin in the middle of a word and be interrupted by spaces and punctuation. For example: The Canadians were victorious in hockey once again. Can you find the names of ten fabrics hidden in the sentences below?

1. Vile Hilda was displeased with the taste of bat wing in her soup, so she added an apricot to neutralize the flavour.
2. Ringo worked out melody and harmony, longing for the day when he'd have a band to sing with.
3. The landscape was uniquely African—vast savannas stretching to the baked horizon.
4. After Kyle was crowned Bird King, hummingbirds darted excitedly around his head, while cheering penguins and emus lined his path.
5. June gasped, for there, nestled inside the jade box, was a tiny gem.
6. Later, whilst wandering through the ornamental garden, I met Felicity, taking her afternoon stroll.
7. The entire party succumbed to the volcano's toxic ash mere feet from the safety of their cabin.
8. Our hearts beating like jackhammers, our brows dripping with sweat, we edged our way along the deadly precipice.
9. Face the window, raise the cleaner, spray once, then polish with the chamois until your hands are sore.
10. The crops stretched for acre after acre—peas, lentils, beans, and a host of other choice legumes.

230.

SKILLATHON

The goal is to find as many words as possible made up of the letters in the word or phrase below. Words must be made of four or more letters. No plurals allowed. Only one tense or form of a verb is permitted (if you find WALK, you can't also have WALKS, WALKED, WALKING, etc.). The exception is when two forms have different meanings—e.g., BORE and BORED.

BARBECUE

Try to beat our experts. They found 20 words.

231.

WORD JIGSAW

The words in these quotes and quips have been sliced up into pieces, so you can no longer see where one word begins and another ends. The order of the letters inside each piece is unchanged. Can you reassemble the word pieces and figure out the original phrase?

1. _ _ _'_ _   _ _ _ _ _   _ _ _ _ _   _ _ _   _
_ _ _ _ _ _   _ _ _ _   _ _   _ _ _   _ _ _   _ _
_ _ _   _ _ _ _ _ _ _ _ _ _ _!   _ _ _ _ _ _ _ _.

ERGU ESSW ETRIS EWAYT HOIBUM LNEV OONTH OTHEO PEDINT PTOM TEVER YONE YOUL

2. _ _ _ _   _   _ _ _ _ _   _ _ _ _   _ _
_ _ _ _   _ _ _ _ _,   _ _ _   _ _ _ _ _ _ _   _
_ _ _ _ _ _ _   _ _ _ _   _ _ _ _   _ _ _ _. —
_ _ _ _ _ _ _   _ _ _ _ _ _ _

APSAS BIRDWI DPERH ECHIN EINYO ESEPR GREE INGING KEEPA LLCOM NTRE OVERB RTAN URHEA

3. _ _   _ _ _ _ _ _   _ _   _ _   _ _ _ _ _ _ _,
_ _ _   _ _   _ _ _   _ _ _ _   _ _   _ _ _   _ _ _
_ _ _ _ _ _ _?

BIEIS ETOBU IFBAR OUHAV RIENDS SOPOP ULARWH YDOY YHERF

4. _   _ _ _ _   _ _ _ _ _   _ _ _ _   _ _
_ _ _   _ _ _ _   _ _ _ _,   _ _ _ _   _ _ _ _
_ _ _ _   _ _ _   _ _ _ _. — _ _ _ _ _ _
_ _ _ _ _ _ _ _ _ _

ATIFY EFOU ELIF EWI IHAV LLLO NDTH NSTEIN OULO RRUBI RTHU UBACKA VELIF VEYO

5. _ _   _ _ _   _ _ _   _ _   _ _ _ _ _ _ _ _,

_ _ _   _ _ _ _ _ _ _   _ _ _ _ _ _ _ _   _ _ _

_ _ _ _ _ _ _ _ _   _ _ _   _ _ _ _ _ _ _

_ _ _ _ _ _ _ _   _ _ _ _   _ _   _ _ _ _ _ _ _ _

_ _   _ _ _ _ _ _ _ _ _ _,   _ _ _ _   _ _

_ _ _ _   _ _ _ _ _ _ _ _ _   _ _ _ _ _ _

_ _ _ _   _ _ _   _ _   _ _ _   _ _ _

_ _ _ _ _ _ _   _ _ _ _ _ _. —_ _ _ _ _

_ _ _ _ _ _

AGEAME BYTH CEONTE DREDTH DAC DURI EAGEO EENT EMOCCU EONEO FEIGHT FFSER FTHENH HASWI HEAVER IESS IOLEN LEVISI LPLAYO NGGAM ONMOS OUSAN RICAN RRING SEDT TEVER TNES TOFTH TSOFV USHIN WOHUN

6. _ _ _ _ _   _ _ _   _ _ _   _ _ _ _ _,   _ _ _ _

_ _   _ _ _   _ _ _ _   _ _   _ _ _ _ _   _ _   _

_ _ _ _ _ _. —_ _ _ _ _   _ _ _ _ _ _ _ _

ACAC ANDON ARSEV CHFOR ENIFY NGACRE OUHA REA SANLO THEST TUSSU VETOST

QUIZ

What time and day is it in Fredericton, New Brunswick, when it is 11:00 p.m. on Monday in Victoria, British Columbia?

[Answer: It is 3:00 a.m. Tuesday in Fredericton.]

232.

CRYPTOGRAM

Each of the quotes below has been encrypted, with each letter of the alphabet substituted for a different letter. The substitutions are different for each puzzle. Use your code-breaking skills to discover the original quotation! (Hints: Start with short words—a one-letter word is usually A or I. Count the number of each letter—the commonest letter in English is E, followed by T, A, O, I, and N, while the most common three-letter word is THE.)

1. J R M Y M ' W   H L J R K H F   E K P M   E L L P K H F   C J

_ _ _ _ _ ' _   _ _ _ _ _ _ _   _ _ _ _   _ _ _ _ _ _ _   _ _

D C U C J K L H   A K U J I Y M W   J L   A I J   F I M W J W

_ _ _ _ _ _ _ _   _ _ _ _ _ _ _ _   _ _   _ _ _   _ _ _ _ _ _

K H   C   J Y C D M E E K H F   X L L S .

_ _   _   _ _ _ _ _ _ _ _ _ _   _ _ _ _ .

2. Q J Y G Y ' U   L I Y   C L L Z   Q J X I C   P W L D Q

_ _ _ _ _ ' _   _ _ _   _ _ _ _   _ _ _ _ _   _ _ _ _ _

U I L S :   X Q   K P B Y U   A L D G   T P S I   T L L B

_ _ _ _ :   _ _   _ _ _ _ _   _ _ _ _   _ _ _ _   _ _ _ _

P U   I X E Y   P U   A L D G   I Y X C J W L D G ' U .

_ _   _ _ _ _   _ _   _ _ _ _   _ _ _ _ _ _ _ _ _ ' _ .

3. F M   B J M K F G T   S H T F G K ,   V M K K M S   B M R G

_ _   _ _ _ _ _ _ _   _ _ _ _ _ _ ,   _ _ _ _ _ _   _ _ _ _

R M T G I   Z N G   H T   B A K H T X . — S . P .   Y M X F C

_ _ _ _ _   _ _ _   _ _   _ _ _ _ _ _ . — _ . _ .   _ _ _ _ _

4. OAEEZB VUB AN LYBQ KWS'DB
NAGGAQU VG YWOB WQ V NVGSDEVK
QAUYG VQE GYB GBZBCYWQB DAQUN
VQE KWS YWCB AG ANQ'G XWD KWS.—
WUEBQ QVNY

5. BDKO KRE JO R TVVZ NORAOF, JLB
DB'I R AVLIE JORLBDMDRY.—RLBNVF
LYSYVQY

6. WQKBJ, B PBD IDQGIAK QD PJ KQQY
BDK BZIAK VQY B ZPBHH KQDBWMQD
WQCBYKZ WSA HQGBH ZCMPPMDT OQQH.
M TBXA SMP B THBZZ QV CBWAY.

233.

CASTLES

All the words in the list below are hidden somewhere in the grid of letters. See if you can find them! Words may run in any direction, including diagonally, and spaces are ignored. When you've crossed off all the words, read the leftover letters in the grid (running left to right, from top to bottom) to reveal a hidden quote related to the puzzle's theme.

```
G A R D E N S T O N E K H A D
C N T R O S D N I W Q I E R E
N H G U R W A L L G L U A E L
D I A E R F S A F L A G E S P
N R W P A R L H T S O T G E M
A O O I E U E O U N W A E N N
T S R L C L P T E A R O Y A L
H Y O A S N I U R C E M R M N
H G R U B N I D E G N T E D W
E D K N I G H T A I S A A H O
C S C I S S C I H A L L L H R
N P O M D D R A Y T R U O C C
I E R A N R P A L A C E S T L
R A M P A R T S I E G E A R L
P R E C S T N E M E L T T A B
```

ARMS
BARON
BATTLEMENTS
CARRIAGE
CHAPEL
CHATEAU
COURTYARD
CRAGS
CROWN
DRACULA
DRAGON
EARL
EDINBURGH
FAIRY
FLAG
GARDENS
GATE
HALL
HILLTOP
KEEP
KNIGHT
LANCE
LORD
MOAT
PALACE
PRINCE
QUEEN
RAMPARTS
ROCK
ROYAL
RUINS
SAND
SIEGE
SPEAR
STONE
SWORD
TOWERS
TURRET
WALL
WAR
WINDSOR

EXPERT 2

DOUBLE-DOUBLE TAKE

Spot the difference: can you find the 12 changes?

© BanksPhotos/iStock

FUN AND GAMES

Santa Says

This is a good game for young children. It's Simon Says, but now the leader is Santa. (The players can be elves.) Santa stands in front of a group and explains what the players must do. However, they must obey only those commands that begin with the words "Santa says." If Santa simply says "Whistle," without first saying "Santa says," players must not whistle. Those who do whistle are out. The last player to remain is the winner and becomes the next Santa. (Trick question: Santa may want to begin the game by saying, "If you're ready to play, raise your hands.")

Holiday Memory Game

Randomly arrange 10 holiday-themed objects on a table. (Examples may include a ribbon, a candle, and a tree decoration.) Give the guests one minute to memorize the objects. Then remove the tray and have everyone write down as many items as they can remember, setting a timer at 30 seconds. The person who remembers the most items is the winner.

Anagrammed

Rearrange the letters in each word group to give you a single holiday-related word. (Example: lousier not = resolution.)

A. key rut
B. wire forks
C. vain taco
D. a bigger nerd
E. change map

SOLUTION EXPERT 2

Answers:
A. turkey, B. fireworks, C. vacation, D. gingerbread, E. champagne

234.

AT THE SKI LODGE

All the words in the list below are hidden somewhere in the grid of letters. See if you can find them! Words may run in any direction, including diagonally, and spaces are ignored. When you've crossed off all the words, read the leftover letters in the grid (running left to right, from top to bottom) to reveal a hidden quote related to the puzzle's theme.

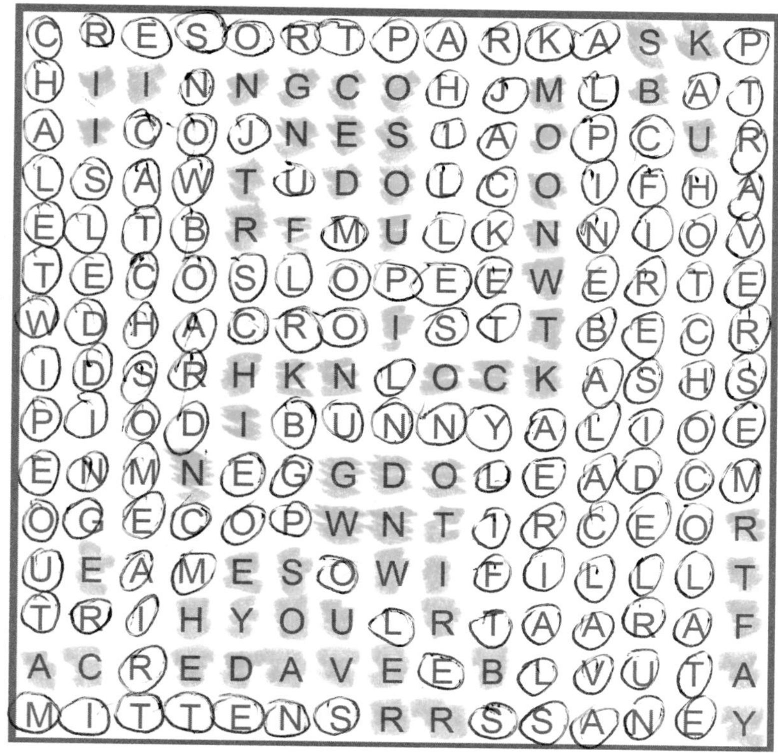

ACRO
AERIALS
ALPINE
BALACLAVA
BUNNY
CAP
CATCH SOME AIR
CHALET
FIRESIDE
HILL
HOT CHOCOLATE
JACKET
JUMP
LIFT
MITTENS
MOGULS
PARKA
POLES
RACE
RESORT
RUN
SLALOM
SLEDDING
SLOPE
SNOWBOARD
TRAVERSE
WIPE OUT

235.

15 × 15 CROSSWORD

ACROSS

1. Cause of ruin
5. Comfort
9. Kind of fund
14. Type of lily
15. Cut coupons
16. Ristorante order
17. Doorway part
18. Not in favour
19. Dolt
20. Head of a monastery
22. "The Sound of Music" setting: Abbr.
23. Writing style
24. Add
26. More powerful
28. Diabolical
32. Openly gay
33. Matchless
35. Buddy, to a cowboy
39. Bolivian high points
40. Free TV ad
41. About the forearm
42. Placed down
43. Country east of the Philippines
45. Droid cousin
46. Sleepy
47. Chart-topper's prize
52. No longer working: Abbr.
53. Edmonton hockey player
54. Slurp drink
56. Likewise
60. Cancel a mission
61. Bill passers
63. Bambi, e.g.
64. Quash
65. Schlep
66. Type of acid
67. Land across the Styx
68. Once, in former times
69. Narrow road

DOWN

1. ___ California (Mexican peninsula)
2. Breed of horse
3. Desensitize
4. Received into affections
5. European rocket launcher
6. "The King and I" lady
7. Spot, in law
8. Lettered
9. Tap
10. Filled with cargo
11. Utilizing
12. Mall tenant
13. Lover's antithesis
21. North African capital
25. School in Cambridge
27. Regret
28. Old phone or TV part
29. Province of Sicily
30. Below-the-knee skirt
31. Admit defeat
34. Science degree
35. Unlimited
36. Standards org.
37. Shower
38. Burden
41. Not married
43. Time to get back to work: Abbr.
44. Galley gear
45. Deliveries
47. Cook with water
48. Follower of Virgo
49. How children read
50. Succinct
51. Rob Ford, for one
55. Teacher's favourites
57. "Gone with the Wind" mansion
58. Duplicate
59. Some time ago
62. Harden, as plaster

1	2	3	4	■	5	6	7	8	■	9	10	11	12	13
14				■	15				■	16				
17				■	18				■	19				
20				21	■	22			■	23				
■	■	■	24		25	■	26		27					
28	29	30				31	■	32			■	■	■	■
33							34			■	35	36	37	38
39					■	40			■	41				
42				■	43				44					
■	■	■	■	45			■	46						
47	48	49	50				51	■	52			■	■	■
53					■	54		55	■	56		57	58	59
60					■	61			62	■	63			
64					■	65				■	66			
67					■	68				■	69			

236.

WORDS × SIX

This puzzle is similar to a crossword, but the six-letter answer to each clue is written twice—both across and down. So, if the solution to clue 1 is GOBLIN, you would write GOBLIN into the grid twice, from left to right and from top to bottom.

1	2	3	4	5	6
2					
3					
4					
5					
6					

1. Yawning gaps in the land
2. Danish prince
3. Current measure
4. Toboggan or hammer
5. Joining of companies
6. Guides a vehicle

237.

WORDS × SIX

This puzzle is similar to a crossword, but the six-letter answer to each clue is written twice—both across and down. So, if the solution to clue 1 is GOBLIN, you would write GOBLIN into the grid twice, from left to right and from top to bottom.

1	2	3	4	5	6
2					
3					
4					
5					
6					

1. Brought in gradually
2. Move fast
3. Fall on
4. Position
5. Bring forth
6. Remove

238.

FUN IN THE SNOW

All the words in the list below are hidden somewhere in the grid of letters. See if you can find them! Words may run in any direction, including diagonally, and spaces are ignored. When you've crossed off all the words, read the leftover letters in the grid (running left to right, from top to bottom) to reveal a hidden quote related to the puzzle's theme.

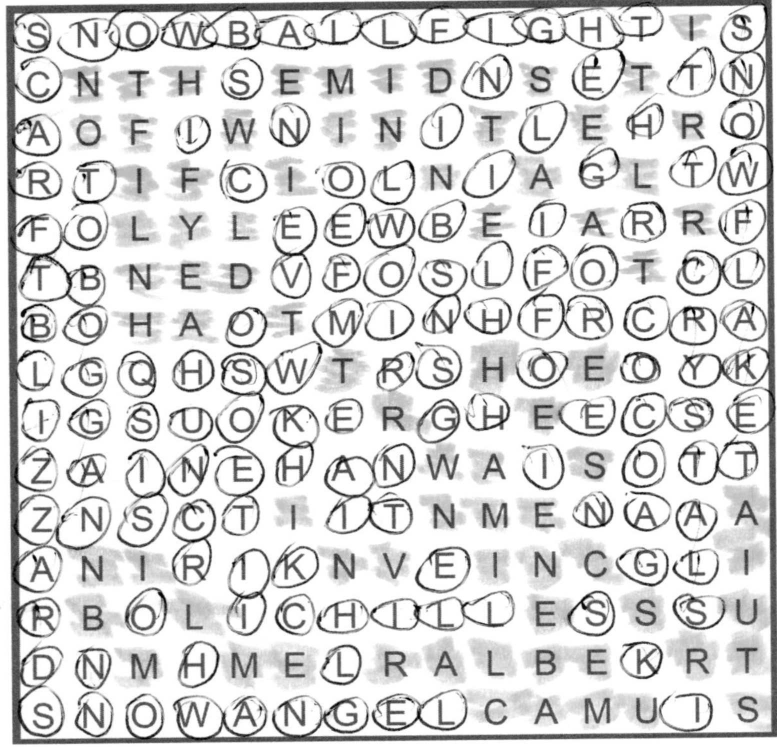

BLIZZARD
CHILL
COCOA
CRYSTALS
FORT
FROST
HIKING
ICE FISHING
ICICLE
NORTHERN LIGHTS
SCARF
SHOVELING
SKATE
SKI
SNOW ANGEL
SNOWBALL FIGHT
SNOWFLAKE
SNOWMOBILE
SNOWSHOE
TOBOGGAN
TOQUE

WINTER OLYMPICS

1. Snowboarding, an increasingly common extreme sport, became an official Olympic Games sport at which Winter Olympics?

   A. Nagano (1998)
   B. Calgary (1988)
   C. Salt Lake City (2002)
   D. Sochi (2014)
   E. Lake Placid (1980)

2. Summer and Winter Games were traditionally held in the same year until the International Olympic Committee voted to hold them in alternating even-numbered years. The first Winter Olympics to be held in a different year than the Summer Games took place in

   A. St. Moritz, Switzerland (1948)
   B. Lake Placid, New York (1980)
   C. Albertville, France (1992)
   D. Lillehammer, Norway (1994)
   E. Turin, Italy (2006)

3. This winter sport, which traces its origins to an exercise for Norwegian soldiers, combines cross-country skiing and rifle shooting.

4. What is the name given to a sled with metal runners but no steering apparatus or brakes that is ridden in a seated or face-up reclining position?

[Answers: 1. = A. Nagano (1998); 2. = D. Lillehammer (1994); 3. biathlon; 4. luge]

239.

SKILLATHON

The goal is to find as many words as possible made up of the letters in the word or phrase below. Words must be made of four or more letters. No plurals allowed. Only one tense or form of a verb is permitted (if you find WALK, you can't also have WALKS, WALKED, WALKING, etc.). The exception is when two forms have different meanings—e.g., BORE and BORED.

SASKATCHEWAN

Try to beat our experts. They found 145 words.

240.

BEFORE AND AFTER

The words in each group have one thing in common: they all frequently appear either immediately before or immediately after the solution word. For example, if the group includes CHRISTMAS, APPLE, TRUNK, HOUSE, and FAMILY, the solution might be TREE (CHRISTMAS TREE, APPLE TREE, TREE TRUNK, TREE HOUSE, FAMILY TREE). When you've figured out all the solutions, read the first letter of each to discover the puzzle's secret theme.

1.	ALIEN	HOME	BRITISH	_ _ _ _ _ _ _ _ _
	NORMANDY	MASSIVE	FORCE	
	PRIVACY	ROUTE	IRAQI	
2.	BIRD	COMFORTABLE	COZY	_ _ _ _
	EMPTY	LITTLE	LITTLE	
	LOVE	RAT	WASP	
3.	BEE	DRAMATIC	DRUG	_ _ _ _ _
	EYES	FBI	SCORPION	
	SHARP	UNDERCOVER	WASP	
4.	BLUE	CLOSED	DARTED	_ _ _ _
	FIXED	FOCUSED	GREEN	
	HAZEL	NARROWED	WIDE	
5.	ALONG	FORWARD	INSIDE	_ _ _ _ _
	SKIN	SLOWLY	SPACE	
	STROKE	UNDERNEATH	WORMS	
6.	BIT	DOT	FRACTION	_ _ _ _
	LITTLE	MINORITY	SPECK	
	TEENY	TIM	VILLAGE	

241.

SUDOKU: HARD

A sudoku puzzle is a type of logic puzzle. Although it uses numbers, no mathematics is involved. The grid below is divided into nine large squares, each of which is divided into nine smaller squares. Each large square contains all the digits from 1 to 9, with each digit appearing exactly once. Each horizontal row of the puzzle also contains each digit exactly once, and so does each vertical row. By carefully observing which numbers are missing from each row, column, or square, see if you can figure out which numbers go where. There's only one possible solution to each puzzle.

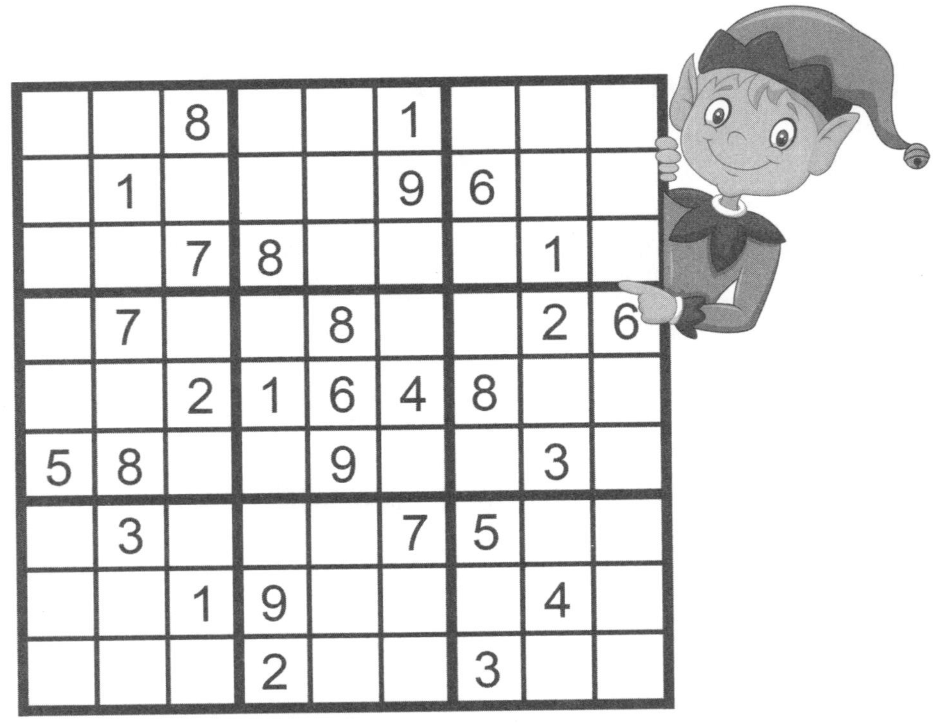

		8			1			
	1				9	6		
		7	8				1	
	7			8			2	6
		2	1	6	4	8		
5	8			9			3	
	3				7	5		
		1	9				4	
			2			3		

242.

SUDOKU: HARD

A sudoku puzzle is a type of logic puzzle. Although it uses numbers, no mathematics is involved. The grid below is divided into nine large squares, each of which is divided into nine smaller squares. Each large square contains all the digits from 1 to 9, with each digit appearing exactly once. Each horizontal row of the puzzle also contains each digit exactly once, and so does each vertical row. By carefully observing which numbers are missing from each row, column, or square, see if you can figure out which numbers go where. There's only one possible solution to each puzzle.

	1			9	7	6		
		2	8			9	3	
								1
	5	7			2			
3			7		1			4
			6			8	7	
4								
	7	5			8	2		
		8	5	7			1	

243.

LUNAR CROSSWORD

ACROSS

1. Morning drops
4. Boot material
8. On the rise
12. Bad situation
13. It's known as "the fifth taste"
15. Grabbed affectionately
16. Duds
18. Brother of Cain
19. Nada
20. Danish money
21. "Your point is?"
22. Kick out
23. Down on one's luck
24. Rank below Lt.
25. ___ Pak
28. Struck down
31. Sweetie pie
32. State south from BC
33. Leave out
34. North Sea bird
35. Sea nymph
38. Appropriately named fruit
39. Adidas alternative
41. North Sea bird
43. What something might be blown to
46. Vancouver path
47. Novel

DOWN

1. #1 guys
2. And so on
3. One of the five Ws
4. Beam at, perhaps
5. Barenaked Ladies title girl
6. Outback runner
7. "Pacific ___" (2013 film)
8. Importance
9. Hundred-Acre Woods resident
10. Bothersome person
11. Fed, in a noir film
12. Not-quite-square shape
14. Spring bloom
15. 1992 Neil Young song
17. Ink follower
20. Most clever
23. Bug catcher
26. One into boarding
27. They're worn
29. Sense of self?
30. "The Open Window" writer
32. Obscure, like a film
34. "Rock of ___" (musical)
36. Nile wader
37. Pamper, with "on"
38. Coffee maker
40. Name shouted by Kirk
41. Slippery as an ___
42. Go smoothly
44. Milk source, sometimes
45. Tartar, perhaps

244.

CATCH A WORD: CURRENCY

In this type of puzzle, the answer appears in its correct order but may begin in the middle of a word and be interrupted by spaces and punctuation. For example: The Canadi<u>ans were</u> victorious in hockey once again. Can you find the names of ten currencies hidden in the sentences below?

1. The winning bidders on the antique doll aren't happy with the condition of the china.
2. A strong current from Squid Bay pushed the rower up Eel Creek.
3. During her trip to the zoo, Sarah saw a hippo under a tree.
4. When the teacher passed out markers, Farrah chose a purple one.
5. He ran down the hallway to reach his class on time.
6. The electrician wouldn't let his apprentice handle any of the advanced equipment, saying she would learn what it was for in time.
7. Billy Bishop, the renowned flying ace, dived through the clouds.
8. The concept of choosing our destiny appears often in contemporary literature.
9. The wine connoisseur only had eyes for the expensive vintage red.
10. The thieves' guild eroded the foothold of the local merchant collective.

245.

HOLIDAY DINNER

All the words in the list below are hidden somewhere in the grid of letters. See if you can find them! Words may run in any direction, including diagonally, and spaces are ignored. When you've crossed off all the words, read the leftover letters in the grid (running left to right, from top to bottom) to reveal a hidden quote related to the puzzle's theme.

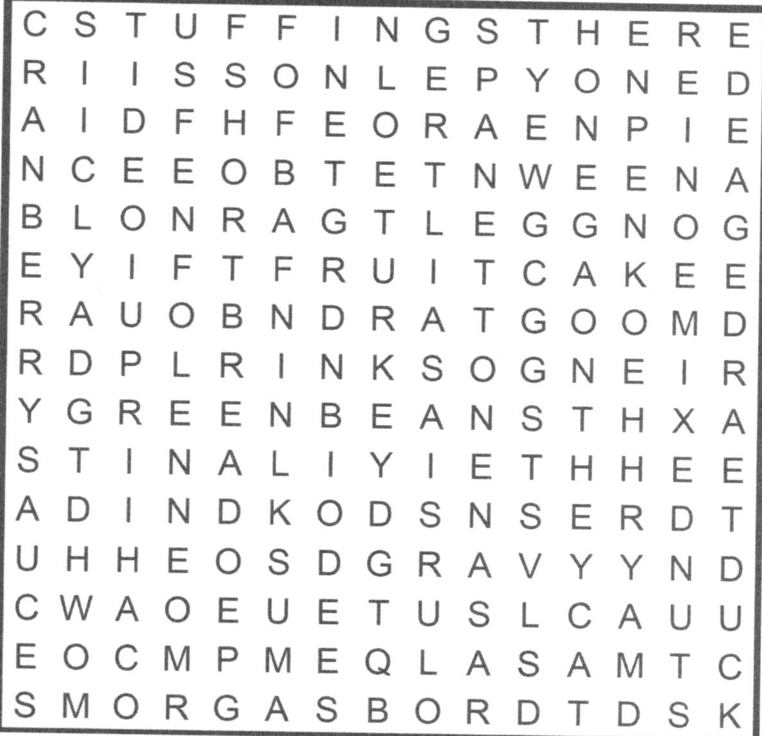

C S T U F F I N G S T H E R E
R I I S S O N L E P Y O N E D
A I D F H F E O R A E N P I E
N C E E O B T E T N W E E N A
B L O N R A G T L E G G N O G
E Y I F T F R U I T C A K E E
R A U O B N D R A T G O O M D
R D P L R I N K S O G N E I R
Y G R E E N B E A N S T H X A
S T I N A L I Y I E T H H E E
A D I N D K O D S N S E R D T
U H H E O S D G R A V Y Y N D
C W A O E U E T U S L C A U U
E O C M P M E Q L A S A M T C
S M O R G A S B O R D T D S K

CIDER
COOKIES
CRANBERRY SAUCE
DUCK
EGGNOG
FRUITCAKE
GRAVY
GREEN BEANS
HAM
MIXED NUTS
PANETTONE
PIE
POTATOES
PUDDING
SALAD
SHORTBREAD
SMORGASBORD
SQUASH
STUFFING
TURKEY
YAM
YULE LOG

246.

PYRAMID POWER

The pyramid is made up of a series of words, each one containing the letters used in the word directly above it (the order of the letters may be changed) plus one new letter. Solve the clues to fill in the pyramid!

1. Modern -ticket, -book, or -bank
2. Poet Cummings's initials
3. Mrs. Adam
4. Always
5. Rhyme
6. Food bringer
7. Backward travel
8. Keep
9. Delays in sentences

DOLLARS TO DOUGHNUTS

1. Canada's one-dollar coin, the loonie, was introduced in
   - A. 1967
   - B. 1977
   - C. 1987
   - D. 1997

2. The Tim Hortons chain was founded in 1964. In what year did the chain introduce the Timbit?
   - A. 1966
   - B. 1976
   - C. 1986
   - D. 1996

[Answers: 1. = C. 1987; 2. = B. 1976]

247.

WORD SUDOKU: HARD

A word sudoku is a logic puzzle that works in exactly the same way as a regular number sudoku; however, instead of using nine different numbers in each square, row, and column, it uses nine different letters. The letters are anagrams (jumbled versions) of a single word. When you've solved the puzzle, you'll find the secret word in one of the puzzle's rows.

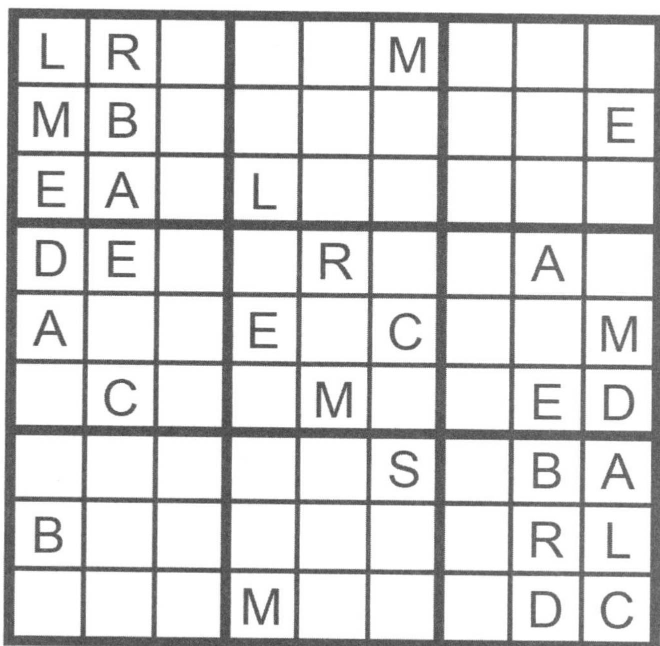

L	R				M			
M	B							E
E	A		L					
D	E			R			A	
A			E		C			M
	C			M			E	D
					S		B	A
B							R	L
			M				D	C

248.

WORD JIGSAW

The words in these quotes and quips have been sliced up into pieces, so you can no longer see where one word begins and another ends. The order of the letters inside each piece is unchanged. Can you reassemble the word pieces and figure out the original phrase?

1. _ _ _   _ _ _ _   _ _   _   _ _ _ _ ,   _ _ _
_ _ _ _   _ _   _ _ _   _ _ _ _ _ ,   “ _ _ _   _ _ _
_ _ _   _ _ _ _ ,   _ ’ _ _   _ _ _ _ _ ! ”

ATAN AYSTO HERY ISHIN KONES NSILLD OUMAN RIVE THEGU THEOT TWOF

2. _ _ ’ _   _ _ _ _ _ _   _ _ _ _ _ _ _ _   _ _ _ _ _ _
_ _ _   _ _ _ _ .   _ _   _ _   _ _ _ _ ’ _ _
_ _ _ _ _   _ _   _ _ _ _ _   _ _ _ _
_ _ _ _ _ _ _ _ ’ _   _ _ _ _ _ _ _ _ _ ,
_ _ _ _ ’ _   _ _ _   _ _ _ _   _ _   _ _   _ _ .

ARKES AWNS IGHBO IMET INGTOS ITSAL ODOIT OIFYO ORETHED OURNE URSNEW RTHAT SPAPE STHET TBEF TEALY UREGO WAYSD

3. _ _ _ _   _ _ _ _   _ _ _ _   _ _ _
_ _ _ _ _ _ _ _ _ _   _ _   _ _ _ _   _ _ _
_ _ _ _ _ _ _ _ _ _   _ _ _ _ ,   _ _ _   _ ’ _
_ _ _ _ _   _ _ _   _ _ _ _ _ _ _ _ _ .

BIV DSHER ECOG EGETA LSAI LUBBU MEFRO MTHEV NIZED ORE RIANC SGIR THER THI TIDNE VERME

4. _ _ _ _ _ _ _ _ _ _   _ _   _   _ _ _   _ _ _
_ _ _   _ _ _ _   _ _ _   _ _ _ _ _ _ _ _ _ ,
_ _ _   _ _ _ _ _ ' _ .

AGENT ANPLAYT ESNT HEACCO ISAMA LEMAN NWHOC RDIONB UTDO

5. _ _ _ _ - _ _ _ _ _ _ _ _ ,   _ _ _ _ _ _ _ _ ,
_ _ _ _ _ _ _ _ ,   _ _ _ _ _ _ _ _ ,
_ _ _ _ _ _ _ _ ,   _ _ _ _ _ _ _ ,
_ _ _ _ _ _ _ _ ,   _ _ _ _ _ _ _ _ _ _ _ _ _ _ _
_ _ _ _ _ _ _ ,   _ _ _ _ _ _ _ _ _ _ _ _ ,
_ _ _ _ _ _ _ _ . . . . _ _ _ _ _ _ _ _ _ _   _ _ _ _
_ _   _ _ _ _   _ _ _ _ _ _   _ _ _ _ _ _ _ .

DUCTIN ENCER ESKA GELSE GEVER HIGHS HINGS ISJUS KECON NGCHA NGFIGH NGTRI OOKI OUGHIN PEARI PPING RGINGH SLAS SPOR TERFER TFIGUR TICKI TING TINGUN TSMANLI YTHIN

LARGEST IN THE WORLD

1. The world's largest lobster, a 9-tonne sculpture, is located in

- **A.** Summerside, Prince Edward Island
- **B.** Tatamagouche, Nova Scotia
- **C.** Baker's Tickle, Newfoundland and Labrador
- **D.** Shediac, New Brunswick

2. The largest single concentration of harmless garter snakes in the world is in

- **A.** Kincardine, Ontario
- **B.** Narcisse, Manitoba
- **C.** Moncton, New Brunswick
- **D.** Baie Comeau, Quebec
- **E.** Estevan, Saskatchewan

[Answers: 1. = D. Shediac, New Brunswick; 2. = B. Narcisse, Manitoba]

249.

CANADIAN AUTHORS CROSSWORD

ACROSS

1. Green Gables creator
11. Spot for a yacht
15. An American who has not roamed
16. The big screen
17. Resolve
18. Leak (through)
19. Part of a golf club
20. Grain
21. Dustin in "Midnight Cowboy"
22. To be in Montreal
23. Desert in Israel
25. Big letters in fashion
28. Dish after the first course, at an Italian restaurant
32. ____ emergency
37. Author of "The Handmaid's Tale"
38. Light blue
39. Cast ingredient
41. To me, en Paris
42. James novella "The ____ Papers"
44. Writer who popularized the term "Generation X"
46. Author of "Nonsense Novels"
48. Unclosed, to a poet
49. Stags and does
51. Dextrous prefix
55. Some pens
58. Suffix in taxonomy
60. Scottish Robert
62. Test for a prospective lawyer
63. Wish evil on
65. "I'll pay!"
66. Flush with embarrassment
67. Head honcho
68. Where Robb Stark is king

DOWN

1. Command to a husky
2. Leg extended, in ballet
3. Type of explosion
4. One who corners an animal upwards
5. Typesetter proofs
6. Egg prefix
7. "Send ____ Flowers" (Jewison film)
8. Of the same region as the first olympics
9. Remainders (Fr.)
10. Groups of ft.
11. Negative assertion
12. "____ a traveller from an antique land"
13. Actresses West and Questel
14. Trade show
21. Angular beginning
24. Get ready, colloquially
26. Medium's meeting place
27. Place, abbr.
29. Miniature pony
30. "The Banks O' ____" (60 Across poem)
31. "It was me!"
32. Apple date-maker
33. TSX rival
34. Cloak for a matador
35. Stories by 46 Across, e.g.
36. Canadian fashion network
40. Win in tic-tac-toe
43. Some eggs
45. Red and white legume
47. Former Austrian coins
50. City in Germany
52. Jumbo partner
53. Prickly patch
54. Embedded photo
55. Formless lump
56. "There ____ try" (Yoda)
57. Smashes into
59. Greenland settlement
61. Brother of Abel
63. "Entourage" character Gold
64. A-frame bldg.

1	2	3	4	5	6	7	8	9	10	■	11	12	13	14
15										■	16			
17										■	18			
19					■	20			■	21				
■	22				■	■	23		24			■	■	■
■	■	■	■	25	26	27	■	28				29	30	31
32	33	34	35				36	■	37					
38				■	39			40		■	41			
42				43		■	44			45				
46						47	■	48			■	■	■	■
■	■	■	49				50	■	■	51	52	53	54	■
55	56	57			■	58		59	■	60				61
62				■	63				64					
65				■	66									
67				■	68									

250.

SUDOKU: HARD

A sudoku puzzle is a type of logic puzzle. Although it uses numbers, no mathematics is involved. The grid below is divided into nine large squares, each of which is divided into nine smaller squares. Each large square contains all the digits from 1 to 9, with each digit appearing exactly once. Each horizontal row of the puzzle also contains each digit exactly once, and so does each vertical row. By carefully observing which numbers are missing from each row, column, or square, see if you can figure out which numbers go where. There's only one possible solution to each puzzle.

2			8		3		6	
		8	7					9
	5					8		
	2		9				5	
		7				2		
	6				4		7	
		5					3	
4					7	9		
	3		4		9			1

251.

SUDOKU: HARD

A sudoku puzzle is a type of logic puzzle. Although it uses numbers, no mathematics is involved. The grid below is divided into nine large squares, each of which is divided into nine smaller squares. Each large square contains all the digits from 1 to 9, with each digit appearing exactly once. Each horizontal row of the puzzle also contains each digit exactly once, and so does each vertical row. By carefully observing which numbers are missing from each row, column, or square, see if you can figure out which numbers go where. There's only one possible solution to each puzzle.

8					5			
	5				4	3		
	2			1		7	5	
	8		1					
1	4		8		3		7	6
					7		1	
	7	3		8			9	
		9	3				8	
			2					1

252.

CRYPTOGRAM

Each of the quotes below has been encrypted, with each letter of the alphabet substituted for a different letter. The substitutions are different for each puzzle. Use your code-breaking skills to discover the original quotation! (Hints: Start with short words—a one-letter word is usually A or I. Count the number of each letter—the commonest letter in English is E, followed by T, A, O, I, and N, while the most common three-letter word is THE.)

1. B N J A   C N M T U I   Q M T   I M   X G   Q M T   C P P

J F   P F I J F D P O P J   F X E J U   P J A X F D   J F

P F I J F D P O P I   H U J F A ?

2. R K J K W Q K J U   K F D   Z D J D F K H H C

Q J W Q U I Q J Z A Q U P K X H D   Y F B T   K T D F Q R K J U ,

K J W   I P D   U A F D U I   O K C   B Y   I D H H Q J Z

I P D   I O B   K M K F I   Q U   I B   T K N D   I P K I

B X U D F L K I Q B J   I B   K   R K J K W Q K J .

—F Q R P K F W   U I K Q J D U

3. L D O   D R K   B I I G :   D   K D W ' G   P F Y Q   E F Y   D   Z L A Z Q B R ,   D   S A E B M A O B   Z F O O A M O B R M   E F Y   D   N A I .

4. Z U   L K F   J B X V M C   K F G   M A A   G O V   J M P C   Z P   P K X G O   M U X Z I M ,   Z G   D K F A C   I K E V X   G O V   J M O M X M   C V J V X G .

5. Z   Y M D Q   T G Z Q C B L   O Y V   L O Q M G   X Y Q K   B G Q M W   Z C   P V A V N G ;   Z   L M K   Z X ' L   U N L X   M   E Z J W Q C X   V T   X Y Q Z G   Z W M J Z C M X Z V C .

6. J ' X W   E W L J E W E   C D   T W Y Y   N S   X G L M M N   L Y W G B W K . . . O W Y Y ,   J C   O G T   V M T C   L D Y Y W L C J B R   E M T C . — C J N   X J B W

253.

HERBS AND SPICES

All the words in the list below are hidden somewhere in the grid of letters. See if you can find them! Words may run in any direction, including diagonally, and spaces are ignored. When you've crossed off all the words, read the leftover letters in the grid (running left to right, from top to bottom) to reveal a hidden quote related to the puzzle's theme.

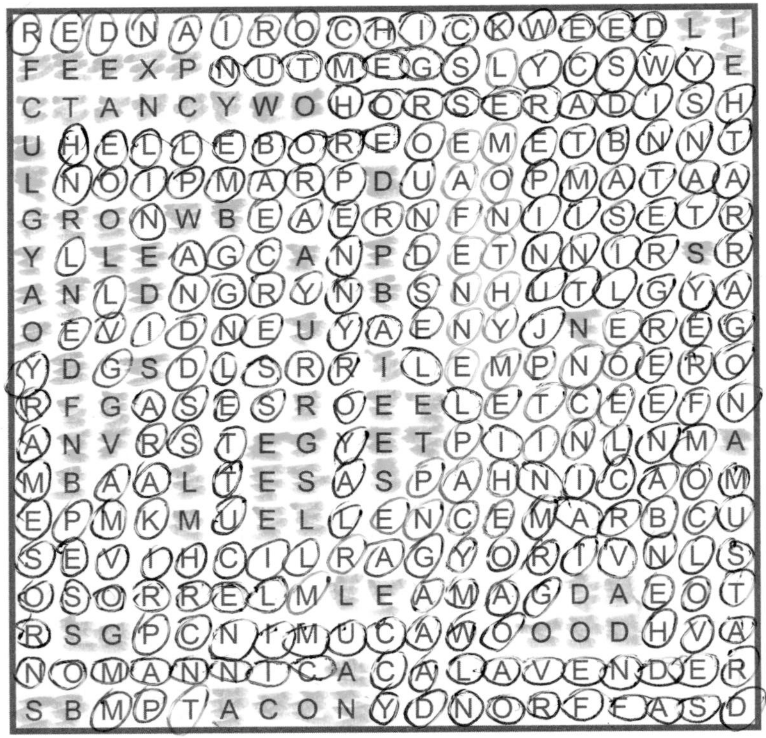

ANISE
BASIL
BAY
CAMOMILE
CAPERS
CARAWAY
CATMINT
CAYENNE
CHICKWEED
CHICORY
CHIVES
CINNAMON
CLOVES
COMFREY
CORIANDER
CRESS
CUMIN
DILL
ENDIVE
GARLIC
GENTIAN
GINGER
GROUNDSEL
HELLEBORE
HENBANE
HORSERADISH
JUNIPER
LAVENDER
LEMON THYME
LETTUCE
MACE
MARIGOLD
MUSTARD
NUTMEG
OREGANO
PAPRIKA
PARSLEY
PENNY ROYAL
PEPPERMINT
RAMPION
ROSEMARY
RUE
SAFFRON
SAGE
SEA FENNEL
SESAME
SORREL
TANSY
TARRAGON
VANILLA
WINTER GREEN

CHRISTMAS SONGS

1. Which Christmas carol includes the lyrics "Deep and crisp and even"?

2. Which Christmas carol includes the lyrics "A song, a song, high above the trees"?

3. Who has a corncob pipe, a button nose, and two eyes made of coal?

4. In the song "Winter Wonderland," who do we pretend the snowman is?

5. Name the Christmas songs whose names have these initials:

   A. LISLISLIS
   B. TMWTOTY
   C. HYAMLC
   D. SCICTT

6. What is the error in the lyrics of the traditional Christmas carol "I Saw Three Ships"?

   A. Ships never sail in threes.
   B. Ships never sail on Christmas Day.
   C. Bethlehem doesn't have a port.

[Answers: 1. "Good King Wenceslas"; 2. "Do You Hear What I Hear?"; 3. Frosty the Snowman; 4. Parson Brown; 5. A. = "Let It Snow! Let It Snow! Let It Snow!"; B. = "The Most Wonderful Time of the Year"; C. = "Have Yourself a Merry Little Christmas"; D. = "Santa Claus Is Coming to Town"; 6. = C. Bethlehem doesn't have a port.]

254.

REBUS

In these puzzles, the arrangement of the letters and symbols suggests a common word or expression. For example, this combination

COVER
GOING

is "going undercover" (the word GOING is under the word COVER—literally). See how many you can figure out.

1. **MOVE**

2. ⟶ WING

3. PACING
↕
PACING

4. ans.

5. V A R I E T Y

255.

ANTLERGRAM

The goal of antlergrams is to form as many words as you can using the letters in the moose's nose and antlers. Each letter can be used only once, which means you can form a word with two Ts only if there are two Ts in the puzzle. Each word must be three or more letters long and must contain the letter in the nose, along with any combination of the letters from the antlers. For the ultimate challenge, see if you can find the one 9-letter word that contains ALL the letters in the puzzle.

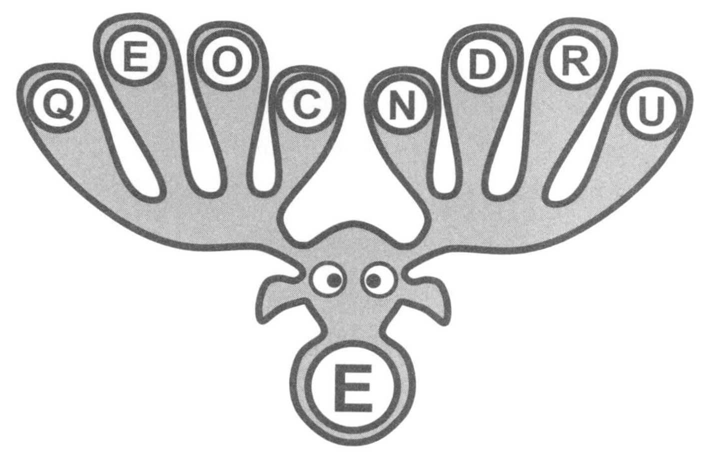

256.

13 × 13 CROSSWORD

ACROSS

1. C, E, G, e.g.
6. Engine part
9. Just right
12. Pâté base
13. Playing card
14. Skilled person
15. Insect phase
16. Earth-friendly prefix
17. Whack
18. Trainee
21. Breather
24. Tear
25. Footnote notation
26. Great time
27. Classic Volkswagen
29. Nude
31. Aviator
35. Marco Polo area
37. Saloon order
38. Slimy critter
41. Bag
42. Do nothing
43. Far-flung
46. Eliminate
47. Movie studio
48. "Knock it off!"
52. Get older
53. Timber wood
54. Jet detector
55. Ontario capital (abbr.)
56. Turkish bigwig
57. Flee to wed

DOWN

1. 151 on a monument
2. Her's partner
3. Biological eggs
4. Fit for a king
5. Go down
6. Spenser's "The ___ Queen"
7. Green light
8. Times Square sign
9. Prey for a ladybug
10. Payment
11. Pole in BC
19. Incline
20. Piece of cake
21. Romanian money
22. Coffee holder
23. Lot of eau
27. Oppose
28. Afire
30. Theatre section
32. Screwy
33. Above ___ (primarily)
34. Word before a maiden name in wedding announcements
36. Coarse, as humour
38. Perspire
39. Specialized talk
40. What a milking machine connects to
42. Perfect
44. Block
45. Piece of land
49. Hassle
50. Enfeeble
51. Prior to, poetically

1	2	3	4	5	■	6	7	8	■	9	10	11
12					■	13			■	14		
15					■	16			■	17		
■	■	■	18		19				20			
21	22	23		■	24			■	25			
26			■	27				28		■	■	■
29			30			■	31			32	33	34
■	■	■	35			36			■	37		
38	39	40		■	41			■	42			
43				44				45		■	■	■
46			■	47			■	48		49	50	51
52			■	53			■	54				
55			■	56			■	57				

257.

WORDS × FIVE

This puzzle is similar to a crossword, but the five-letter answer to each clue is written twice—both across and down. So, if the solution to clue 1 is FLAME, you would write FLAME into the grid twice, from left to right and from top to bottom.

1	2	3	4	5
2				
3				
4				
5				

1. Horse
2. Glittering headpiece
3. Keen
4. Standing
5. Pub game

EXPERT 3

DOUBLE-DOUBLE TAKE

Spot the difference: can you find the 12 changes?

HOLIDAY BABIES

1. Identify these well-known people, all born on December 25:

    A. She won an Academy Award for her portrayal of country-and-western singer Loretta Lynn.

    B. She is half of the British music duo known as the Eurythmics.

    C. He is Canada's second-youngest prime minister.

    D. Rick Blaine and Sam Spade were two of his famous roles.

    E. Her song "Black Velvet" was a tribute to Elvis Presley.

2. This Christmas baby said, "What goes up must come down":

    A. Isaac Newton

    B. Galileo Galilei

    C. Albert Einstein

    D. Johannes Kepler

    E. Nicolaus Copernicus

3. Born October 31, his movies include *Home Alone* and *Uncle Buck*:

    A. Martin Short

    B. Eugene Levy

    C. John Candy

    D. Mike Myers

    E. Leslie Nielsen

4. These three Canadians were born on July 1:

    A. Jim Carrey, Alice Munro, Ryan Gosling

    B. Dan Aykroyd, Pamela Anderson, Geneviève Bujold

    C. Rick Moranis, Christopher Plummer, Margaret Atwood

    D. Roberta Bondar, Mary Pickford, Mario Lemieux

    E. Shania Twain, Andre De Grasse, William Shatner

5. Who wasn't born on December 24?

    A. Actress Ava Gardner

    B. Singer Ricky Martin

    C. Newfoundland premier Joey Smallwood

    D. Movie director James Cameron

    E. *Twilight* author Stephenie Meyer

SOLUTION EXPERT 3

Answers:
1. A. Sissy Spacek, B. Annie Lennox, C. Justin Trudeau (Joe Clark was younger), D. Humphrey Bogart (the roles were in *Casablanca* and *The Maltese Falcon*), E. Alannah Myles;
2. A. Isaac Newton;
3. C. John Candy;
4. B. Dan Aykroyd, Pamela Anderson, Geneviève Bujold;
5. D. Movie director James Cameron;

258.

WORDS × FIVE

This puzzle is similar to a crossword, but the five-letter answer to each clue is written twice—both across and down. So, if the solution to clue 1 is FLAME, you would write FLAME into the grid twice, from left to right and from top to bottom.

1	2	3	4	5
2				
3				
4				
5				

1. Presents
2. Fool
3. Large bill
4. Sum
5. Fashion

259.

MAPLE LEAF

The goal of this puzzle is to form as many words as you can using the letters contained in the leaf. Each letter can be used only once, so you can create a word with two Ts only if there are two Ts in the leaf. Each word must be three or more letters long, and all words must contain the large central letter of the leaf, along with any mix of the letters around the outside. For the ultimate challenge, see if you can find the one 10-letter word that contains ALL the letters in the leaf.

260.

REBUS

In these puzzles, the arrangement of the letters and symbols suggests a common word or expression. For example, this combination

COVER
GOING

is "going undercover" (the word GOING is under the word COVER—literally). See how many you can figure out.

1. Begin
Begin

2. 

3. ALL ALL ALL ALL ALL ALL WELL
WELL THAT

4. 

5.

261.

SUDOKU: HARD

A sudoku puzzle is a type of logic puzzle. Although it uses numbers, no mathematics is involved. The grid below is divided into nine large squares, each of which is divided into nine smaller squares. Each large square contains all the digits from 1 to 9, with each digit appearing exactly once. Each horizontal row of the puzzle also contains each digit exactly once, and so does each vertical row. By carefully observing which numbers are missing from each row, column, or square, see if you can figure out which numbers go where. There's only one possible solution to each puzzle.

5	6		8	7		2		
			4			7	9	
				1				
	3				1			2
		4				8		
9			6				3	
				2				
	5	7			4			
		3		6	7		4	1

262.

SUDOKU: HARD

A sudoku puzzle is a type of logic puzzle. Although it uses numbers, no mathematics is involved. The grid below is divided into nine large squares, each of which is divided into nine smaller squares. Each large square contains all the digits from 1 to 9, with each digit appearing exactly once. Each horizontal row of the puzzle also contains each digit exactly once, and so does each vertical row. By carefully observing which numbers are missing from each row, column, or square, see if you can figure out which numbers go where. There's only one possible solution to each puzzle.

					4			1
			3	7			9	4
4	3		5	9			2	
				1	3		6	5
5								9
2	6		9	4				
	9			5	6		3	2
8	5			3	7			
3			4					

263.

URBAN LIFE

All the words in the list below are hidden somewhere in the grid of letters. See if you can find them! Words may run in any direction, including diagonally, and spaces are ignored. When you've crossed off all the words, read the leftover letters in the grid (running left to right, from top to bottom) to reveal a hidden quote related to the puzzle's theme. This city is what it is because our citizens are what they are

ALLEY
AVENUE
BUSINESS
BUSTLE
COMMUTERS
CONCRETE JUNGLE
CONSTRUCTION
CROSSWALK
DOWNTOWN
FASHION DISTRICT
MULTICULTURAL
NINE TO FIVE
PIGEON
SHOPS
SIDEWALK
SKYSCRAPER
SMOG
SUBWAY
TAXI
TOURISM
TRAFFIC
TRAIN
TRENDY

264.

CATCH A WORD: FRUITS

In this type of puzzle, the answer appears in its correct order but may begin in the middle of a word and be interrupted by spaces and punctuation. For example: The Canadians were victorious in hockey once again. Can you find the names of ten fruits hidden in the sentences below?

1. Professor Anari specialized in urban analysis, with a focus on nodal development.
2. Interpol and the RCMP trap plenty of criminals together.
3. However much you gripe, aches and pains do not recede without proper care.
4. Gwen thought it would prove difficult to connect Ari, needy as he was, with a blind date.
5. Who knows the havoc a dog can cause, cohabiting with a ferret.
6. Anders was not sure whether to trust his shoulder devil or angel.
7. Despite her friend's bedazzlement, Beatriz hoped she could slap Rico to his senses.
8. The mailman got through his rounds, despite the delivery van blowout.
9. Tina got beef from the butcher, rye bread from the baker, and pine-scented candles from the candlestick maker.
10. They visited Guatemala, Honduras, and Nicaragua, vacationed on a West Indian isle, then took a returning flight to Mexico.

265.

15 × 15 CROSSWORD

ACROSS

1. Persian fairy
5. Went underwater
9. Finnish island group
14. Cosmetics brand
15. Philippine port
16. Generous one
17. South American pigs
19. Scamp
20. "Indiana Jones" quest
21. Anticipated
23. Past
24. French sovereign
25. Feminizing suffix
26. Degrassi High, e.g.
30. Set-tos
32. Jumped
33. Hold up
34. Dance in a grass skirt
38. Lounge
39. Muck
40. Love deity
41. Sleigh pullers
42. Moneyed Brits
43. Germany's Third ___
44. Up there
46. Hummable, perhaps
47. Lang. of Isr.
50. Recording giant
51. Sweetheart
52. Pottery
55. Word before and after "-à-"
58. Hoard
59. Garbo film "Queen ___"
61. 1988 Olympics site
62. Gorges
63. Artist Warhol
64. Complete
65. Eye malady
66. Dudes

DOWN

1. One of the three bears
2. "Happily ___ after"
3. Popular music
4. "Monsters, ___" (Disney film)
5. Dead Sea document
6. Bizarre
7. Influence
8. Explodes
9. Able
10. Carpet weaver
11. Rolling Stones hit: 1973
12. They can be common or proper
13. Vestiges
18. Happening
22. Car style
26. Lost traction
27. Relinquish
28. In good health
29. "La Bohème" or "La Traviata"
30. Buy off
31. Bed spread
33. Ontario and Quebec
35. Acid related to gout
36. Ness or Lomond
37. Washed-out
39. Fairy tale figure
43. Grades
45. Envisioned
46. Cherry shade
47. Nobel novelist Hermann
48. Food after one does 62 Across
49. Offspring
51. Group
53. Genuine
54. "Come again?"
55. Italian wine
56. "500" race
57. Talks
60. Typewriter key

1	2	3	4	■	5	6	7	8	■	9	10	11	12	13
14				■	15				■	16				
17				18					■	19				
20			■	21					22					
■	■	■	■	23			■	24			■	25		
26	27	28	29			■	30				31	■	■	■
32					■	33				■	34	35	36	37
38				■	39					■	40			
41				■	42				■	43				
■	■	■	44	45				■	46					
47	48	49	■	50			■	51			■	■	■	■
52			53				54				■	55	56	57
58					■	59					60			
61					■	62				■	63			
64					■	65				■	66			

266.

WORDS × SIX

This puzzle is similar to a crossword, but the six-letter answer to each clue is written twice—both across and down. So, if the solution to clue 1 is GOBLIN, you would write GOBLIN into the grid twice, from left to right and from top to bottom.

1	2	3	4	5	6
2					
3					
4					
5					
6					

1. Paper glues
2. Quantity
3. At a closer time
4. Permafrost region
5. Get-up-and-go
6. Lost dogs

267.

WORDS × SIX

This puzzle is similar to a crossword, but the six-letter answer to each clue is written twice—both across and down. So, if the solution to clue 1 is GOBLIN, you would write GOBLIN into the grid twice, from left to right and from top to bottom.

1	2	3	4	5	6
2					
3					
4					
5					
6					

1. Fearful
2. Film spot
3. Reply
4. Make changes
5. Climb out
6. Less bright

268.

MAPLE LEAF

The goal of this puzzle is to form as many words as you can, using the letters contained in the leaf. Each letter can be used only once, so you can create a word with two Ts only if there are two Ts in the leaf. Each word must be three or more letters long, and all words must contain the large central letter of the leaf, along with any mix of the letters around the outside. For the ultimate challenge, see if you can find the one 10-letter word that contains ALL the letters in the leaf.

LET IT SNOW!

1. The biggest one-day snowfall measured in Canada occurred in

- **A.** British Columbia
- **B.** Quebec
- **C.** Nunavut

2. Canada's snowiest large cities are

- **A.** Montreal, Quebec; Winnipeg, Manitoba
- **B.** St. John's, Newfoundland and Labrador; Saguenay, Quebec
- **C.** Regina, Saskatchewan; Thunder Bay, Ontario

3. The classic Christmas movie *A Christmas Story* was filmed in and around Toronto during a snow-free January. Which of the following substances was *not* used to create snow for the Christmas morning backyard scene?

- **A.** fire-fighting foam
- **B.** potato flakes
- **C.** flour

[Answers: 1. = A. British Columbia—in 1999, about 145 centimetres fell in Tahtsa Lake, B.C., within a 24-hour period; 2. = B. St. John's, Newfoundland and Labrador, ranks first for total amount of snow; Saguenay, Quebec, has the most days with fresh snowfall; 3. = C. flour]

269.

CLUE CROSSWORD

ACROSS

1. Shortstop Turner
5. Knife
9. Sweet 48 Down
14. Skimmed
15. Pakistani coin
16. Poet Nash
17. Poreless, as a plant
19. Pillages
20. A winning deduction, with 36 and 55 Across
22. Diner dessert
23. E-organizer
24. South American tree
25. One who works in a colony
26. Unagi, at a sushi restaurant
27. Hwys.
28. Functions
31. Brit. decorations
33. Miniature orchid
36. See 20 Across
40. Clean freak
41. California wine valley
43. The Beatles' "Back in the ___"
44. Certain snack biscuit
47. Cooking unit
48. Easy mark
51. "A Midsummer Night's Dream" character
53. Carbon-fibre material, for short
54. ___ king
55. See 20 Across
57. Word on the street
59. Banana lurker
60. Dispatch boat
61. Military orbiter
62. Electrical minist.
63. Drink that doesn't wake you up
64. Cheek
65. Norms: Abbr.

DOWN

1. Barged (in)
2. Is a citizen of
3. Is excluded from the lunch table, say
4. Troubles
5. Simon Pegg sitcom
6. Predecessors to gods
7. Ticks, taxonomically
8. Cord in a Victorian house
9. Shock
10. Freudian subject
11. Treatment described in Oliver Sacks's "Awakenings"
12. Invite, as a vampire
13. Commencement
18. Skype, e.g., for short
21. Artist's stand
29. Norse goddess of medicine
30. Shortly
32. Traffic jam on the autobahn
33. Comic book writer Greg
34. "On ___ can it be right to do an injustice . . ."
35. Colourfully enraged
37. Alts.
38. Chinese canyon
39. Catholic hats
42. Seems to be
44. Colourful fish
45. Doffs one's cap
46. Normandy city
48. Caesar or Waldorf
49. Pearl Jam single
50. ___ at the Disco (band)
52. Tibet's capital
55. Canine interjection
56. Country paths
58. Citroen family vehicle

1	2	3	4		5	6	7	8		9	10	11	12	13
14					15					16				
17				18						19				
20									21			22		
23				24								25		
26				27				28		29	30			
31			32				33					34	35	
	36			37	38	39								
	40										41			42
			43					44	45	46		47		
48	49	50			51		52					53		
54				55							56			
57			58			59								
60						61					62			
63						64					65			

270.

WORDS × FIVE

This puzzle is similar to a crossword, but the five-letter answer to each clue is written twice—both across and down. So, if the solution to clue 1 is FLAME, you would write FLAME into the grid twice, from left to right and from top to bottom.

1	2	3	4	5
2				
3				
4				
5				

1. Diced
2. The way words are employed
3. Lapel decoration
4. Urged on
5. Accomplishments

271.

MAPLE LEAF

The goal of this puzzle is to form as many words as you can, using the letters contained in the leaf. Each letter can be used only once, so you can create a word with two Ts only if there are two Ts in the leaf. Each word must be three or more letters long, and all words must contain the large central letter of the leaf, along with any mix of the letters around the outside. For the ultimate challenge, see if you can find the one 10-letter word that contains ALL the letters in the leaf.

272.

SYLLABLANK

The solution to each of the following puzzles is a single nine-letter word. We've chopped each word up into the smaller words listed below. Place the smaller words into the right positions on the blanks to discover the original words.

A A ABLE ABLE AT BID CAR DEN FOR FUR HIS I ICE IN IRE IS IT JUST KING LIT ME NU ON OR PAL PART PART PEN PLAY PUT RAT RE RED RED SO SOP THE TRY TRY

1. WELL-REGARDED __ __   __ __ __   __ __ __ __
2. CARD GAME TIME KILLER __ __   __ __ __   __   __ __ __
3. WRONGDOING __ __   __ __ __ __   __ __ __
4. TASTY __ __ __   __ __   __ __ __ __
5. SHOW AGAIN __ __ __   __ __   __ __ __ __
6. ADVANCED __ __ __   __ __ __   __ __ __
7. WOODWORK __ __ __   __ __ __   __ __ __
8. JOINING THE MEAL __ __ __ __   __   __ __ __ __
9. SPLIT UP __ __ __ __   __ __   __   __ __
10. PROHIBITED __ __ __   __ __ __   __ __ __
11. WELL-WORDED FALSEHOOD __ __ __   __ __ __   __ __ __
12. FRACTION TOP __ __   __ __   __ __ __   __ __

CHRISTMAS MEMORY GAME

This game is for small groups. You'll need a sheet of paper and a pencil for each player. Place 10 to 15 Christmas items (for example: a card, tinsel, different ornaments) on a tray. Give people one minute to memorize the items and then take the tray away. Participants have one minute to write down the name of as many items as they can remember.

273.

ANTLERGRAM

The goal of antlergrams is to form as many words as you can using the letters in the moose's nose and antlers. Each letter can be used only once, which means you can form a word with two Ts only if there are two Ts in the puzzle. Each word must be three or more letters long and must contain the letter in the nose, along with any combination of the letters from the antlers. For the ultimate challenge, see if you can find the one 9-letter word that contains ALL the letters in the puzzle.

274.

SUDOKU: HARD

A sudoku puzzle is a type of logic puzzle. Although it uses numbers, no mathematics is involved. The grid below is divided into nine large squares, each of which is divided into nine smaller squares. Each large square contains all the digits from 1 to 9, with each digit appearing exactly once. Each horizontal row of the puzzle also contains each digit exactly once, and so does each vertical row. By carefully observing which numbers are missing from each row, column, or square, see if you can figure out which numbers go where. There's only one possible solution to each puzzle.

					4	1	5	
		2	1	9				
		4		2	7		3	
	3	7						
9		6				4		5
						3	6	
	8		6	7		5		
				1	5	9		
	9	5	4					

275.

SUDOKU: HARD

A sudoku puzzle is a type of logic puzzle. Although it uses numbers, no mathematics is involved. The grid below is divided into nine large squares, each of which is divided into nine smaller squares. Each large square contains all the digits from 1 to 9, with each digit appearing exactly once. Each horizontal row of the puzzle also contains each digit exactly once, and so does each vertical row. By carefully observing which numbers are missing from each row, column, or square, see if you can figure out which numbers go where. There's only one possible solution to each puzzle.

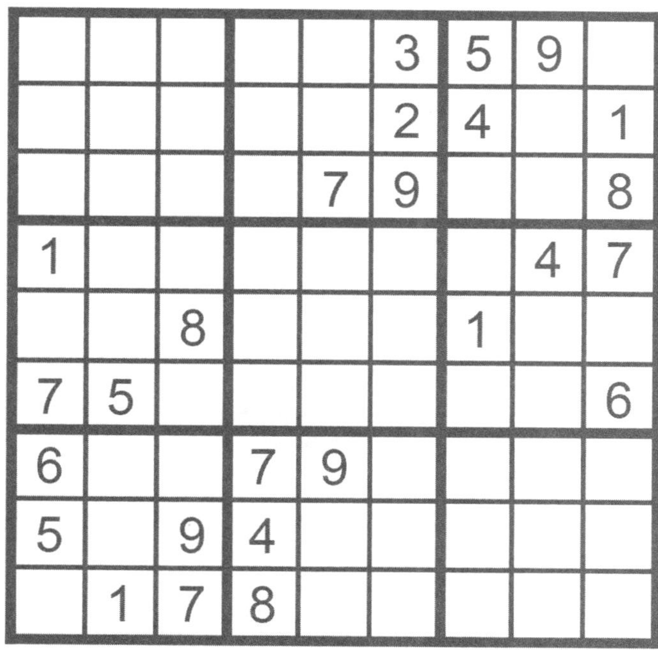

					3	5	9	
					2	4		1
				7	9			8
1							4	7
		8				1		
7	5							6
6			7	9				
5		9	4					
	1	7	8					

276.

SUPER GROUP CROSSWORD

ACROSS

1. Common rhyming scheme
5. American territory
9. Nick
13. Small iPods
15. Japanese woman
16. Quarterback Tony
17. Demand
18. Made an entrance
20. #1 hit of 1974
22. Activity for data or coal
23. Bun
24. Italian gulf city
25. Like pants in the 1970s
29. A song in this puzzle, perhaps
30. Polloi starter
31. Group behind 20, 43, and 46 Across and 8 and 60 Down
35. Firm up
36. California valley
40. Member of one's fam.
41. Computer peripheral protocol
43. #1 hit of 1975
44. Online refund
46. #1 hit of 1976
50. Pippa's mother, and others
53. Blue in Madrid
54. "The Love Affairs of Nathaniel P" author Waldman
55. Spot for a no-parking sign
59. Station tuner
61. Curtain fabric
62. R&B singer Foxx
63. Actress Falco
64. Hotsy partner
65. Home turf
66. Rhode Island rebellion
67. Capital of Okinawa

DOWN

1. Start fresh
2. Bing lead-in
3. Thing that's picked
4. Tenor Andrea
5. Become more lenient
6. "___ the Fourth Generation" (Asimov story)
7. "That's -___"
8. #1 hit of 1975
9. Island nation northeast of Venezuela
10. Thinker sculptor
11. What's made, if successful
12. Small drum
14. Lights at the disco
19. Worse, to François
21. ___-tzu
24. "Roger Rabbit," for one
25. Marshes
26. Type of pwr.
27. Cholesterols
28. "___ Promise You" (*NSYNC)
32. Scottish bank, in a way
33. ___ noire
34. BC soccer coach Marcina
37. If necessary
38. Spots (abbr.)
39. Following
42. Worship, as a hero
45. Gold ingots
47. Bobby's greeting
48. Tool for a carpenter
49. Black Sabbath spinoff band
50. West Indies resident
51. Turkish city
52. Ancient counsels
55. Expo
56. Temple-style pillar
57. Grub
58. New Age singer
60. Repeated, #1 hit of 1975

1	2	3	4	■	■	5	6	7	8	■	9	10	11	12
13				14	■	15				■	16			
17					■	18				19				
20					21			■	22					
■	■	■	23				■	24						
25	26	27					28					■	■	■
29					■	■	30			■	31	32	33	34
35			■	36	37	38				39	■	40		
41			42	■	43			■	■	44	45			
■	■	■	46	47				48	49					
50	51	52					■	53				■	■	■
54						■	55					56	57	58
59						60			■	61				
62				■	63				■	64				
65				■	66				■	■	67			

277.

SUPERHEROES

All the words in the list below are hidden somewhere in the grid of letters. See if you can find them! Words may run in any direction, including diagonally, and spaces are ignored. When you've crossed off all the words, read the leftover letters in the grid (running left to right, from top to bottom) to reveal a hidden quote related to the puzzle's theme.

G F A N T A S T I C F O U R X
R B W O N D E R W O M A N D W
E L I T H H A W K E Y E E N S
E A G H O S T R I D E R A R U
N C G R R E P A L T P M E W P
L K A O E S P I R I T G W O E
A W E Q R E V C D A N O X L R
N I P M U E N E B E S G M V M
T D R U D A E H V A R T E E A
E O R E N M M A O F E M N R N
R W R S O I P A K R A O A I T
N A N T H S S S N I N L B N M
D I A L I U A H U L K E C E A
F L A S H M L T E R O H T O N
I R O N M A N K Y R O B I N N

ANTMAN
AQUAMAN
ATOM
AVENGERS
BATMAN
BLACK WIDOW
DAREDEVIL
FALCON
FANTASTIC FOUR
FLASH
GHOST RIDER
GREEN HORNET
GREEN LANTERN
HAWKEYE
HULK
IRON MAN
MASK
PUNISHER
RED X
ROBIN
SPIDER-MAN
SPIRIT
SUPERMAN
THOR
WOLVERINE
WONDER WOMAN
X-MEN

278.

JACK

All the words in the list below are hidden somewhere in the grid of letters. See if you can find them! Words may run in any direction, including diagonally, and spaces are ignored. When you've crossed off all the words, read the leftover letters in the grid (running left to right, from top to bottom) to reveal a hidden quote related to the puzzle's theme.

M	P	H	I	T	T	H	E	R	O	A	D	W	I	T
A	M	U	O	F	A	L	L	T	R	A	D	E	S	H
C	O	M	D	Y	S	E	U	N	G	L	F	A	S	S
K	N	E	S	D	I	O	N	R	I	M	J	L	A	C
E	T	K	N	N	I	R	I	O	O	S	T	R	A	W
R	E	C	A	H	E	N	N	B	F	O	L	B	N	P
E	R	D	J	K	L	R	G	I	H	L	S	L	A	O
L	E	N	C	U	E	S	W	N	E	S	I	A	P	T
H	Y	A	O	T	M	U	T	S	A	T	O	C	E	T
H	R	E	N	A	M	P	S	O	R	E	C	K	S	L
C	I	A	D	M	F	U	I	N	T	E	L	A	T	U
F	L	A	S	H	R	A	N	N	S	P	O	T	D	M
O	D	A	N	D	J	I	L	L	G	L	C	A	A	B
S	I	X	T	L	A	D	D	E	R	E	K	R	W	E
Y	I	N	T	H	E	B	O	X	K	N	I	F	E	R

ADAMS
ANAPES
AND JILL
BLACK
CRACKER
DANIEL
DAW
FLAP
FLASH
HIT THE ROAD
IN THE BOX
JUMPING
KNIFE
LADDER
LUMBER
MACKEREL
MONTEREY
O'CLOCK
O'LANTERN
OF ALL TRADES
OF HEARTS
POT
PUDDING
ROBINSON
RUSSELL
STEEPLE
STRAW
TAR

279.

LUCKY CROSSWORD

ACROSS

1. Conventional
6. Dispatches from the dog house
11. Jewellery box content
12. Set on fire
14. Good luck charms, appropriate for this puzzle
17. Sea bird
18. British pirate of note
19. Comfort
20. Out of the ordinary
21. Wrath that's drawn
22. Floor covering
23. Got one's hands on
25. Metric volume
27. Remainder, old-fashionedly
28. Toll-less road
30. Playful composition
32. Sea wriggler
33. Grassy spot
34. Nest builders
38. Mystic chants
42. Deck members
43. Comic sound effect
45. Rough fabric
46. Adaptable truck: Abbr.
47. Something positive
48. Wrestling announcer Marshall
49. Footy suffix
51. "____ the End of Time" (Timberlake/Beyonce duet)
53. Toyota coupe
54. Slim chance in searching, like 14 Across
57. Font option
58. Maverick's portrayer
59. One of the seven deadlies
60. Tooth lead-in

DOWN

1. Bed on wheels
2. The olden days
3. Candidate, for short
4. Chilled
5. One of three virtues
6. Nettings
7. Check out
8. Lennon's S. O.
9. A handful?
10. Broccoli container
11. Be on edge
13. Counterfeit
14. Give feudal land
15. Cab driver's due
16. Begin
24. Younger years
25. Makes barren, as earth
26. Splendour, en Tours
27. Under, poetically
29. Tiny
31. Miss Prissy was one
34. Finnish football club
35. Leggy creatures
36. Prepares for a third draft, say
37. Florentine ingredient
38. Madmen
39. Let go
40. Punish, financially
41. Give a piece of one's mind
44. Reluctant
50. Aldehyde
51. Police task force
52. Constellation containing Vega
53. ____ the pot
55. U.N. grp.
56. Teaching temp

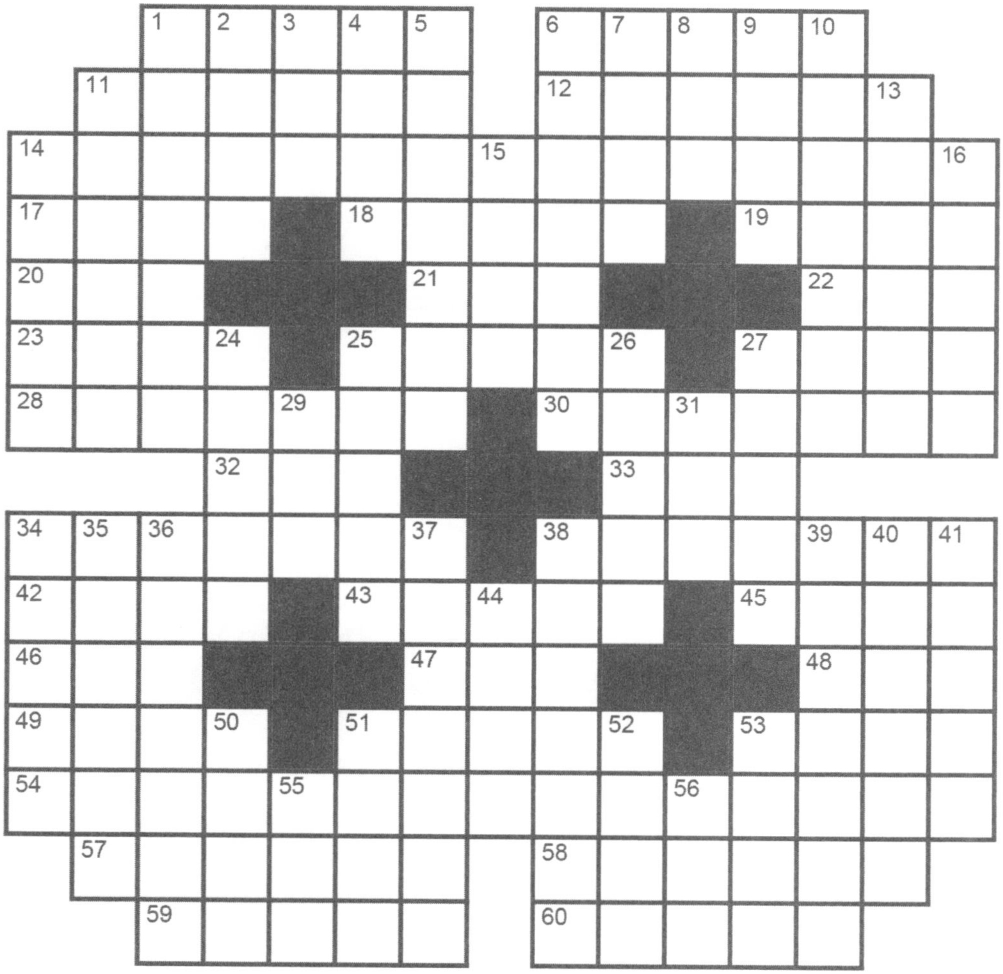
1
2
3
4
5
6
7
8
9
10
11
12
13
14
15
16
17
18
19
20
21
22
23
24
25
26
27
28
29
30
31
32
33
34
35
36
37
38
39
40
41
42
43
44
45
46
47
48
49
50
51
52
53
54
55
56
57
58
59
60

280.

REBUS

In these puzzles, the arrangement of the letters and symbols suggests a common word or expression. For example, this combination

COVER
GOING

is "going undercover" (the word GOING is under the word COVER—literally). See how many you can figure out.

1. T H E B L O C K

2. 1,000,(1)000

3. doubt

4. fortune **favours**

5. **link link link** link

SOLUTIONS

SOLUTION 1

1. CROSS-COUNTRY SKIING
2. SNOWBALL FIGHT
3. FIGURE SKATING
4. TOBOGGANING
5. SNOWSHOEING
6. BUILDING A SNOWMAN
7. ICE FISHING
8. DOGSLED RACING

SOLUTION 2

EVE
EVEN
EVER
EVERGREEN
NERVE
NEVER
REEVE
REVENGE
REVERE
VEER
VENEER
VERGE
VERGER

SOLUTION 3

P	E	C	O	S	■	A	R	F	E	D	■	A	N	A
O	M	A	N	I	■	R	O	U	G	E	■	C	O	N
L	A	D	E	N	■	A	S	N	O	W	B	A	N	K
I	C	E	■	A	L	L	E	N	■	Y	O	D	E	L
T	I	N	S	I	L	I	T	I	S	■	M	I	T	E
E	A	C	H	■	M	A	T	E	O	■	B	A	S	T
S	T	E	E	D	■	■	E	S	S	E	S	■	■	■
T	E	D	■	O	A	R	■	T	O	R	■	M	O	B
■	■	■	C	E	L	E	B	■	■	A	R	E	N	A
S	U	M	O	■	A	F	O	O	T	■	A	M	E	N
U	S	E	R	■	R	I	B	B	O	N	H	O	O	D
R	U	M	P	S	■	N	O	S	E	Y	■	R	N	A
F	R	O	S	T	B	I	T	E	■	A	N	I	O	N
E	E	R	■	A	R	N	I	S	■	L	I	A	N	A
D	R	Y	■	D	O	G	E	S	■	A	X	L	E	S

SOLUTION 4

1. CLUB
2. FILE
3. BOUND
4. JERK
5. WELL
6. BUG
7. LEFT
8. BARK
9. FORGE

SOLUTION 5

R
RE
REP
PERU
PURER
RUPERT
RAPTURE
APERTURE
DEPARTURE
RECAPTURED

SOLUTION 6

E
EN
NET
RENT
TUNER
NEUTER
TENURED
RETURNED
UNDERRATE
ADVENTURER

SOLUTION 7

W	H	I	T	E	C	H	R	I	S	T	M	A	S	D
S	T	R	I	F	I	R	S	T	N	O	E	L	A	N
S	I	L	V	E	R	B	E	L	L	S	G	D	S	S
D	E	C	K	T	H	E	H	A	L	L	I	L	A	G
S	O	O	F	S	T	R	E	E	I	V	L	T	T	R
A	L	H	L	I	G	H	T	A	A	E	N	L	P	E
N	E	O	S	E	V	E	S	N	B	A	O	N	A	E
T	T	L	S	T	O	S	Z	E	S	R	P	L	T	N
A	I	Y	I	G	A	I	L	E	A	H	T	S	A	S
B	T	N	B	W	L	G	B	C	L	I	N	K	P	L
A	S	I	L	E	N	T	N	I	G	H	T	A	A	E
B	N	G	F	I	S	O	B	R	I	G	H	T	N	E
Y	O	H	J	U	R	R	E	D	A	N	D	G	R	V
E	W	T	M	U	S	L	E	I	G	H	R	I	D	E
W	E	T	H	R	E	E	K	I	N	G	S	E	N	S

Hidden Phrase:
"Strings of street lights, even stoplights /
Blink a bright red and green"

SOLUTION 8

1. O Holy Night
2. New Year's countdown
3. Snowball
4. Angels We Have Heard On High
5. Broken resolution

SOLUTION 9

ACME
ACRE
AERIE
AIMER
AMERCE
CAME
CARE
CERAMIC
CERIC
CIRCA
CRAM
CREAM
CRIME
EMIR
MACE
MARE
MECCA
MERE
MICA
MIRE
RACE
RACEME
RACEMIC
RAMIE
REAM
RECCE
RICE
RIME

SOLUTION 10

ACORN
ACORNS
ACT
ACTION
ACTIONS
ACTOR
ACTORS
ACTS
ANCHOR
ANCHORS
ANTICS
ARC
ARCH
ARCS
ATOMIC
CAM
CAN
CANS
CANT
CANTO
CAR
CARS
CART
CARTON
CARTONS
CARTS
CASH
CAST
CAT
CATION
CATIONS
CATS
CHAIN
CHAINS
CHAIR
CHAIRS
CHAMOIS
CHANT
CHANTS
CHAOS
CHAR
CHARIOT
CHARIOTS
CHARM
CHARMS
CHARS
CHART
CHARTS
CHASM
CHAT
CHATS
CHI
CHIN
CHINA
CHINS
CHOIR
CHOIRS
COAST
COAT
COATS
COIN
COINS
COMA
CON
CORN
CORNS
COST
COT
COTS
CRAM
CRAMS
CRASH
CRIMSON
HARMONIC
HARMONICS
ICON
ICONS
INCH
ITCH
MACHO
MACINTOSH
MACRON
MANIC
MARCH
MASCOT
MASONIC
MATCH
MICA
MICRON
MICRONS
MONARCH
MONARCHIST
MONARCHS
MONASTIC
MOSAIC
NOTCH
OSTRICH
RACISM
RACIST
RANCH
RICH
ROACH
ROMANTIC
ROMANTICS
SCAN
SCANT
SCAR
SCORN
SIC
SNATCH
SONIC
STOIC
STOMACH
TONIC
TONICS
TORCH

SOLUTION 11

C	A	R	O	L
A	L	I	B	I
R	I	S	E	N
O	B	E	S	E
L	I	N	E	N

SOLUTION 12

T	R	E	E	S
R	E	V	E	L
E	V	E	R	Y
E	E	R	I	E
S	L	Y	E	R

SOLUTION 13

1. Mail your packages early so the post office can lose them in time for Christmas. —Johnny Carson
2. Laughter is the sun that drives winter from the human face.—Victor Hugo
3. For it is good to be children sometimes, and never better than at Christmas, when its mighty Founder was a child Himself.—Charles Dickens
4. People ask me what I do in winter when there's no baseball. I'll tell you what I do. I stare out the window and wait for spring.—Rogers Hornsby
5. I stopped believing in Santa Claus when I was six. Mother took me to see him in a department store and he asked for my autograph.—Shirley Temple
6. Then the Grinch thought of something he hadn't before! What if Christmas, he thought, doesn't come from a store. What if Christmas . . . perhaps . . . means a little bit more! —Dr. Seuss

SOLUTION 14

8	2	5	4	3	6	1	7	9
1	6	3	7	9	2	5	8	4
9	4	7	1	8	5	6	3	2
4	8	1	6	7	9	3	2	5
5	9	6	3	2	8	7	4	1
7	3	2	5	1	4	9	6	8
2	5	4	9	6	7	8	1	3
6	1	9	8	4	3	2	5	7
3	7	8	2	5	1	4	9	6

SOLUTION 15

7	1	3	2	4	5	6	9	8
2	6	4	1	8	9	7	3	5
5	8	9	7	3	6	2	1	4
3	2	1	5	7	8	4	6	9
4	5	8	9	6	2	1	7	3
6	9	7	4	1	3	5	8	2
8	4	2	6	9	1	3	5	7
1	3	5	8	2	7	9	4	6
9	7	6	3	5	4	8	2	1

SOLUTION 16

CAKE
SAKE
SATE
SITE
SITS
PITS
PIES

COLD
FOLD
FOOD
FOOL
FOUL
SOUL
SOUP
SOAP
SNAP

SOLUTION 17

1. BANANA
2. BOWLED
3. UPSHOT
4. SOILED
5. MARINA
6. POTION
7. LITANY
8. PATINA
9. AMULET
10. ERRATA
11. DIGITS
12. ORATOR

SOLUTION 18

T	O	R	O	N	T	O	■	O	N	T	A	R	I	O
R	Y	E	R	S	O	N	■	R	I	O	T	A	C	T
U	S	S	T	E	E	L	■	P	L	U	M	M	E	T
D	T	H	■	C	R	O	C	H	E	T	■	B	H	A
E	E	O	C	■	R	A	G	A	S	■	P	L	O	W
A	R	O	O	M	■	N	I	N	■	L	E	E	L	A
U	S	T	O	U	R	■	■	■	L	A	R	S	E	N
■	■	■	K	A	A	■	■	■	A	K	C	■	■	■
M	O	P	I	N	G	■	■	■	W	H	E	L	A	N
A	C	I	N	G	■	C	I	D	■	S	P	E	K	E
S	A	N	G	■	C	A	G	E	S	■	T	A	W	T
O	R	B	■	M	A	N	D	A	T	E	■	R	A	F
N	I	A	G	A	R	A	■	R	A	V	E	N	A	L
I	N	L	A	Y	E	R	■	T	R	I	P	O	L	I
C	A	L	G	A	R	Y	■	H	A	L	I	F	A	X

SOLUTION 19

1. I detest life-insurance agents: they always argue that I shall someday die, which is not so.—Stephen Leacock
2. Honesty may be the best policy, but it's important to remember that apparently, by elimination, dishonesty is the second-best policy.—George Carlin
3. I went to a therapy group to help me cope with loneliness, but no one else turned up.—Stewart Francis
4. Any fool can criticize, condemn, and complain, and most fools do. —Benjamin Franklin
5. Politics is the skilled use of blunt objects.—Lester B. Pearson
6. When my kids become wild and unruly, I use a nice, safe playpen. When they're finished, I climb out.—Erma Bombeck

SOLUTION 20

1. Fair bear
2. Fleet treat
3. Frailer tailor
4. Defence suspense
5. Bantam phantom
6. Fake drake
7. Granite planet
8. Baboon tycoon
9. Tearful earful
10. Handsome ransom

SOLUTION 21

1. MASTIFF
2. BASENJI
3. PUG
4. HOVAWART
5. BORZOI
6. DALMATIAN
7. BOXER
8. PEKINGESE
9. BRAQUE FRANÇAIS
10. GREYHOUND

SOLUTION 22

1. CASE
2. KEEP
3. PRIME
4. ANGLE
5. KEY
6. BACK
7. BAND
8. BAT
9. VAULT

SOLUTION 23

1. POD
2. BORE
3. PUNT
4. BOLT
5. FLAG
6. WAX
7. BALL
8. POST
9. VICE

SOLUTION 26

ACT
ACTS
ARC
ARCH
ARCS
CAM
CAMS
CAR
CARS
CART
CARTS
CASH
CAST
CASTS
CAT
CATS
CHAIR
CHAIRS
CHAR
CHARM
CHARMS
CHARS
CHART
CHARTS
CHASM
CHASMS
CHAT
CHATS
CHI
CHRISTMAS
CRAM
CRAMS
CRASH
CRASS
ITCH
MARCH
MATCH
MICA
MISCAST
RACISM
RACIST
RACISTS
RICH
SAC
SCAR
SCARS
SCHISM
SIC
TIC

SOLUTION 29

E
ED
END
SEND
NEEDS
TENSED
DENOTES
SOFTENED
FESTOONED

SOLUTION 33

1. A bus station is where a bus stops. A train station is where a train stops. On my desk, I have a work station.
2. How does anything ever get done at the bubble wrap factory?
3. I want a job cleaning mirrors. It is something I could really see myself doing.
4. You know you're getting old when you sink your teeth into a steak—and they stay there.
5. How do you stop bacon from curling in the frying pan? Take away their brooms.

SOLUTION 24

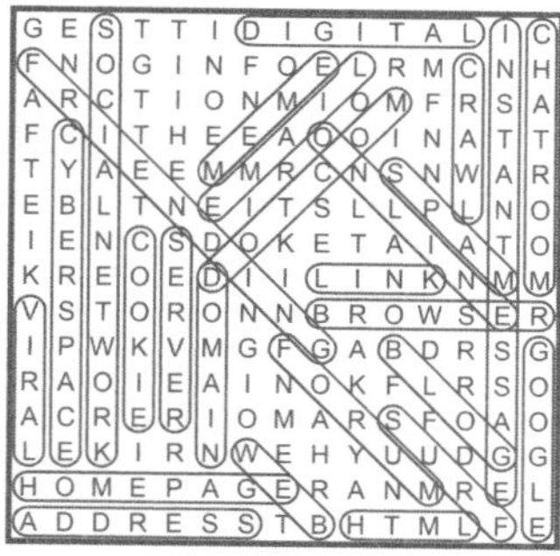

Hidden phrase:
"Getting information off the Internet is like taking a drink from a fire hydrant"

SOLUTION 27

ABOUND
BABOON
BAND
BANG
BAUD
BONA
BOND
BONG
BONGO
BOOB
BOON
BOUND
BUBO
BUGABOO
BUNG
DANG
DODO
DUNG
GOAD
GOBO
GONAD
GOOD
GOON
GUANO
NABOB
UNDO

SOLUTION 30

1. GOLEM
2. DRAGON
3. GOBLIN
4. GHOST
5. LEVIATHAN
6. DWARF
7. GIANT
8. FAIRY
9. TROLL
10. CHUPACABRA

SOLUTION 34

I'D LIKE SOMETHING SHORT AND SIMPLE ON MY TOMBSTONE. LIKE "BACK IN FIVE MINUTES."

SOLUTION 35

1. Go out on a limb
2. Greatest show on earth
3. What's the big idea
4. Shrink wrap
5. Light at the end of the tunnel

SOLUTION 25

1. FRESH
2. LEAVES
3. ORANGE
4. WATER
5. EXPRESSION
6. ROMANCE

Secret Theme: FLOWER

SOLUTION 28

A
RA
ARC
ACRE
CRANE
NECTAR
CERTAIN
REACTION
CONTRAIRE
RECREATION

SOLUTION 31

C A R D S
A W A R E
R A V E N
D R E S S
S E N S E

SOLUTION 32

B A L S A
A V O I D
L O B E D
S I E G E
A D D E R

SOLUTION 36

■	S	A	R	I	■	■	S	W	I	P	E	■
T	H	R	O	N	E	■	W	E	R	E	N	T
A	R	O	U	N	D	■	A	L	K	A	L	I
P	E	S	T	■	D	I	N	T	■	S	A	M
S	W	E	E	P	I	N	G	■	B	A	R	E
■	■	■	■	R	E	S	■	B	A	N	G	S
■	B	R	E	A	S	T	P	L	A	T	E	■
C	R	E	A	M	■	E	I	D	■	■	■	■
R	A	P	T	■	L	A	N	G	U	A	G	E
I	N	T	■	F	A	D	E	■	S	L	U	G
E	D	I	T	O	R	■	A	Q	U	I	L	A
D	O	L	O	U	R	■	L	U	R	K	E	D
■	N	E	W	L	Y	■	■	A	Y	E	S	■

SOLUTION 37

9	8	3	2	4	1	7	5	6
2	6	5	7	8	3	4	1	9
4	7	1	6	9	5	8	3	2
3	4	6	9	5	7	2	8	1
5	9	8	1	2	4	3	6	7
1	2	7	3	6	8	5	9	4
7	1	4	5	3	6	9	2	8
8	5	9	4	1	2	6	7	3
6	3	2	8	7	9	1	4	5

SOLUTION 38

1	5	8	6	9	7	3	4	2
9	3	7	2	4	8	6	5	1
4	6	2	1	3	5	8	7	9
6	4	1	5	8	9	2	3	7
3	8	9	4	7	2	5	1	6
2	7	5	3	6	1	4	9	8
7	9	6	8	5	4	1	2	3
8	2	4	7	1	3	9	6	5
5	1	3	9	2	6	7	8	4

SOLUTION 39

1. Holidays are all different depending on the company and time of your life.—Dominic Monaghan
2. Kindle the taper like the steadfast star / Ablaze on evening's forehead o'er the earth, And add each night a lustre till afar / An eightfold splendor shine above thy hearth.—Emma Lazarus
3. Now is the winter of our discontent made glorious summer by this sun of York.—William Shakespeare
4. Then all the reindeer loved him / As they shouted out with glee / Rudolph the red-nosed reindeer / You'll go down in history!—Johnny Marks
5. We cannot live only for ourselves. A thousand fibres connect us with our fellow men.—Henry Melvill
6. Who sings "Love Me Tender" and makes Christmas toys? Santa's little Elvis.

SOLUTION 40

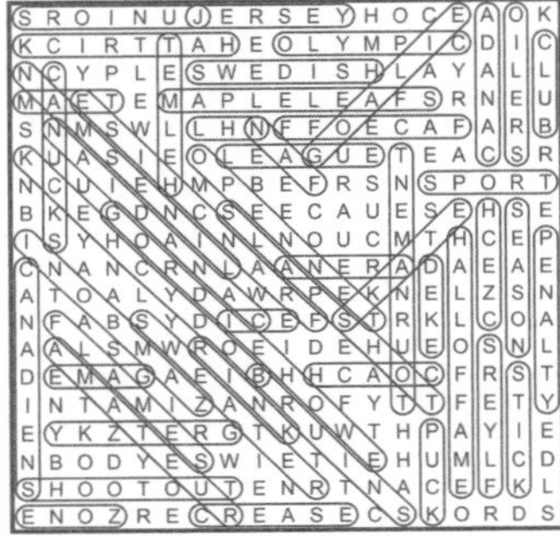

Hidden Phrase:
"Hockey players wear numbers because you can't always identify the body with dental records"

SOLUTION 41

1. BARBARIAN
2. COALITION
3. SLITHERED
4. PERCOLATE
5. PENTAGRAM
6. HEARTBEAT
7. ENDORSING
8. AMBUSHERS
9. ARTIFACTS
10. HOUSEMAID
11. CONCURRED
12. CURTAILED

SOLUTION 42

I
IN
GIN
SIGN
RINGS
GRAINS
RASPING
SPARKING
SPARKLING

SOLUTION 43

I
SI
SIR
RISE
SIREN
RESIGN
FINGERS
REFUSING
FIGURINES

SOLUTION 44

ACTION
ACTS
ANTIC
ASCOT
ASIA
ASIAN
AVIAN
AVOCATION
CANST
CANT
CANTO
CANVAS
CASINO
CASITA
CAST
CATION
CIAO
COAST
COAT
COIN
COON
COOT
COST
ICON
INCA
INTO
IOTA
NASTIC
NITS
NOVA
OATS
OCTAVO
ONTIC
ONTO
OVATION
SAINT
SATANIC
SATIN
SAVANT
SCAN
SCANT
SCAT
SCION
SCOOT
SCOT
SNIT
SNOOT
SNOT
SONATA
SONIC
SOON
SOOT
STAIN
STOIC
TACO
TANS
TONIC
TONS
VACANT
VACATION
VAIN
VAST
VATICAN
VINO
VISA
VISTA
VOCATION

SOLUTION 45

FIRE
FORE
CORE
COLE
COLL
COAL

SNUG
SNOG
SNOT
SOOT
COOT
CONT
CONY
COZY

SOLUTION 46

1. Nice rice
2. Marriage carriage
3. French bench
4. Llama drama
5. Civet pivot
6. Tacky lackey
7. Direction correction
8. Palace malice
9. Serpentine turpentine
10. Dynamic ceramic

SOLUTION 47

1. INTEREST
2. PUMP
3. HOST
4. BATTER
5. MUG
6. PAD
7. MOULD
8. PITCH
9. PORT

SOLUTION 48

1. FLUKE
2. PUNCH
3. BOWL
4. BLOW
5. HIP
6. GIG
7. LEAN
8. ALIGHT
9. MEAN

SOLUTION 49

1. Up on the Housetop
2. Shortbread
3. Right down Santa Claus Lane
4. Cup of cheer
5. Little Drummer Boy

SOLUTION 50

ACE
ACES
ACRE
ACRES
ARC
ARCS
ASCRIBE
BASIC
BRACE
BRACES
BRIEFCASE
CAB
CABS
CAFE
CAFES
CAR
CARE
CARES
CARIES
CARS
CASE
CEASE
CERISE
CRAB
CRABS
CREASE
CRIB
CRIBS
CRIES
FABRIC
FABRICS
FACE
FACES
FACIES
FAECES
FARCE
FARCES
FECES
FIERCE
ICE
ICES
RACE
RACES
RICE
RICES
SAC
SCAB
SCAR
SCARE
SCARF
SCREE
SCRIBE
SIC

SOLUTION 51

1. TOURIST
2. ROAD
3. AIR
4. VACATION
5. EXPENSE
6. LOCATION

Secret Theme: TRAVEL

SOLUTION 52

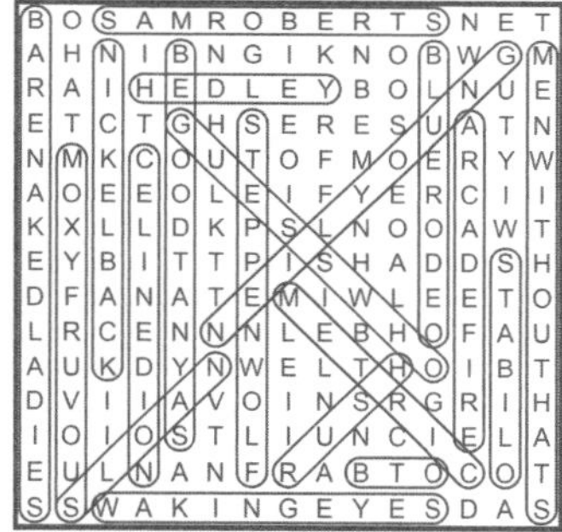

Hidden Phrase:
"One thing I know about the rest of my life, I know that I'll be living it in Canada"

SOLUTION 53

1. AUTOMATON
2. BUSHINESS
3. FORECASTING
4. PRESENTED
5. REMORSELESS
6. RESULTANT
7. SCRAMBLED
8. SCAVENGER
9. STRANGEST
10. TEARFULLY
11. TEACHINGS
12. THANKLESS

SOLUTION 54

1. MINCE PIES
2. CHRISTMAS PUDDING
3. ROASTED TURKEY
4. CRANBERRY SAUCE
5. GINGERBREAD HOUSE
6. PUMPKIN PIE
7. CANDY CANES
8. MASHED POTATO

SOLUTION 55

1. The greatest pleasure of a dog is that you may make a fool of yourself with him, and not only will he not scold you, but he will make a fool of himself, too.—Samuel Butler
2. Definition of an engineer: someone who solves a problem you didn't know you had, in a way you don't understand.
3. The more you eat, the less flavour; the less you eat, the more flavour.—Chinese proverb
4. Middle age is when you choose your cereal for the fibre, not the toy.—Author unknown
5. The most remarkable thing about my mother is that for thirty years she served the family nothing but leftovers. The original meal was never found.—Calvin Trillin
6. The play was a great success, but the audience was a disaster.—Oscar Wilde

SOLUTION 56

SOLUTION 57

I M P A C T
M U E S L I
P E R S O N
A S S E T S
C L O T H E
T I N S E L

SOLUTION 58

A C C E S S
C O R S E T
C R A T E R
E S T A T E
S E E T H E
S T R E E T

SOLUTION 59

4	9	5	1	3	7	2	6	8
8	7	3	2	5	6	9	4	1
2	1	6	4	8	9	7	5	3
5	6	9	8	2	1	4	3	7
3	8	4	7	6	5	1	2	9
7	2	1	9	4	3	6	8	5
9	4	2	3	7	8	5	1	6
6	3	7	5	1	4	8	9	2
1	5	8	6	9	2	3	7	4

SOLUTION 60

5	9	8	2	7	6	1	4	3
3	6	7	1	9	4	5	8	2
1	2	4	8	3	5	9	7	6
4	7	3	5	1	2	6	9	8
6	8	1	3	4	9	2	5	7
9	5	2	7	6	8	3	1	4
7	3	6	4	5	1	8	2	9
8	1	9	6	2	7	4	3	5
2	4	5	9	8	3	7	6	1

SOLUTION 61

1. POSTURE STORE UP TROUPES
2. SLAIN NAILS SNAIL
3. SNARE EARNS NEARS
4. PARSEC CAPERS SCRAPE
5. SANDLER SLANDER SNARLED
6. CARTER CRATER TRACER
7. SATIN SAINT STAIN
8. SINGER REIGNS RESIGN
9. SPEAR REAPS SPARE
10. TIMERS MERITS MISTER

SOLUTION 62

ABET
ABLE
BALE
BALL
BALLET
BALLOT
BAT
BATCH
BATE
BATH
BATHE
BATTLE
BEACH
BEAT
BELCH
BELL
BELT
BET
BETA
BETH
BLAH
BLEACH
BLEAT
BLOAT
BLOC
BLOT
BLOTCH
BOA
BOAT
BOLA
BOLE
BOLL
BOLT
BOTCH
BOTH
BOTTLE
CAB
CABLE
COB
COBALT
HOB
LAB
LABEL
LOB
LOBE
OBLATE
TAB
TABLE
TABLECLOTH
TABLET

SOLUTION 63

1. Lightning strike
2. Holey grey L (Holy Grail)
3. Long past due
4. Front lines
5. Trace amounts

SOLUTION 64

ALIGN
ALONG
ANION
ANNO
ANNUL
GAOL
GILA
GLIA
GLUON
GOAL
GUANO
LAIN
LINGO
LINGUA
LINO
LION
LOAN
LOANING
LOGIN
LOIN
LONG
LUNG
NAIL
NOUN
QUAIL
QUANGO
QUIN
QUINOA
ULNA
UNGAIN
UNIO

SOLUTION 65

1. COUNTIES
2. DISCREET
3. DURATION
4. FOUNDERS
5. MISHEARD
6. MOTHERED
7. NOSINESS
8. PLOTTERS
9. POINTERS
10. ROUNDERS
11. SEAWARDS
12. SPROUTED

SOLUTION 66

1. If you don't get everything you want, think of the things you don't get that you don't want.—Oscar Wilde
2. My grandfather is hard of hearing. He needs to read lips. I don't mind him reading lips, but he uses one of those yellow highlighters.—Brian Kiley
3. He who believes that the past cannot be changed has not yet written his memoirs. —Torvald Gahlin
4. Lead me not into temptation; I can find the way myself.—Rita Mae Brown
5. The large print giveth, but the small print taketh away.—Tom Waits
6. I asked the doctor, "Do you have anything for wind?" He gave me a kite.

SOLUTION 67

B	A	B	E		E	C	O	N		C	U	D	D	Y
A	G	E	D		L	U	B	A		A	G	R	E	E
T	H	E	D	I	V	E	I	N		S	H	E	B	A
H	A	S	A	T	I	T		A	L	I		W	T	S
				A	R	I	A		U	N	J	U	S	T
T	H	E	W	R	A	P	P	I	N	G	S			
G	E	T	A	T			E	R	G		B	E	I	
I	R	O	N		S	O	L	E	S		A	L	D	A
	A	N	D		C	H	I			A	C	L	E	F
			A	C	O	O	K	I	E	S	H	E	E	T
I	N	K	S	I	N		E	M	M	E				
D	A	N		C	E	E		O	C	E	A	N	I	C
L	O	O	S	E		B	A	K	E	D	H	E	R	E
E	M	B	E	R		B	L	A	E		E	V	I	L
D	I	S	C	O		S	A	Y	S		M	I	S	S

SOLUTION 68

1. Why can't you hear a pterodactyl going to the bathroom? Because the P is silent.
2. A politician is one who shakes your hand before elections and your confidence after.
3. Winter is not a season; it's an occupation.—Aristotle
4. True terror is to wake up one morning and discover that your high school class is running the country.—Kurt Vonnegut
5. Two can live as cheaply as one, and they generally have to.
6. Youth is a wonderful thing. What a crime to waste it on children.—George Bernard Shaw

SOLUTION 69

1. GODFATHER
2. PANTOMIME
3. PENTHOUSE
4. HUMANKIND
5. DISHONOUR
6. LEGISLATE
7. FEATHERED
8. MODERATOR
9. DRAGONFLY
10. NEWSPAPER
11. PERISCOPE
12. COMBATANT

SOLUTION 70

1. BURDEN
2. TO SAY THE LEAST
3. BUCKSKIN
4. BAREHEADED
5. ROULETTE WHEEL
6. BUCHANAN
7. BUNYAN
8. BREACHED
9. BROAD LEAVED
10. BEDOUIN
11. TOPMAST
12. RESTYLE
13. BRIGADIER GENERAL
14. BRIDGEHEAD
15. BURN
16. BEAUTICIAN

SOLUTION 71

GOLD
FOLD
FOND
FIND
RIND
RING

GIFT
GIRT
DIRT
DART
CART
CARD

SOLUTION 72

1. Cash stash
2. Mutiny scrutiny
3. Surveyor betrayer
4. Pedantic romantic
5. Savanna banana
6. Major wager
7. Argent sargeant
8. Salmon shaman
9. Blue glue
10. Snarky marquis

SOLUTION 73

A
A T
S A T
S A L T
S T E A L
C A S T L E
S C A R L E T
C L E A R E S T
B R A C E L E T S
C E L E B R A T E S

SOLUTION 74

E
E N
N E T
T E E N
E A T E N
B E A T E N
T E N A B L E
E N D T A B L E
B L A N K E T E D

SOLUTION 75

1. Camping: the art of getting closer to nature while getting farther away from the nearest cold beverage, hot shower, and flush toilet.
2. We know we're getting old when the only thing we want for our birthday is not to be reminded of it.
3. Safety slogan: Watch out for schoolchildren, especially if they are driving cars.
4. Shin: a device for finding furniture in the dark.
5. Friends are those rare people who ask how you are and then wait for the answer.
6. Some people hear voices. Some see invisible people. Others have no imagination whatsoever.

SOLUTION 76

ABED
ABUNDANCE
ACED
AND
BAD
BADE
BAND
BANNED
BAUD
BEAD
BED
BEND
BUD
CAD
CANED
CANNED
CUBED
CUD
CUED
DAB
DACE
DANCE
DAUB
DEAN
DEN
DUB
DUE
DUN
DUNCE
DUNE
END
NED
NUANCED
NUDE
UNBEND

SOLUTION 77

1. RUDOLPH THE RED-NOSED REINDEER
2. ANGELS WE HAVE HEARD ON HIGH
3. SILENT NIGHT
4. ALL I WANT FOR CHRISTMAS IS YOU
5. SANTA CLAUS IS COMING TO TOWN
6. THE LITTLE DRUMMER BOY
7. WINTER WONDERLAND
8. FROSTY THE SNOWMAN

SOLUTION 78

5	9	6	4	3	2	1	7	8
7	1	4	5	6	8	3	9	2
2	8	3	7	9	1	5	6	4
3	6	7	8	2	9	4	5	1
4	2	1	6	5	3	7	8	9
9	5	8	1	4	7	6	2	3
8	7	9	3	1	6	2	4	5
6	3	5	2	8	4	9	1	7
1	4	2	9	7	5	8	3	6

SOLUTION 79

6	4	1	5	2	7	9	3	8
3	8	7	9	6	1	2	4	5
5	9	2	3	8	4	1	6	7
8	3	4	1	9	5	7	2	6
1	6	5	7	3	2	4	8	9
2	7	9	6	4	8	5	1	3
4	2	3	8	7	9	6	5	1
7	1	8	2	5	6	3	9	4
9	5	6	4	1	3	8	7	2

SOLUTION 80

S	L	O	B		D	A	Y	S		P	R	I	A	M
P	O	L	L		A	R	E	S		R	E	T	I	E
U	G	L	I		N	I	L	E		A	V	E	N	S
D	E	A	T	H	C	A	P		A	N	I	M	U	S
			Z	E	E	S		O	N	C	E			
C	A	R	E	E	R		S	I	N	E	W	A	V	E
O	M	E	N	S		M	A	N	O	R		M	I	X
M	A	A			P	I	N	K	Y			A	X	E
E	N	T		C	A	R	T	S		G	A	Z	E	R
T	I	A	M	A	R	I	A		D	E	C	E	N	T
			A	M	E	N		C	A	N	T			
D	O	N	N	E	R		M	U	S	T	A	R	D	S
O	D	O	U	R		S	E	P	H		B	E	A	U
P	E	D	R	O		E	R	I	E		L	A	I	R
E	S	S	E	N		D	V	D	R		E	L	S	E

SOLUTION 81

1. Silver Bells
2. Babes in Toyland
3. Came upon a Midnight Clear
4. Rockin' Around the Christmas Tree
5. Joy to the World

SOLUTION 82

1. MOUNT
2. DUB
3. ASH
4. CLIP
5. DIE
6. PERCH
7. HOP
8. PORTER
9. LAST

SOLUTION 83

1. HATCH
2. COUNT
3. GUM
4. PAWN
5. BAR
6. PEDAL
7. LONG
8. BRIDGE
9. GRAVE

SOLUTION 84

EWE	RENEW	WEE	WIN	WITTIER
EWER	TWEE	WEIR	WINE	WREN
MEW	TWEEN	WENT	WINTER	WRIT
NEW	TWEET	WERE	**WINTERTIME**	WRITE
NEWER	TWIN	WET	WIRE	WRITTEN
NEWT	TWINE	WETTER	WIT	
NITWIT	TWIT	WIENER	WITTER	

SOLUTION 85

Hidden Phrase:
"Oh dreidel, dreidel, dreidel, I made you out of clay / And when you're dry and ready, oh dreidel we shall play"

SOLUTION 86

AKIN	KING	SIGN	SNIT	STINK
ASKING	KNIT	SING	STAG	TAKING
GAIN	SAINT	SINK	STAIN	TANG
GAIT	SANG	SKIN	STAKING	TANK
GIANT	SANK	SKINT	STANG	TASK
GIST	SATIN	SKIT	STANK	TASKING
GNAT	SATING	SNAG	STING	

SOLUTION 87

IT IS A CLICHÉ THAT MOST CLICHÉS ARE TRUE, BUT THEN LIKE MOST CLICHÉS, THAT CLICHÉ IS UNTRUE.

SOLUTION 88

1. THRONES HORNETS SHORTEN
2. CORSETS SECTORS ESCORTS
3. CHALETS SATCHEL LATCHES
4. CLOSE TO OCELOTS COOLEST
5. TERRACE CATERER RETRACE
6. TAMERS MASTER STREAM
7. SUCROSE COURSES CROESUS
8. HUSTLES LUSHEST SLEUTHS
9. UPSCALE CAPSULE LACEUPS
10. SIDEBAR AIRBEDS SEABIRD

SOLUTION 89

1. ABOARD
2. NAVY
3. CARGO
4. HOLD
5. OVERBOARD
6. RIVER

Secret Theme: ANCHOR

SOLUTION 90

F	R	O	S	T
R	I	F	L	E
O	F	T	E	N
S	L	E	P	T
T	E	N	T	S

SOLUTION 91

E	L	V	E	S
L	L	A	M	A
V	A	L	E	T
E	M	E	R	Y
S	A	T	Y	R

SOLUTION 92

1. Most Texans think Hanukkah is some sort of duck call.—Richard Lewis
2. The Bermuda Triangle got tired of warm weather. It moved to Alaska. Now Santa Claus is missing.—Steven Wright
3. Even in winter an isolated patch of snow has a special quality.—Andy Goldsworthy
4. Snow and adolescence are the only problems that disappear if you ignore them long enough.—Earl Wilson
5. So I've started wearing sweatpants to bed because I really don't need Santa seeing me in my underwear.—*Diary of a Wimpy Kid*
6. When it snows, you have two choices: shovel or make snow angels.

SOLUTION 93

SOLUTION 94

1. SUPERVISE	UV
2. BETWIXT	WX
3. REKINDLE	KL
4. PETRIFY	EF
5. EXACERBATE	AB
6. AMBIANCE	MN
7. NINJA	IJ
8. CATALYZES	YZ
9. DESSERTS	ST
10. LENGTHEN	GH
11. HOROSCOPE	OP
12. BLOCKADE	CD
13. INQUIRY	QR

SOLUTION 95

1. LONDON
2. OTTAWA
3. DUBLIN
4. CAIRO
5. HELSINKI
6. BUDAPEST
7. AMSTERDAM
8. KINGSTON
9. MADRID
10. ATHENS

SOLUTION 96

4	5	3	1	2	7	9	6	8
1	6	2	9	8	3	5	7	4
8	9	7	6	5	4	2	3	1
6	1	4	7	3	2	8	9	5
3	8	5	4	9	6	1	2	7
7	2	9	8	1	5	6	4	3
2	7	6	5	4	8	3	1	9
9	3	8	2	7	1	4	5	6
5	4	1	3	6	9	7	8	2

SOLUTION 97

7	4	2	8	5	6	1	3	9
9	8	5	2	1	3	7	4	6
3	1	6	4	7	9	8	2	5
2	3	8	7	6	5	4	9	1
5	9	4	1	3	2	6	7	8
1	6	7	9	4	8	2	5	3
4	7	9	5	8	1	3	6	2
8	2	3	6	9	4	5	1	7
6	5	1	3	2	7	9	8	4

SOLUTION 98

1. ALTOGETHER
2. SEASONALLY
3. DEMOLITION
4. AMMUNITION
5. CAPITALIST
6. BUTTONHOLE
7. PORTCULLIS
8. HIGHWAYMEN
9. PASSAGEWAY
10. RELENTLESS
11. NOTICEABLE
12. BEFOREHAND

SOLUTION 99

GEL
GILT
GIRL
GIRLIE
GLEN
GLINT
GLITTER
GLITTERING
INLET
LEG
LENT
LET
LETTING
LIE
LIEN
LIGER
LIGNITE
LINE
LINER
LINGER
LINT
LIRE
LIT
LITRE
LITTER
LITTERING
NIL
NITRILE
RELIT
RINGLET
TILE
TILER
TILING
TILT
TILTING
TINGLE
TITLE
TITLING

SOLUTION 100

G	R	O	U	N	D	S	Q	U	I	R	R	E	L	I
G	U	I	L	L	E	M	O	T	S	F	I	T	G	S
M	U	S	K	O	X	E	O	T	T	E	R	T	R	N
O	S	N	O	W	G	O	O	S	E	U	S	U	E	G
P	W	H	S	N	O	W	Y	O	W	L	N	N	E	M
O	O	N	S	E	Y	L	Y	N	X	I	O	D	N	L
L	L	L	P	K	L	A	F	S	Y	T	W	R	L	T
L	V	C	A	M	U	H	E	E	P	N	S	A	A	E
E	E	A	B	R	O	A	O	A	U	R	H	S	N	R
M	R	R	E	O	B	O	T	L	F	W	O	W	D	N
M	I	I	R	H	W	E	S	P	F	A	E	A	S	O
I	N	B	M	L	E	H	A	E	I	L	H	N	H	O
N	E	O	I	T	E	D	E	R	N	R	A	D	A	R
G	Y	U	N	A	R	W	H	A	L	U	R	W	R	C
R	A	V	E	N	I	L	S	O	D	S	E	N	K	A

Hidden Phrase:
"If it's enough money, I'll play the North Pole"
—Teddy Wilson

SOLUTION 101

T	O	O	T	T	A	T	E	H	E	C	B	A	N	A
D	F	I	O	D	D	A	N	O	T	A	B	M	O	C
O	L	P	C	R	A	N	G	E	F	M	T	U	O	R
R	E	R	A	F	R	A	W	H	C	N	E	R	T	B
D	E	F	S	O	I	O	D	K	A	N	T	D	A	S
N	T	S	L	R	P	U	N	V	E	R	E	S	N	S
A	L	E	O	A	T	A	Y	M	U	C	E	I	I	E
N	T	R	W	Y	R	C	Y	C	O	N	P	C	K	M
C	L	O	M	A	R	A	E	R	I	E	M	N	C	N
E	L	T	A	Y	I	N	A	L	R	S	A	L	A	E
I	E	S	R	K	E	T	S	W	I	L	C	V	T	Z
E	H	R	C	L	I	E	A	N	F	D	E	S	K	W
I	S	T	H	O	H	E	O	U	T	T	D	A	N	H
E	K	G	N	I	W	N	N	R	E	T	R	E	A	T
D	E	M	O	B	I	L	I	Z	E	M	I	F	T	E

SOLUTION 102

1. A bank is a place that will lend you money, if you can prove that you don't need it.—Bob Hope
2. A bargain is something you don't need at a price you can't resist.
3. A bus is a vehicle that runs twice as fast when you are after it as when you are in it.
4. A business that makes nothing but money is a poor business.—Henry Ford
5. A cauliflower is a cabbage with a college education.—Mark Twain
6. A dog teaches a boy fidelity, perseverance, and to turn around three times before lying down.—Robert Benchley

SOLUTION 103

O
ON
TON
NOTE
TONER
CORNET
CITROEN
DOCTRINE
REDACTION
COORDINATE
DECORATIONS

SOLUTION 104

O
NO
ONE
NERO
SNORE
TENORS
TREASON
RESONANT
ORNAMENTS

SOLUTION 105

THREE
THREW
SHREW
SHRED
SHIED
SHIES
SHIPS
LIVE
WIVE
WILE
WILL
WELL

SOLUTION 106

COMING FROM CANADA, BEING A WRITER AND JEWISH AS WELL, I HAVE IMPECCABLE PARANOIA CREDENTIALS.

SOLUTION 107

O	A	S	I	S	■	S	H	A	M	■	S	C	A	D
F	L	E	S	H	■	T	A	X	I	■	O	R	L	E
F	E	N	N	elf	L	O	W	E	R	■	L	E	D	A
E	X	I	T	■	Y	A	K	■	R	A	I	D	E	R
N	I	L	■	F	I	T	■	W	O	N	D	E	R	S
D	A	E	M	O	N	■	B	elf	R	Y	■	N	M	I
■	■	A	N	G	E	L	A	■	■	■	E	Z	E	R
■	A	S	I	T	■	A	U	R	■	A	S	A	N	■
A	N	U	N	■	■	T	R	E	A	T	S	■	■	■
D	G	G	■	M	G	M	T	■	B	R	U	G	E	S
S	elf	A	W	A	R	E	■	P	A	Y	■	O	S	I
P	A	R	O	L	E	■	D	I	S	■	M	O	T	S
A	L	P	O	■	T	W	elf	T	H	N	I	G	H	T
C	L	E	F	■	E	T	T	A	■	A	L	L	E	E
E	S	A	S	■	L	A	S	S	■	T	O	E	R	R

SOLUTION 108

M U S I C
U L T R A
S T E A K
I R A T E
C A K E S

SOLUTION 109

W H I T E
H Y D R A
I D E A S
T R A C E
E A S E S

SOLUTION 110

1. Larval marvel
2. Cloth broth
3. Camper stamper
4. Package trackage
5. Cheddar shredder
6. Bug mug
7. Sick pick
8. Weird beard
9. Tractor actor
10. Tabasco fiasco

SOLUTION 111

1. RECHECK, CHECKER
2. DESIGN, SIGNED
3. ALIGNS, SIGNAL
4. VIEWER, REVIEW
5. ARCHES, SEARCH
6. COUNTER, RECOUNT
7. LAMENT, MENTAL
8. DELIGHT, LIGHTED
9. REBOUND, BOUNDER
10. DESPOIL, SPOILED

SOLUTION 112

AVALANCHE
CALVE
CAVE
HALVA
HALVE
HAVE
HAVEN
LAVA
LAVE
NAVAL
NAVE
NAVEL
VALANCE
VALE
VAN
VANE
VEAL
VENAL

SOLUTION 113

1. LATTE
2. MOCHA
3. CARAMEL
4. MATCHA
5. PUMPKIN
6. CHAI TEA
7. VANILLA
8. JAVA
9. CINNAMON
10. TOFFEE

SOLUTION 114

AESIR
AIRIEST
AIRS
AIRTIME
ARISE
ARMS
ARSE
EAST
EATS
EMIR
EMITS
IRATE
IRIS
ITEM
MAIM
MARE
MARMITE
MARS
MART
MASER
MAST
MASTER
MATE
MATER
MEAT
MERIT
MESA
METIS
MIASM
MIME
MIMER
MIRE
MISER
MIST
MISTER
MISTIER
MITE
MITRE
RAISE
RAMS
RATE
REAM
REST
RIME
RIMS
RISE
RITES
SAME
SAMITE
SARI
SATE
SATIRE
SEAM
SEAR
SEAT
SEMI
SERAI
SIMMER
SIRE
SITAR
SMARM
SMART
SMEAR
SMITE
SMITER
STAIR
STAMMER
STAR
STARE
STEAM
STEM
STIR
STREAM
TAME
TAMER
TARE
TASER
TEAM
TEAR
TEAS
TERM
TIES
TIME
TIMER
TIRE
TRAM
TRIES
TRIM
TSAR

SOLUTION 115

Hidden Phrase:
"I'm not always going to keep waiting for a fairy tale ending"

SOLUTION 116

1. Baby, It's Cold Outside
2. Snow-capped
3. Ski slope
4. The First Noel
5. Wrapping paper

SOLUTION 117

3	1	2	8	7	6	4	9	5
8	6	4	9	3	5	2	1	7
9	5	7	1	4	2	3	6	8
2	9	6	7	8	3	1	5	4
1	4	3	5	6	9	7	8	2
5	7	8	2	1	4	9	3	6
7	3	5	6	2	1	8	4	9
4	8	9	3	5	7	6	2	1
6	2	1	4	9	8	5	7	3

SOLUTION 118

1	5	2	4	8	7	9	6	3
7	3	4	2	9	6	5	1	8
8	9	6	3	1	5	4	7	2
2	7	9	6	5	3	1	8	4
3	4	1	9	2	8	7	5	6
6	8	5	7	4	1	3	2	9
9	6	8	1	7	4	2	3	5
4	1	3	5	6	2	8	9	7
5	2	7	8	3	9	6	4	1

SOLUTION 119

1. A CHRISTMAS STORY
2. IT'S A WONDERFUL LIFE
3. MIRACLE ON THIRTY-FOURTH STREET
4. THE POLAR EXPRESS
5. THE BISHOP'S WIFE
6. DIE HARD
7. HOW THE GRINCH STOLE CHRISTMAS
8. EDWARD SCISSORHANDS

SOLUTION 120

1. REVIEWED
2. INCURRED
3. BARITONE
4. PENTAGON
5. MARIGOLD
6. HOMELESS
7. CAPACITY
8. INFANTRY
9. DONATION
10. PUNISHED
11. HOLOGRAM
12. DOORBELL

SOLUTION 121

1. Each age has deemed the new-born year the fittest time for festal cheer.—Walter Scott
2. We cannot destroy kindred: our chains stretch a little sometimes, but they never break. —Marquise de Sévigné
3. At a dinner party one should eat wisely but not too well, and talk well but not too wisely.—W. Somerset Maugham
4. And now we welcome the new year. Full of things that have never been.—Rainer Maria Rilke
5. Remember, George: No man is a failure who has friends.—*It's a Wonderful Life*
6. I never thought it was such a bad little tree. It's not bad at all, really. Maybe it just needs a little love.—*A Charlie Brown Christmas*

SOLUTION 122

O	A	H	U			T	O	E			T	A	R	O
U	S	E	S		E	A	R	N		C	A	M	E	L
C	H	E	S	T	N	U	T	S		A	N	I	S	E
H	Y	D	R	A	N	T	S		T	E	N	N	I	S
				C	U	E		L	E	S	I	O	N	
R	O	A	S	T	I	N	G	O	N	A	N			
O	A	S	I	S			I	G	O	R		E	A	R
S	T	I	R		F	A	V	O	R		O	G	R	E
A	H	A		P	I	L	E			A	V	A	I	L
			A	Y	E	A	R	A	N	D	A	D	A	Y
	S	P	U	R	N	S		L	O	I				
T	U	R	G	I	D		O	P	E	N	F	I	R	E
S	P	O	U	T		R	E	A	L	F	O	C	U	S
P	R	O	S	E		A	C	C	S		R	O	B	E
S	A	F	T			I	D	A			A	N	E	S

SOLUTION 123

1. PELT
2. FLUSH
3. JAM
4. FRET
5. BLUFF
6. POUND
7. BETTER
8. JAR
9. MISS

SOLUTION 124

APING
GAP
GAWP
GRIP
NAP
NAPPING
NIP
PAIN
PAIR
PAN
PANG
PAP
PAR
PARING
PAW
PAWING
PAWN
PAWNING
PIG
PIN
PING
PINUP
PIP
PRANG
PRAWN
PRIG
PRUNING
PUG
PUN
PUP
PUPA
PURI
RAP
RAPING
RAPPING
RIP
UNPIN
UNWRAP
UNWRAPPING
WARP
WARPING
WRAP
WRAPPING

SOLUTION 125

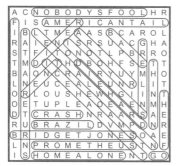

A	C	N	O	B	O	D	Y	S	F	O	O	L	H	R
F	I	S	A	M	E	R	I	C	A	N	T	A	I	L
I	B	L	T	M	E	A	A	S	B	C	A	R	O	L
R	A	I	E	N	I	S	R	S	U	A	C	G	H	A
S	T	F	I	T	O	N	O	T	L	P	B	R	R	O
T	M	D	O	T	H	D	B	O	H	F	S	E	T	T
B	A	O	N	C	R	A	I	R	Y	U	Y	M	H	O
L	N	E	U	C	E	A	L	E	U	N	R	L	I	T
O	R	L	O	U	S	H	E	W	H	G	I	I	N	T
O	E	T	U	P	L	E	A	O	E	A	E	N	M	H
D	T	C	R	A	S	H	N	R	A	A	R	S	A	E
R	U	B	R	A	Z	I	L	D	V	M	P	D	N	R
B	R	I	D	G	E	T	J	O	N	E	S	O	A	E
L	N	P	R	O	M	E	T	H	E	U	S	T	N	F
I	S	H	O	M	E	A	L	O	N	E	N	T	G	O

Hidden Phrase:

"*A Christmas Carol* is such a foolproof story you can't louse it up"—Leonard Maltin

SOLUTION 126

If God did not intend for us to eat animals, then why did He make them out of meat?

SOLUTION 127

A C C U S E
C H O S E N
C O B A L T
U S A B L E
S E L L E R
E N T E R S

SOLUTION 128

D I S C O S
I M P U R E
S P R E A D
C U E I N G
O R A N G E
S E D G E S

SOLUTION 129

PEACE
PEACH
BEACH
BEATH
BERTH
BIRTH
GIRTH
GARTH
EARTH
PIPER
PAPER
PARER
PORER
PORES
PORKS
DORKS
DORMS
DOUMS
DRUMS

SOLUTION 130

EMIT
ENTER
ENTIRE
INERT
INTER
ITEM
MEET
MERIT
MERRIMENT
MET
METE
METER
METIER
METRE
MINT
MITE
MITRE
NET
NIT
NITRE
REINTER
REMIT
RENT
RENTER
RETIE
RETIRE
RETRIM
RITE
TEE
TEEM
TEEN
TEN
TERM
TERN
TERRINE
TIE
TIER
TIME
TIMER
TIN
TINE
TIRE
TREE
TRIM
TRIMMER
TRIN
TRIREME

SOLUTION 131

1. It's a scientific fact that your body will not absorb cholesterol if you take it from another person's plate.—Dave Barry
2. Just remember, once you're over the hill, you begin to pick up speed.—Charles Schulz
3. Happiness? That's nothing more than health and a poor memory.—Albert Schweitzer
4. Middle age is when a narrow waist and a broad mind begin to change places. —Author unknown
5. You know you're getting old when all the names in your black book have M.D. after them.—Arnold Palmer
6. Money will buy you a pretty good dog, but it won't buy the wag of his tail. —Henry Wheeler Shaw

SOLUTION 132

5	8	4	7	6	9	2	1	3
7	3	1	2	4	5	8	6	9
2	6	9	8	3	1	5	4	7
6	4	2	3	1	7	9	8	5
8	7	5	9	2	4	1	3	6
1	9	3	6	5	8	7	2	4
4	1	7	5	8	3	6	9	2
3	5	6	1	9	2	4	7	8
9	2	8	4	7	6	3	5	1

SOLUTION 133

1	5	9	8	3	4	7	6	2
8	4	6	7	9	2	1	5	3
2	3	7	5	6	1	4	8	9
5	2	8	6	1	9	3	4	7
6	7	3	4	2	5	9	1	8
4	9	1	3	7	8	6	2	5
3	8	4	9	5	6	2	7	1
7	6	2	1	8	3	5	9	4
9	1	5	2	4	7	8	3	6

SOLUTION 134

1. BEIGE
2. BLACK
3. INDIGO
4. ORANGE
5. YELLOW
6. WHITE
7. OLIVE
8. PINK
9. GREY
10. PURPLE

SOLUTION 135

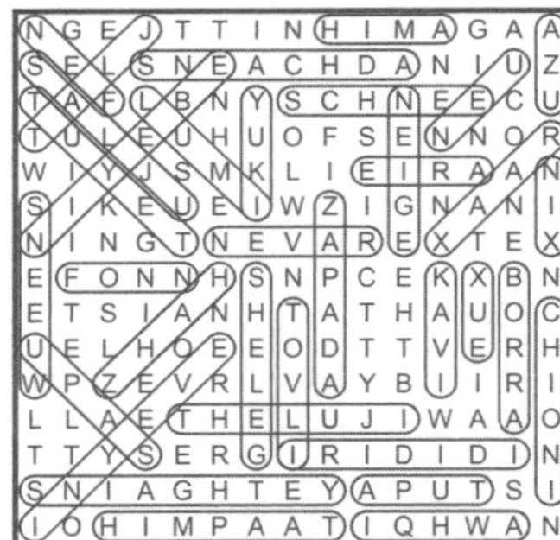

Hidden Phrase:
"Getting an inch of snow is like winning ten cents in the lottery"—Bill Watterson

SOLUTION 136

1. PLANE ALPEN NEPAL
2. SEDUCER REDUCES RESCUED
3. WHITER WITHER WRITHE
4. TEASER EASTER RESEAT
5. AMBLE MELBA BLAME
6. SEDAN ANDES DANES
7. DANGLE ANGLED GLENDA
8. GLEAN ANGEL ANGLE
9. LAMBED BEDLAM BLAMED
10. LUSTRE RESULT RUSTLE

SOLUTION 137

I
PI
TIP
SPIT
POSIT
POSTIT
TIPTOES
STEPONIT
PETITIONS
POINSETTIA

SOLUTION 138

E
LE
ESL
LIES
ISLET
TITLES
TOILETS
TIMESLOT
MISTLETOE

SOLUTION 139

1. CHEMISE, CHEMIST
2. COLLAGEN, COLLAGES
3. ENCOURAGE, ENTOURAGE
4. HIDEOUS, HIDEOUT
5. WINDED, WINKED
6. KARATE, KARATS
7. ROUTING, ROUTINE
8. WASHES, WASTES
9. CAROUSAL, CAROUSEL
10. REVENGE, REVENUE

SOLUTION 140

1. SATIRE
2. FOREGO
3. ISSUES
4. TARTAN
5. RETINA
6. BEACON
7. HEALED
8. TEETHE
9. MADAME
10. MARGIN
11. FINALE
12. POTATO

SOLUTION 141

F	C	A		R	E	L	A	T	E	S		P	A	R
O	O	S		U	N	A	W	A	R	E		A	V	E
R	H	I	N	E	S	T	O	N	E	S		L	I	E
D	E	M	O			I	L	K	S		C	O	A	L
S	N	O	W	M	A	N				O	R	A	T	E
		V	I	O	L	A		A	C	R	Y	L	I	C
			S	O	B		A	G	A	R		T	O	T
L	O	R	E		E	S	T	E	R		T	O	N	S
O	R	E		P	I	P	E		R	H	O			
C	A	N	T	A	T	A		C	O	O	P	S		
A	T	E	A	M				E	T	C	H	I	N	G
T	O	W	N		K	H	A	N			A	M	I	R
I	R	A		H	E	A	R	T	H	S	T	O	N	E
O	I	L		E	R	I	T	R	E	A		N	E	E
N	O	S		N	U	R	S	E	R	Y		E	S	T

SOLUTION 142

1. What do you call the fear of getting stuck while sliding down a chimney? Santa Claus-trophobia.
2. Why do giraffes get Christmas presents every year? They are so good—they'll stick their necks out for anyone.
3. I bought my brother some gift-wrap for Christmas. I took it to the gift-wrap department and told them to wrap it, but in a different print so he would know when to stop unwrapping.—Phyllis Diller
4. It is a fair, even-handed, noble adjustment of things, that while there is infection in disease and sorrow, there is nothing in the world so irresistibly contagious as laughter and good humour.—Charles Dickens
5. Gifts of time and love are surely the basic ingredients of a truly merry Christmas. —Peg Bracken
6. Christmas is like a day at the office—you do all the work, and the fat guy in the suit gets all the credit.

SOLUTION 143

ACTOR
AORTIC
ATOP
ATOPIC
CAPTOR
CARP
CART
CIAO
COAT
COIR
COPRA
CORIA
CRAP
CROP
IOTA
OPTIC
ORCA
PACT
PAIR
PAROTIC
PART
PATIO
PICA
PICOT
PICT
PITA
PORT
RAPT
RATIO
RIOT
ROTA
ROTI
TAPIR
TARO
TOPIC
TORI
TRAP
TRIO
TRIP
TROPIC

SOLUTION 144

1. On thin ice
2. Winter break
3. Frostbitten
4. White out
5. Christmas cracker

SOLUTION 145

G A M E S
A V A I L
M A N G O
E I G H T
S L O T H

SOLUTION 146

C H E E R
H E L L O
E L B O W
E L O P E
R O W E D

SOLUTION 147

2	7	9	5	6	3	1	8	4
6	8	3	4	1	2	9	7	5
1	4	5	8	7	9	6	3	2
8	5	1	9	2	6	7	4	3
3	9	2	7	4	1	5	6	8
7	6	4	3	8	5	2	1	9
5	3	7	6	9	4	8	2	1
4	2	6	1	5	8	3	9	7
9	1	8	2	3	7	4	5	6

SOLUTION 148

3	5	1	8	2	7	6	4	9
4	8	9	1	6	3	2	5	7
6	7	2	9	4	5	1	3	8
8	9	5	4	1	6	3	7	2
1	4	3	7	9	2	8	6	5
2	6	7	5	3	8	9	1	4
9	2	4	3	5	1	7	8	6
5	3	8	6	7	9	4	2	1
7	1	6	2	8	4	5	9	3

SOLUTION 149

1. Hey yogurt, if you're so cultured, how come I never see you at the opera?—Stephen Colbert
2. The digital camera is a great invention because it allows us to reminisce . . . instantly.—Demetri Martin
3. If nature had arranged that husbands and wives should have children alternatively, there would never be more than three in a family.—Laurence Housman
4. Only two things are infinite, the universe and human stupidity. And I'm not sure about the former.—Albert Einstein
5. A puck is a hard rubber disc that hockey players strike when they can't hit one another.—Jimmy Cannon
6. I lent my friend eight thousand dollars for plastic surgery. Now I don't know what he looks like.—Emo Philips

SOLUTION 150

C	S	D	A	E	R	I	A	L	Y	K	D	I	B	I
R	N	O	G	I	S	T	H	E	E	R	O	N	I	S
O	M	G	N	N	L	Y	K	S	A	P	O	G	A	K
S	O	S	O	O	R	C	T	O	W	T	N	S	T	I
S	G	L	R	H	O	E	B	R	E	I	E	N	H	J
C	U	E	D	H	Y	W	O	L	T	U	D	O	L	O
O	L	D	I	S	O	P	E	A	E	E	N	W	O	R
U	D	R	C	N	A	K	K	N	L	A	R	S	N	I
N	M	A	S	A	S	S	G	S	N	U	D	H	A	N
T	L	C	E	G	E	N	B	T	O	B	G	O	B	G
R	R	E	E	R	I	O	A	K	A	N	A	E	A	R
Y	M	A	U	L	B	N	D	A	L	E	G	A	N	N
O	N	G	R	F	R	E	E	S	T	Y	L	E	D	Y
M	I	U	S	K	I	B	A	L	L	E	T	O	Y	U
F	C	S	S	P	E	E	D	S	K	A	T	I	N	G

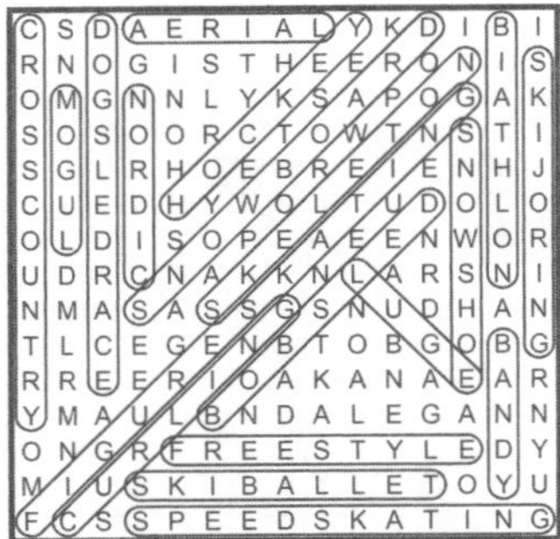

Hidden Phrase:
"Skiing is the only sport where you spend an arm and a leg to break an arm and a leg"
—Anonymous

SOLUTION 151

1. SUSPECT
2. ENIGMA
3. CLOSE
4. RITUAL
5. ENVELOPE
6. TOP

Secret Theme: SECRET

SOLUTION 152

						■						
					■	O	■					
				■	O	T	A	■				
			■	O	P	A	L	S	■			
		■	T	R	E	N	T	O	N	■		
		■	■	■	N	N	E	■	■	■		
			■	A	H	E	R	N	■			
		■	S	T	E	N	C	I	L	■		
	■	D	A	T	A	B	A	S	E	S	■	
■	D	E	C	O	R	A	T	I	O	N	S	■
■	■	■	■	■	T	U	E	■	■	■	■	■
				■	H	M	S	■				
				■	■	■	■	■				

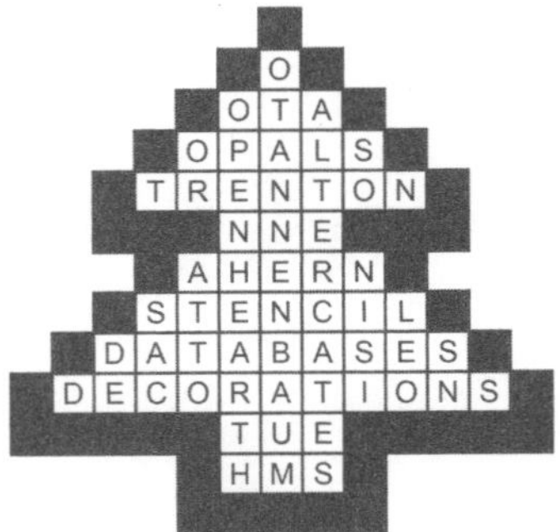

SOLUTION 153

COG
COMING
COOING
ECHOING
EGO
GEM
GIN
GNOME
GONE
GOO
GOON
HEMMING
HINGE
HOEING
HOG
HOMECOMING
HOMING
MOOCHING
MOOING
NIGH
NOG
OOHING

SOLUTION 154

PURE
SURE
SORE
SORT
SOOT
SHOT
SHOW
SNOW
GOOD
MOOD
MOLD
MILD
WILD
WILL

SOLUTION 155

1. SWEDEN
2. ARGENTINA
3. RUSSIA
4. FRANCE
5. VIETNAM
6. ENGLAND
7. CHINA
8. CANADA
9. WALES
10. MEXICO

SOLUTION 156

AFIRE
CAFE
CALF
CLEF
ELF
FACE
FACILE
FAERIE
FAIL
FAIR
FAR
FARCE
FARE
FEAR
FECAL
FEE
FEEL
FERAL
FIE
FIERCE
FILE
FIR
FIRE
FIREPLACE
FLAIR
FLAP
FLARE
FLEA
FLEE
FLIER
FLIP
FRAIL
FREE
LEAF
LIFE
PREFACE
REEF
RELIEF
RIFE
RIFLE

SOLUTION 157

E
ER
EUR
PERU
ERUPT
RUPERT
RAPTURE
APERTURE
PREMATURE
EARTRUMPET
TEMPERATURE

SOLUTION 158

E
EW
NEW
SEWN
WINES
SINEWS
WITNESS
SNOWIEST
SNOWTIRES

SOLUTION 161

N	I	P	■	■	P	I	V	O	T	■	P	A	R	K
B	L	E	U	■	A	N	I	T	A	■	A	M	O	I
C	O	R	N	S	T	A	R	C	H	■	Y	A	Y	S
■	■	F	I	T	S	I	N	■	I	R	E	N	A	■
Y	O	U	V	E	■	D	A	S	T	A	R	D	L	Y
M	A	M	E	T	S	■	■	C	I	V	■	A	L	E
A	K	E	R	■	E	B	R	O	■	E	A	S	Y	A
■	■	■	S	T	A	R	B	O	A	R	D	■	■	■
P	A	C	E	R	■	A	C	T	I	■	D	L	I	X
I	N	U	■	E	D	S	■	■	R	E	S	O	R	T
C	O	S	T	A	R	I	C	A	■	M	U	S	K	S
■	I	T	I	S	A	■	A	B	R	U	P	T	■	■
S	N	A	P	■	F	A	L	S	E	S	T	A	R	T
O	T	R	O	■	T	U	L	I	P	■	O	R	E	O
A	S	D	F	■	S	K	A	T	S	■	■	K	I	D

SOLUTION 159

S	E	A	B	E	D
E	N	C	O	D	E
A	C	Q	U	I	T
B	O	U	N	C	E
E	D	I	C	T	S
D	E	T	E	S	T

SOLUTION 160

A	P	P	E	A	L
P	O	O	D	L	E
P	O	L	I	C	E
E	D	I	T	O	R
A	L	C	O	V	E
L	E	E	R	E	D

SOLUTION 162

1. ALGERIA
2. JAPAN
3. SPAIN
4. EGYPT
5. ITALY
6. GERMANY
7. INDIA
8. PERU
9. TAIWAN
10. PORTUGAL

SOLUTION 163

Hidden Phrase:
"If you asked me for my New Year resolution, it would be to find out who I am"
—Cyril Cusack

SOLUTION 164

1. Many hands make light work
2. Every cloud has a silver lining
3. Running around in circles
4. Split pea soup
5. Stepladder

SOLUTION 165

There is no great invention, from fire to flying, which has not been hailed as an insult to some god.

SOLUTION 166

DEER
DELI
DENIER
DENIES
DENS
DENSE
DENSER
DESIRE
DESIRES
DEWIER
DEWINESS
DEWLESS
DEWS
DIES
DIESEL
DINE
DINER
DIRE
DIRENESS
DRESS
DREW
DRIES
EELS
EIDER
ELDER
ELIDE
ELSE
ENDER
ENDLESS
ENDS
ENDWISE
ERNE
ESNE
EWER
EWES
IDES
IDLE
IDLENESS
IDLER
ISLE
LEER
LEES
LEND
LENDER
LENS
LENSES
LESS
LESSEN
LESSER
LEWD
LEWDER
LEWDNESS
LIDS
LIED
LIEDER
LIEN
LIES
LINE
LINED
LINER
LINES
LINSEED
NEED
NEEDS
NERD
NEREID
NEWEL
NEWER
NEWS
REDNESS
REDS
REED
REEL
REELS
REIN
REINED
RELIES
REND
RENEW
RESEND
RESEW
RESIDE
RESIN
REWED
REWELD
REWIDEN
REWIND
RIDE
RIDES
RIDS
RILE
RILED
RIND
RINSE
RINSED
RISE
RISEN
RISES
SEDER
SEED
SEEDS
SEEN
SEER
SEES
SEND
SENDER
SENDS
SENILE
SENSE
SENSED
SERE
SERIES
SEWER
SEWN
SEWS
SIDE
SIDES
SIDLE
SIDLER
SINE
SINEW
SINS
SIRE
SIRED
SIREN
SIRS
SLED
SLENDER
SLEW
SLID
SLIDE
SLIDER
SLIDES
SNEER
SNIDE
SNIDER
SWEDE
SWINDLE
SWINDLER
SWINE
SWIRL
SWIRLS
WEDS
WEED
WEEDS
WEIR
WEIRD
WEIRDNESS
WELD
WELDER
WEND
WERE
WIDE
WIDEN
WIDENER
WIDENESS
WIDER
WIELD
WIELDER
WIENER
WILD
WILDER
WILDNESS
WILDS
WILE
WILES
WIND
WINDER
WINDLESS
WINDS
WINE
WINED
WINES
WINS
WIRE
WIRED
WIRELESS
WIRES
WISE
WISED
WISER
WREN

SOLUTION 167

A	T	T	■	I	S	I	T	I	■	P	A	L	E	■
P	A	R	T	N	E	R	E	D	■	A	N	I	L	S
E	V	E	R	G	R	E	E	N	■	L	I	K	E	N
S	E	E	S	■	■	S	N	U	B	S	■	E	G	O
U	R	S	■	O	P	T	I	M	O	■	A	M	I	R
I	N	A	B	A	R	■	E	B	B	■	L	A	Z	E
T	A	P	E	T	O	■	R	E	D	R	Y	D	E	R
■	■	■	L	E	M	A	■	R	Y	E	S	■	■	■
G	O	L	D	R	I	N	G	■	L	A	S	E	R	S
U	R	E	A	■	S	A	E	■	A	C	A	D	I	A
I	D	E	M	■	E	G	M	O	N	T	■	I	V	P
L	E	T	■	I	S	A	I	D	■	■	S	T	E	P
T	R	I	P	S	■	S	N	O	W	W	H	I	T	E
S	E	D	A	N	■	T	I	N	O	P	E	N	E	R
■	D	E	N	T	■	A	S	T	R	A	■	G	D	S

SOLUTION 168

4	2	6	5	3	7	1	9	8
7	3	1	9	4	8	5	2	6
5	8	9	6	2	1	3	7	4
1	5	3	2	6	9	4	8	7
8	4	2	1	7	3	9	6	5
9	6	7	8	5	4	2	3	1
6	1	8	4	9	2	7	5	3
2	7	4	3	8	5	6	1	9
3	9	5	7	1	6	8	4	2

SOLUTION 169

4	3	7	2	6	8	9	1	5
5	2	8	1	7	9	4	3	6
1	6	9	4	3	5	8	2	7
9	5	6	7	4	1	2	8	3
7	4	3	6	8	2	1	5	9
8	1	2	5	9	3	7	6	4
3	7	1	8	5	4	6	9	2
6	8	5	9	2	7	3	4	1
2	9	4	3	1	6	5	7	8

SOLUTION 170

1. SUN
2. PLANT
3. RAIN
4. INSECTS
5. NATURE
6. GROW

Secret Theme: SPRING

SOLUTION 171

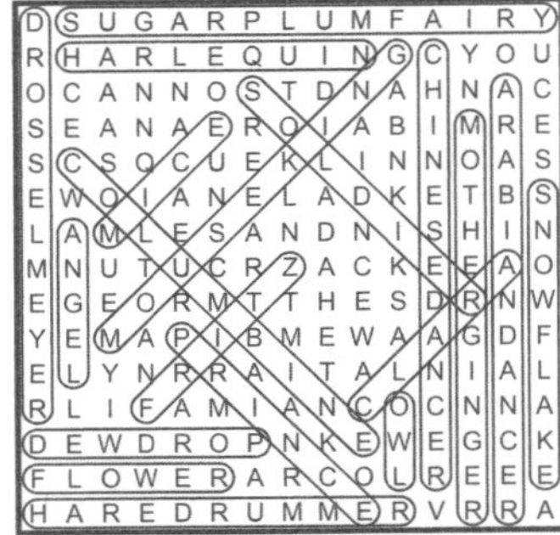

Hidden Phrase:
"You cannot dance an arabesque in Swan Lake and Nutcracker the same way"
—Natalia Makarova

SOLUTION 172

B	R	E	A	D
R	A	L	L	Y
E	L	I	T	E
A	L	T	A	R
D	Y	E	R	S

SOLUTION 173

J	A	C	K	S
A	L	L	O	T
C	L	E	A	R
K	O	A	L	A
S	T	R	A	W

SOLUTION 174

ANEW
AWE
AWED
DAWN
DAWNED
DEW
DOWEL
DOWN
DOWNED
DOWNLAND
DRAW
DRAWL
DRAWLED
DRAWN
DREW
DROWN
DROWNED
ENDOW
LANDOWNER
LAW
LAWN
LOW
LOWER
NEW
NOW
ONWARD
OWE
OWED
OWL
OWN
OWNED
OWNER
RAW
RENOWN
ROW
ROWED
WAD
WADDLE
WADE
WADED
WAN
WAND
WANDER
WANE
WANED
WAR
WARD
WARDEN
WARE
WARN
WARNED
WEAR
WED
WELD
WEND
WOAD
WOE
WON
WONDER
WONDERLAND
WORD
WORDED
WORE
WORLD
WORN
WREN

SOLUTION 175

1. AMIABLE
2. ORIGINS
3. CABINET
4. PENSION
5. BEARING
6. NOWHERE
7. GORILLA
8. OVERAWE
9. WARTIME
10. ABANDON
11. EMPEROR
12. ADAMANT

SOLUTION 176

1. A loyal friend laughs at your jokes when they're not so good, and sympathizes with your problems when they're not so bad.—Arnold H. Glasgow
2. A perfect summer day is when the sun is shining, the breeze is blowing, the birds are singing, and the lawn mower is broken.—James Dent
3. A pessimist sees the difficulty in every opportunity; an optimist sees the opportunity in every difficulty.—Winston Churchill
4. A recipe has no soul. You, as the cook, must bring soul to the recipe.—Thomas Keller
5. Always forgive your enemies; nothing annoys them so much.—Oscar Wilde

SOLUTION 177

F	L	O	R	A		A	B	O		C	U	B	I	T
L	A	T	E	X		R	A	D		A	G	O	N	E
A	M	I	G	O		G	R	E	E	N	L	A	N	D
B	A	C	A	L	A	O		S	T	A	Y			
			L	O	P		T	A	N	S		M	O	R
T	O	G	E	T	H	E	R		A	T	H	O	M	E
U	R	L		L	I	R	A			A	U	D	E	N
R	I	O	T		D	E	I	S	M		T	U	N	E
K	O	R	E	A			P	E	E	L		L	E	G
E	L	I	C	I	T		S	E	T	A	S	I	D	E
Y	E	A		T	A	M	E		R	P	M			
			E	C	R	U		F	O	L	I	A	G	E
N	O	R	T	H	P	O	L	E		A	L	W	A	Y
O	N	I	C	E		N	E	T		N	E	R	V	E
S	O	P	H	S		S	E	A		D	R	Y	E	R

SOLUTION 178

S	T	O	C	K	I	N	G	D	M	E	C	C	K	S
T	I	C	I	C	L	E	H	E	I	H	A	A	L	N
L	S	W	I	T	T	W	H	B	S	O	U	N	P	O
G	L	H	S	Y	O	R	F	S	T	A	R	D	I	W
H	O	A	V	C	L	E	E	L	L	T	Y	Y	N	F
P	S	I	W	A	F	A	A	E	E	I	L	C	E	L
O	N	A	L	N	A	T	L	A	T	N	L	A	C	A
I	O	A	L	D	F	H	A	L	O	S	A	N	O	K
N	W	L	G	L	A	I	L	A	E	E	T	E	N	E
S	M	I	A	E	I	S	G	B	E	L	L	S	E	T
E	E	H	R	S	E	G	S	U	E	A	L	B	O	W
T	N	S	L	E	I	G	H	S	R	E	O	N	T	O
T	B	E	A	J	O	L	L	T	G	E	Y	F	A	L
I	A	L	N	A	L	A	L	N	S	A	S	L	A	L
A	A	L	D	O	R	N	A	M	E	N	T	A	L	A

Hidden Phrase:
"Deck the halls with boughs of holly / Fa la la la la la la la la / 'Tis the season to be jolly / Fa la la la la la la la la"

SOLUTION 179

SANTA
MANTA
MANGA
PANGA
PANGS
PANES
PAVES
EAVES
ELVES
SACK
SICK
SINK
SINS
TINS
TONS
TOYS

SOLUTION 180

DEW
DOWEL
DOWN
ENDOW
EWE
GLOW
GLOWED
GOWN
GOWNED
KNEW
KNOW
KNOWLEDGE
LEWD
LOW
NEW
NEWEL
NOW
OWE
OWED
OWL
OWN
OWNED
WED
WEDGE
WEE
WEED
WEEK
WELD
WEN
WEND
WOE
WOKE
WOKEN
WOLD
WON

SOLUTION 181

1. Cold front
2. Ring in the new year
3. Snowdrift
4. Under the mistletoe
5. We (wee) Three Kings
6. Down the chimney

SOLUTION 182

1	8	2	3	7	5	4	9	6
4	7	5	9	6	1	3	2	8
6	9	3	4	2	8	5	1	7
8	6	1	2	9	3	7	5	4
9	3	4	5	1	7	8	6	2
2	5	7	6	8	4	9	3	1
7	1	6	8	5	9	2	4	3
5	4	8	1	3	2	6	7	9
3	2	9	7	4	6	1	8	5

SOLUTION 183

3	8	7	2	4	9	5	1	6
2	6	1	7	8	5	3	9	4
4	5	9	3	6	1	7	2	8
9	1	6	4	2	3	8	5	7
5	2	3	8	1	7	4	6	9
8	7	4	5	9	6	2	3	1
6	3	8	9	5	4	1	7	2
1	4	5	6	7	2	9	8	3
7	9	2	1	3	8	6	4	5

SOLUTION 184

G
AG
TAG
GNAT
AGENT
GARNET
GREATEN
GENERATE
TEENAGERS
AGREEMENTS

SOLUTION 185

R
RA
EAR
SEAR
MARES
REARMS
FARMERS
FOREARMS
REFORMATS
PERMAFROST

SOLUTION 186

BELL
BELLE
BELLED
BLEED
BLOB
BLOOD
BLOODED
BLUB
BLUE
BLUEBLOOD
BLUEBLOODED
BLUED
BODE
BOLD
BOLDED
BOLE
BOLL
BOLO
BOOB
BOOED
BOULE
BUBO
BULB
BULL
BULLED
DEED
DELL
DELUDE
DODO
DOLE
DOLED
DOLL
DOLLED
DOUBLE
DOUBLED
DUBBED
DUDE
DUEL
DUELLED
DULL
DULLED
EBBED
ELUDE
LOBBED
LOBE
LOBED
LODE
LOUD
LUDO
LULU
OBOE

SOLUTION 187

CEMENT
CENT
CENTIME
CITE
EMCEE
EMETIC
ENTICE
EXCITE
EXCITEMENT
EXTINCT
ICE
MICE
MINCE
NICE
NIECE
TIC

SOLUTION 188

F	E	E	T	■	C	O	L	D	■	■	S	L	E	D
A	I	N	U	■	A	F	O	O	T	■	H	A	V	E
I	N	T	R	■	B	U	R	R	Y	■	O	V	E	N
L	E	E	K	S	■	S	A	N	C	T	U	A	R	Y
■	■	R	E	N	E	E	■	■	H	O	L	■	■	■
Y	E	S	Y	E	S	■	B	L	O	O	D	E	D	■
A	P	I	■	S	T	L	E	O	■	N	E	C	R	O
G	I	N	A	■	S	A	G	T	S	■	R	U	I	N
A	S	T	R	O	■	H	O	H	O	S	■	A	V	E
■	C	O	M	F	O	R	T	■	L	I	E	D	E	R
■	■	■	O	A	R	■	■	S	A	L	V	O	■	■
C	O	P	I	N	G	S	A	W	■	T	I	R	A	N
O	V	E	R	■	A	N	N	E	S	■	N	I	U	E
M	U	S	E	■	N	A	G	A	S	■	C	A	L	L
A	M	O	S	■	■	P	A	T	E	■	E	N	D	S

SOLUTION 189

AN ARCHAEOLOGIST IS THE BEST HUSBAND A WOMAN CAN HAVE. THE OLDER SHE GETS THE MORE INTERESTED HE IS IN HER.

SOLUTION 190

1. A lot of people don't like bumper stickers. I don't mind bumper stickers. To me a bumper sticker is a shortcut. It's like a little sign that says "Hey, let's never hang out." —Demetri Martin
2. Since the house is on fire, let us warm ourselves.—Italian proverb
3. There are secrets I will take to the grave—and others I'd feel safer having cremated. —Robert Brault
4. Doctors tell us there are over seven million people who are overweight. These, of course, are only round figures.
5. I like when good things happen to me, but I wait two weeks to tell anyone because I like to use the word "fortnight."—Demetri Martin
6. Laughter and tears are both responses to frustration and exhaustion. I myself prefer to laugh, since there is less cleaning up to do afterward.—Kurt Vonnegut

SOLUTION 191

1. VARNISH
2. INSTRUMENT
3. OLD
4. LESSONS
5. ITALIAN
6. NECK

Secret Theme: VIOLIN

SOLUTION 192

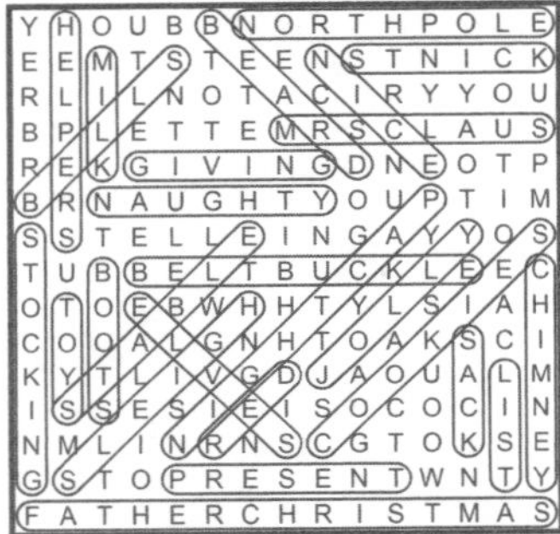

Hidden Phrase:
"You better not cry / you better not pout / I'm telling you why / Santa Claus is coming to town"

SOLUTION 193

1. PANTHER
2. BEAR
3. TOAD
4. GOAT
5. LION
6. COBRA
7. MANDRILL
8. COYOTE
9. TIGER
10. ZEBRA

SOLUTION 194

YULE
MULE
MOLE
MOLS
LOLS
LOGS
DECK
DUCK
HUCK
HULL
HALL

SOLUTION 195

1. GRAZE
2. DUCK
3. BULL
4. LIGHT
5. BASS
6. LOCK
7. PLY
8. FRY
9. PRESS

SOLUTION 196

1. CHECK
2. CAN
3. JACK
4. FLY
5. JET
6. FONT
7. MOLE
8. GAME
9. LINK

SOLUTION 197

8	7	5	2	6	4	1	3	9
4	1	6	8	9	3	7	2	5
3	9	2	5	7	1	8	4	6
5	8	3	1	4	9	6	7	2
6	4	1	7	8	2	9	5	3
7	2	9	6	3	5	4	8	1
1	5	7	9	2	8	3	6	4
9	3	8	4	5	6	2	1	7
2	6	4	3	1	7	5	9	8

SOLUTION 198

2	4	1	5	6	7	3	9	8
3	9	6	1	8	2	5	4	7
5	8	7	4	3	9	6	1	2
1	2	5	9	4	3	7	8	6
4	7	3	6	1	8	9	2	5
8	6	9	2	7	5	1	3	4
6	5	4	8	9	1	2	7	3
9	3	2	7	5	4	8	6	1
7	1	8	3	2	6	4	5	9

SOLUTION 199

D	I	R	T		D	E	N	I	A	L		W	B	A
A	L	A	R		I	S	O	N	T	O		O	R	B
S	I	Z	E		S	T	I	G	M	A		N	I	E
H	A	Z	Y	S	H	A	D	E	O	F		D	A	T
			S	E	O				S	E	D	E	R	S
S	T	E		U	N	I	T			R	R	R		
T	I	M	E	L	O	V	E		I	S	O	L	D	E
E	K	E	S		U	S	A	I	N		N	A	I	L
W	I	N	T	E	R		S	C	A	V	E	N	G	E
		D	O	Y			E	S	M	E		D	S	C
S	O	A	P	E	D				E	R	R			
A	C	T		D	I	S	T	U	R	B	A	N	C	E
P	H	I		R	O	T	I	N	I		V	E	R	A
P	R	O		O	D	I	N	I	C		E	R	O	S
Y	E	N		P	E	R	S	E	A		N	A	P	E

SOLUTION 200

P O S T A L
O C T A V E
S T A K E D
T A K I N G
A V E N G E
L E D G E S

SOLUTION 201

C R I S P S
R E S O R T
I S S U E R
S O U R C E
P R E C I S
S T R E S S

SOLUTION 202

```
F R E N C H H E N S C H R I S
L T M T O D R U M M E R S A S
A S I U L R S D O I N G A L W
Y I T R L U T L L A D I E S A
I E S T Y M O M E T G H G P N
N C I L B M N G E N G N X A S
G O T E I I R A I N I G L R F
M U O D R N R M I R S I E T P
I N O O D G M C D L M F A R E
L T E V S I N L O O N T P I A
K D E E W A O G C R H S I D R
I O C S D G A E R D L E N G T
N W S O M O N E R S O E G E R
G N S C W H U S M A I D S L E
P I P E R S Z E P I P I N G E
```

Hidden Phrase:
"Christmas is doing a little something extra for someone"—Charles Monroe Schulz

SOLUTION 203

ARK	CRANKER	NUKE	RANKER	TEAK
AUK	CREAK	NUTCAKE	TACK	TRACK
CAKE	KART	**NUTCRACKER**	TACKER	TRACKER
CANKER	KEA	RACK	TAKE	TREK
CANUCK	KEAN	RACKET	TAKEN	TRUCK
CRACK	KEN	RAKE	TAKER	TRUCKER
CRACKER	KERN	RAKER	TANK	TRUNK
CRANK	NECK	RANK	TANKER	UKE

SOLUTION 204

1. What's red and bad for your teeth? A brick.
2. There's no such thing as fun for the whole family.—Jerry Seinfeld
3. A booster cable walks into a bar. The barman says, "I'll serve you, but don't start anything."
4. If someone hits you over the head with a coffee cup, have you been mugged?

SOLUTION 205

1. Repeat performance
2. Middle age
3. Cut your losses
4. Written down
5. One small difficulty

SOLUTION 206

CEP	INEPT	PEN	PETRI	PION	PORT	RECEIPT	ROPE
COP	NIP	PENCE	PIE	PIONEER	POT	**RECEPTION**	TIP
COPE	OPEN	PENT	PIECE	PIT	PREEN	RECIPE	TOP
COPIER	OPENER	PER	PIER	POET	PRICE	REOPEN	TOPER
CREEP	OPT	PERCENT	PIERCE	POETIC	PRINCE	REP	TOPIC
CREPE	OPTIC	PERI	PIN	POINT	PRINT	REPENT	TRIP
CREPT	PECTIN	PERT	PINE	POINTER	PRO	RIP	TRIPE
CROP	PEE	PET	PINT	PORCINE	PRONE	RIPE	TROPE
EPIC	PEER	PETER	PINTO	PORE	PROTEIN	RIPEN	TROPIC

SOLUTION 207

U
U R
R U N
T U R N
T U N E R
N A T U R E
C E N T A U R
T R U N C A T E
R E L U C T A N T

SOLUTION 208

E
E H
H E M
M E S H
S H A M E
H A R E M S
M A R C H E S
C A S H M E R E
R E M A T C H E S
M A N C H E S T E R

SOLUTION 209

ADDLE	ANON	DEAD	DOWN	ENFOLD	FENLAND	FLOW	FOUL
AEON	AULD	DEAF	DOWNED	ENWOUND	FEUD	FLOWED	FOULED
AFOUL	AWED	DEAL	DOWNLAND	FADE	FEUDAL	FLOWN	FOUND
ALOE	AWFUL	DEAN	DUAL	FANE	FLAN	FLUE	FOUNDED
ALONE	DADO	DEFUND	DUEL	FANNED	FLAW	FOAL	FOWL
ALOUD	DALE	DOLE	DUNE	FAUN	FLAWED	FOLD	FOWLED
ANEW	DANDLE	DOLED	DUODENAL	FAWN	FLEA	FOLDED	FUEL
ANNUL	DAWDLE	DONE	ELAN	FAWNED	FLED	FOND	FUND
ANODE	DAWN	DONNED	ELAND	FELON	FLEW	FONDLE	FUNDED
ANOLE	DAWNED	DOWEL	ENDOW	FEND	FLOE	FONDUE	FUNNEL

LADE
LADEN
LAND
LANDED
LANE
LAUD
LAUDED
LAWN
LEAD
LEAF
LEAN
LEND
LEWD
LOAD
LOADED
LOAF
LOAN
LOANED
LODE
LONE
LOUD
LOWED
LUDO
LUNE
NEON
NEWFOUND
NODAL
NODE
NODULE
NOEL
NONE
NOUN
NUDE
OLDEN
OWED
OWNED
ULNA
UNDO
UNFED
UNFLAWED
UNFOLD
UNFOLDED
UNLADE
UNLADEN
UNLOAD
UNOWNED
UNWED
WADDLE
WADE
WADED
WAND
WANE
WEAL
WEALD
WEAN
WELD
WEND
WOAD
WOEFUL
WOLF
WOLFED
WOULD
WOUND
WOUNDED

SOLUTION 210

1. REDISCOVER
2. ASTONISHED
3. PRIMORDIAL
4. STARVATION
5. REGENERATE
6. SLUMBERING
7. DISHWASHER
8. PROPERTIES
9. GRAMMARIAN
10. DISHONESTY
11. CONSONANTS
12. INHABITANT

SOLUTION 211

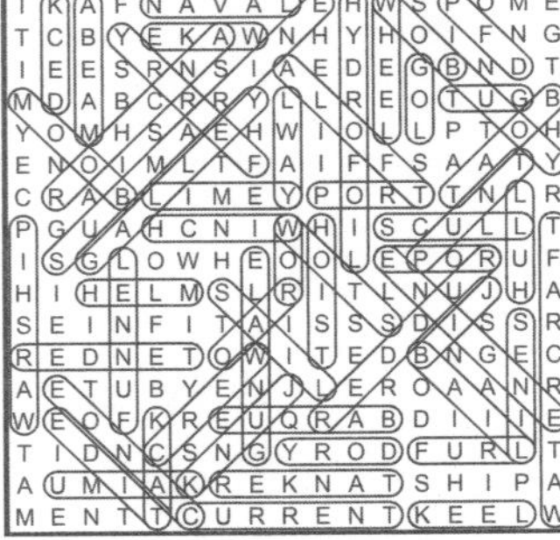

Hidden Phrase:
"If something is sent by ship then it is a cargo while if it is sent by road it is a shipment"

SOLUTION 212

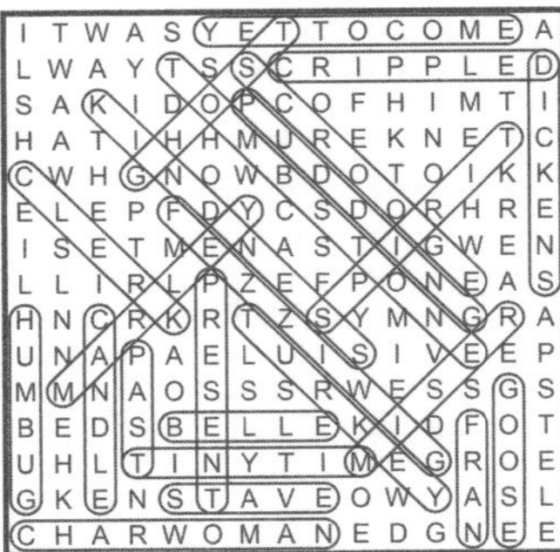

Hidden Phrase:
". . . it was always said of him that he knew how to keep Christmas well, if any man alive possessed the knowledge"
—Charles Dickens, *A Christmas Carol*

SOLUTION 213

C	B	C	■	M	I	S	T	S	■	G	A	U	Z	Y
R	E	L	■	O	N	P	O	P	■	U	N	T	I	E
A	C	A	■	W	O	R	D	O	F	M	O	U	T	H
I	C	I	N	G	■	I	S	O	L	D	■	■	■	■
G	A	M	E	L	A	N	■	F	A	R	■	M	A	G
■	■	■	P	I	N	K	S	■	T	O	B	A	G	O
B	E	L	T	■	A	L	A	S	■	P	O	L	A	R
A	B	O	U	T	■	E	R	E	■	S	N	A	P	S
B	O	R	N	E	■	S	I	V	A	■	B	R	E	E
K	N	E	E	L	S	■	S	E	T	G	O	■	■	■
A	Y	S	■	O	P	E	■	N	O	O	N	D	A	Y
■	■	■	■	M	U	L	E	T	■	O	S	A	G	E
G	I	N	G	E	R	B	R	E	A	D	■	U	R	N
A	R	E	A	R	■	O	N	E	R	A	■	N	E	T
H	O	U	S	E	■	W	O	N	I	T	■	T	E	A

SOLUTION 214

ABET
ACT
ALBEIT
ALTO
APT
ATE
ATOM
ATOMIC
ATOP
BAIT
BAT
BATE
BEAT
BELT
BET
BETA
BIT
BITE
BITMAP
BLEAT
BLOT
BOAT
BOLT
CAT
CITE
CLIMATE
CLOT
COAT
COBALT
COMBAT
COMET
COMPATIBLE
COT
EAT
EMIT
ETA
IMPACT
IOTA
ITEM
LATE
LEAPT
LET
LIT
LOCATE
LOT
MALT
MAT
MATE
MEAT
MELT
MET
METABOLIC
METAL
MITE
MOAT
MOTEL
MOTILE
OBLATE
OCTAL
OMIT
OPIATE
OPT
OPTIC
OPTICAL
OPTIMA
OPTIMAL
PACT
PAT
PATE
PATIO
PEAT
PELT
PET
PETAL
PILOT
PIT
PLATE
PLOT
POET
POETIC
POETICAL
POLECAT
POLITE
POT
TAB
TABLE
TAIL
TALE
TAME
TAP
TAPE
TEA
TEAM
TEMPO
TIE
TILE
TIME
TIP
TOE
TOIL
TOMB
TOME
TOP
TOPIC
TOPICAL

SOLUTION 215

1. CREAM
2. HARD
3. ENTERTAIN
4. EASY
5. SLICE
6. EXPENSIVE

Secret Theme: CHEESE

SOLUTION 216

AEON
ALOE
ALONE
ALTO
ATONE
ATOP
ELATION
EON
INTO
ION
IOTA
LATINO
LEO
LION
LOAN
LOIN
LONE
LOP
LOPE
LOT
NOT
NOTE
OAT
OIL
ONE
OPAL
OPEN
OPIATE
OPT
PATIO
PELOTA
PIANO
PILOT
PINTO
PION
PLOT
POET
POINT
POLE
POLITE
POT
POTENT
POTENTIAL
TALON
TEAPOT
TIPTOE
TOE
TOIL
TOILET
TON
TONAL
TONE
TOP
TOT
TOTAL
TOTE

SOLUTION 217

1. I had a wonderful childhood, which is tough because it's hard to adjust to a miserable adulthood.—Larry David
2. The early bird may get the worm, but the second mouse gets the cheese.
3. The hardness of butter is directly proportional to the softness of the bread.
4. If it's a penny for your thoughts and you put in your two cents' worth, then someone, somewhere is making a penny.—Steven Wright
5. If lawyers are disbarred and clergymen defrocked, doesn't it follow that electricians can be delighted, musicians denoted, cowboys deranged, models deposed, tree surgeons debarked, and dry cleaners depressed?
6. I went to a bookstore and asked the saleswoman where the self-help section was. She said if she told me it would defeat the purpose.—George Carlin

SOLUTION 218

2	4	8	3	7	5	9	1	6
3	7	9	8	1	6	2	4	5
1	6	5	9	2	4	3	7	8
8	2	3	4	9	7	5	6	1
7	9	4	5	6	1	8	2	3
5	1	6	2	8	3	7	9	4
6	5	1	7	3	2	4	8	9
9	3	7	1	4	8	6	5	2
4	8	2	6	5	9	1	3	7

SOLUTION 219

3	9	2	7	8	4	5	1	6
5	8	1	6	2	3	4	7	9
4	7	6	5	9	1	3	2	8
6	1	8	3	4	7	9	5	2
7	2	5	9	1	6	8	4	3
9	4	3	8	5	2	7	6	1
2	6	9	4	7	8	1	3	5
8	3	4	1	6	5	2	9	7
1	5	7	2	3	9	6	8	4

SOLUTION 220

Hidden Phrase:
"The good old hockey game is the best game you can name and the best game you can name is the good old hockey game"

SOLUTION 221

PORT
WORT
WORE
WIRE
WINE

TAPE
TAPS
TOPS
TOWS
BOWS

SOLUTION 222

B	L	E	E	D
L	E	V	E	R
E	V	E	R	Y
E	E	R	I	E
D	R	Y	E	R

SOLUTION 223

C	I	R	C	A
I	D	E	A	L
R	E	A	C	T
C	A	C	H	E
A	L	T	E	R

SOLUTION 224

S	M	A		G	A	L	A			P	L	A	Z	A
T	A	N		L	E	A	S	H		O	I	L	E	D
E	G	G		E	R	N	I	E		M	E	A	D	S
A	P	E	N	N	Y	E	A	R	N	E	D			
M	I	L	A					S	I	L		S	E	A
Y	E	A	R	N	I	N	G		P	O	T	T	E	R
				O	V	A	L				W	I	L	D
	H	A	P	P	Y	N	E	W	Y	E	A	R	S	
I	O	N	E				E	V	A	L				
C	R	I	N	G	E		M	A	N	Y	E	A	R	S
E	N	S		E	R	R					R	H	E	T
			P	L	A	Y	S	I	T	B	Y	E	A	R
U	M	B	R	A		E	L	D	E	R		A	C	E
K	A	R	A	T		S	A	L	S	A		R	T	E
E	Y	E	T	O			B	Y	T	E		T	S	P

SOLUTION 225

A
TA
ATE
MEAT
STEAM
THAMES
ATHEISM
SHIPMATE
STEAMSHIP
SYMPATHIES
METAPHYSICS

SOLUTION 226

I
MI
DIM
MIND
ADMIN
DOMAIN
DIAMOND

SOLUTION 227

1. TASTE
2. OPEN
3. NATIVE
4. GAG
5. UNDER
6. EXTEND

Secret Theme: TONGUE

SOLUTION 228

1. Making a list and checking it twice
2. Black ice
3. Snowbound
4. Twelve Days of Christmas
5. Away in a Manger

SOLUTION 229

1. COTTON
2. NYLON
3. CANVAS
4. MUSLIN
5. SATIN
6. DENIM
7. CASHMERE
8. TWEED
9. RAYON
10. CREPE

SOLUTION 230

ACRE
BABE
BARB
BARE
BEAR
BEAU
BEER
BRACE
CARB
CARE
CRAB
CUBA
CUBE
CUBEB
CURB
CURE
ECRU
RACE
RUBE
UREA

SOLUTION 231

1. You'll never guess who I bumped into on the way to the optometrist! Everyone.
2. Keep a green tree in your heart, and perhaps a singing bird will come.—Chinese proverb
3. If Barbie is so popular, why do you have to buy her friends?
4. I have found that if you love life, life will love you back.
—Arthur Rubinstein
5. By the age of eighteen, the average American has witnessed two hundred thousand acts of violence on television, most of them occurring during game one of the NHL playoff series.
—Steve Rushin
6. Reach for the stars, even if you have to stand on a cactus.
—Susan Longacre

SOLUTION 232

1. There's nothing like looking at vacation pictures to put guests in a travelling mood.
2. There's one good thing about snow: it makes your lawn look as nice as your neighbour's.
3. To shorten winter, borrow some money due in spring.
—W. J. Vogel
4. Middle age is when you're sitting at home on a Saturday night and the telephone rings and you hope it isn't for you.
—Ogden Nash
5. Time may be a good healer, but it's a lousy beautician.
—Author unknown
6. Today, a man knocked on my door and asked for a small donation towards the local swimming pool. I gave him a glass of water.

SOLUTION 233

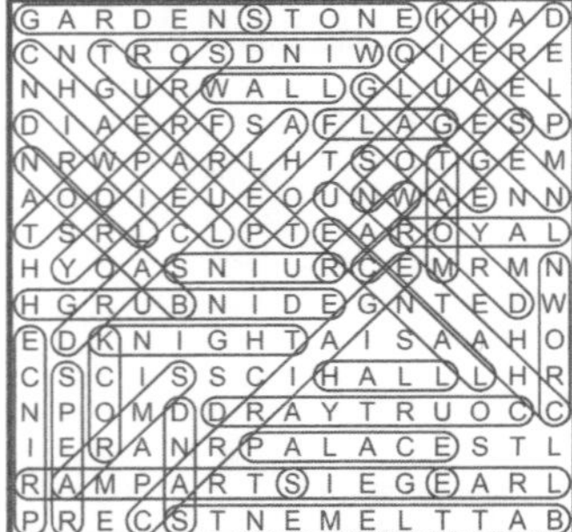

Hidden Phrase:
"An Englishman's home is his castle"

SOLUTION 234

C	R	E	S	O	R	T	P	A	R	K	A	S	K	P
H	I	I	N	N	G	C	O	H	J	M	L	B	A	T
A	I	C	O	J	N	E	S	I	A	O	P	C	U	R
L	S	A	W	T	U	D	O	L	C	O	I	F	H	A
E	L	T	B	R	F	M	U	L	K	N	N	I	O	V
T	E	C	O	S	L	O	P	E	E	W	E	R	T	E
W	D	H	A	C	R	O	I	S	T	T	B	E	C	R
I	D	S	R	H	K	N	L	O	C	K	A	S	H	S
P	I	O	D	I	B	U	N	N	Y	A	L	I	O	E
E	N	M	N	E	G	G	D	O	L	E	A	D	C	M
O	G	E	C	O	P	W	N	T	I	R	C	E	O	R
U	E	A	M	E	S	O	W	I	F	I	L	L	L	T
T	R	I	H	Y	O	U	L	R	T	A	A	R	A	F
A	C	R	E	D	A	V	E	E	B	L	V	U	T	A
M	I	T	T	E	N	S	R	R	S	S	A	N	E	Y

Hidden Phrase:
"Skiing combines outdoor fun with knocking down trees with your face."
—Dave Barry

SOLUTION 235

B	A	N	E		E	A	S	E		S	L	U	S	H
A	R	U	M		S	N	I	P		P	A	S	T	A
J	A	M	B		A	N	T	I		I	D	I	O	T
A	B	B	O	T		A	U	S		G	E	N	R	E
			S	U	M		S	T	R	O	N	G	E	R
D	E	M	O	N	I	C		O	U	T				
I	N	I	M	I	T	A	B	L	E		P	A	R	D
A	N	D	E	S		P	S	A		U	L	N	A	R
L	A	I	D		M	I	C	R	O	N	E	S	I	A
				B	O	T		Y	A	W	N	I	N	G
P	L	A	T	I	N	U	M		R	E	T			
O	I	L	E	R		L	A	P		D	I	T	T	O
A	B	O	R	T		A	Y	E	S		F	A	W	N
C	R	U	S	H		T	O	T	E		U	R	I	C
H	A	D	E	S		E	R	S	T		L	A	N	E

SOLUTION 236

C H A S M S
H A M L E T
A M P E R E
S L E D G E
M E R G E R
S T E E R S

SOLUTION 237

P H A S E D
H U S T L E
A S S A I L
S T A N C E
E L I C I T
D E L E T E

SOLUTION 238

S	N	O	W	B	A	L	L	F	I	G	H	T	I	S
C	N	T	H	S	E	M	I	D	N	S	E	T	T	N
A	O	F	I	W	N	I	N	I	T	L	E	H	R	O
R	T	I	F	C	I	O	L	N	I	A	G	L	T	W
F	O	L	Y	L	E	E	W	B	E	I	A	R	R	F
T	B	N	E	D	V	F	O	S	L	F	O	T	C	L
B	O	H	A	O	T	M	I	N	H	F	R	C	R	A
L	G	Q	H	S	W	T	R	S	H	O	E	O	Y	K
I	G	S	U	O	K	E	R	G	H	E	E	C	S	E
Z	A	I	N	E	H	A	N	W	A	I	S	O	T	T
Z	N	S	C	T	I	I	T	N	M	E	N	A	A	A
A	N	I	R	I	K	N	V	E	I	N	C	G	L	I
R	B	O	L	I	C	H	I	L	L	E	S	S	S	U
D	N	M	H	M	E	L	R	A	L	B	E	K	R	T
S	N	O	W	A	N	G	E	L	C	A	M	U	I	S

Hidden Phrase:
"In the midst of winter I finally learned that there was, in me, an invincible summer"
—Albert Camus

SOLUTION 239

ACHE
ACNE
ANEW
ANKH
ANTE
ASCENT
ASHCAN
ASHEN
ASKANCE
ASKEW
ASSENT
ASSET
AWAKE
AWAKEN
AWAKES
AWASH
CAKE
CANASTA
CANE
CANT
CASE
CASH
CASHEW
CASK
CASKET
CAST
CASTE
CENT
CESS
CHANT
CHASE
CHASSE
CHASTE
CHASTEN
CHAT
CHEAT
CHESS
CHEST
CHEW
EACH
EAST
ENACT
ETCH
HACK
HACKSAW
HAKE
HAST
HASTE
HASTEN
HATE
HAWK
HAWKS
HEAT
HECK
HEWN
KHAN
KHANATE
KNEW
NEAT
NECK
NEST
NEWS
NEWT
SACHET
SACK
SAKE
SANE
SANEST
SANK
SANS
SASH
SATE
SAWN
SAWS
SAWSET
SCAN
SCANT
SCAT
SCATHE
SCENT
SCHWA
SEAT
SECANT
SECT
SENT
SEWN
SHACK
SHAKE
SHAKEN
SKATE
SKETCH
SKEW
SNACK
SNAKE
SNATCH
SNEAK
STACK
STAKE
STANCE
STANCH
STANK
STASH
STEAK
STENCH
STEW
SWAN
SWANK
SWASH
SWAT
SWATH
SWATHE
SWEAT
TACK
TAKE
TAKEN
TANK
TASK
TEACH
TEAK
TECH
TENCH
THAN
THANE
THANK
THAW
THEN
THWACK
TWEAK
WAKE
WAKEN
WANE
WANT
WASH
WASTE
WATCH
WEAK
WEAN
WENCH
WENT
WEST
WHACK
WHAT
WHEAT
WHEN
WHET

SOLUTION 240

1. INVASION
2. NEST
3. STING
4. EYES
5. CRAWL
6. TINY

Secret Theme: INSECT

SOLUTION 241

6	5	8	4	7	1	2	9	3
4	1	3	5	2	9	6	7	8
9	2	7	8	3	6	4	1	5
1	7	4	3	8	5	9	2	6
3	9	2	1	6	4	8	5	7
5	8	6	7	9	2	1	3	4
2	3	9	6	4	7	5	8	1
8	6	1	9	5	3	7	4	2
7	4	5	2	1	8	3	6	9

SOLUTION 242

5	1	3	4	9	7	6	2	8
6	4	2	8	1	5	9	3	7
7	8	9	3	2	6	4	5	1
8	5	7	9	4	2	1	6	3
3	2	6	7	8	1	5	9	4
1	9	4	6	5	3	8	7	2
4	3	1	2	6	9	7	8	5
9	7	5	1	3	8	2	4	6
2	6	8	5	7	4	3	1	9

SOLUTION 243

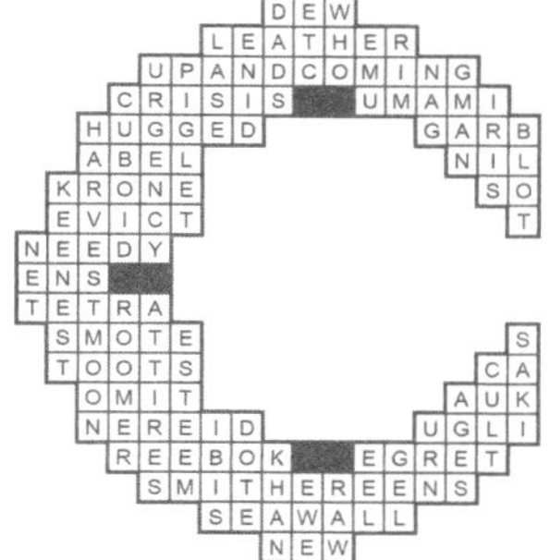

SOLUTION 244

1. DOLLAR
2. RUPEE
3. POUND
4. LEONE
5. RAND
6. FORINT
7. CEDI
8. GOURDE
9. EURO
10. GUILDER

SOLUTION 245

C	S	T	U	F	F	I	N	G	S	T	H	E	R	E
R	I	I	S	S	O	N	L	E	P	Y	O	N	E	D
A	I	D	F	H	F	E	O	R	A	E	N	P	I	E
N	C	E	E	O	B	T	E	T	N	W	E	E	N	A
B	L	O	N	R	A	G	T	L	E	G	G	N	O	G
E	Y	I	F	T	F	R	U	I	T	C	A	K	E	E
R	A	U	O	B	N	D	R	A	T	G	O	O	M	D
R	D	P	L	R	I	N	K	S	O	G	N	E	I	R
Y	G	R	E	E	N	B	E	A	N	S	T	H	X	A
S	T	I	N	A	L	I	Y	I	E	T	H	H	E	E
A	D	I	N	D	K	O	D	S	N	S	E	R	D	T
U	H	H	E	O	S	D	G	R	A	V	Y	Y	N	D
C	W	A	O	E	U	E	T	U	S	L	C	A	U	U
E	O	C	M	P	M	E	Q	L	A	S	A	M	T	C
S	M	O	R	G	A	S	B	O	R	D	T	D	S	K

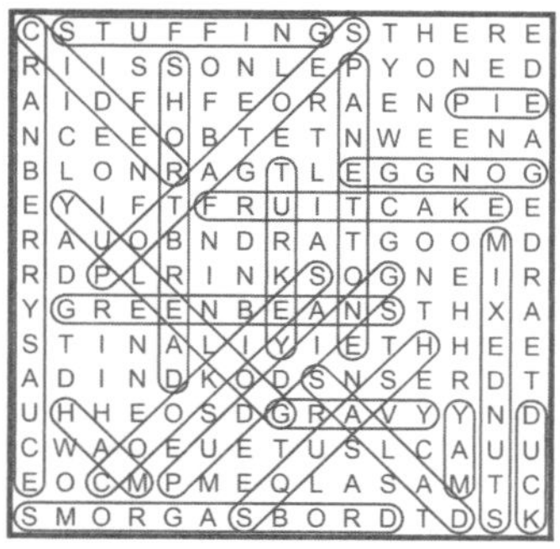

Hidden Phrase:
"There is only one difference between a long life and a good dinner: that, in the dinner, the sweets come last"

SOLUTION 246

E
EE
EVE
EVER
VERSE
SERVER
REVERSE
PRESERVE
REPRIEVES

SOLUTION 247

L	R	D	B	E	M	A	C	S
M	B	S	C	A	R	D	L	E
E	A	C	L	S	D	B	M	R
D	E	M	S	R	L	C	A	B
A	L	B	E	D	C	R	S	M
S	C	R	A	M	B	L	E	D
C	D	E	R	L	S	M	B	A
B	M	A	D	C	E	S	R	L
R	S	L	M	B	A	E	D	C

SOLUTION 248

1. Two fish in a tank, one says to the other, "You man the guns, I'll drive!"
2. It's always darkest before the dawn. So if you're going to steal your neighbour's newspaper, that's the time to do it.
3. This girl said she recognized me from the vegetarian club, but I'd never met herbivore.
4. A gentleman is a man who can play the accordion, but doesn't.
5. High-sticking, tripping, slashing, spearing, charging, hooking, fighting, unsportsmanlike conduct, interference, roughing. . . . Everything else is just figure skating.

SOLUTION 249

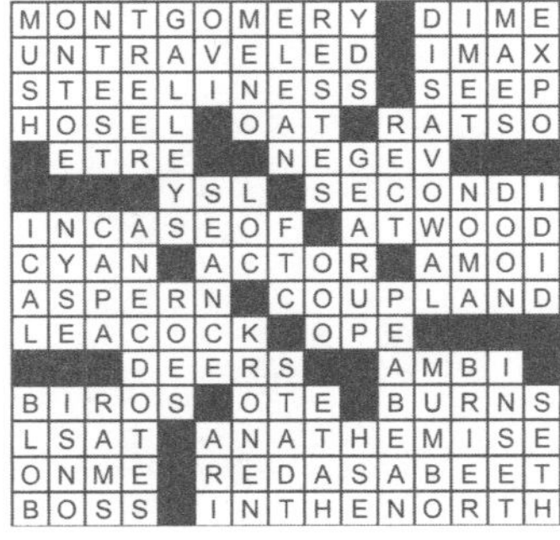

SOLUTION 250

2	9	1	8	4	3	5	6	7
6	4	8	7	2	5	3	1	9
7	5	3	6	9	1	8	4	2
1	2	4	9	7	8	6	5	3
3	8	7	5	1	6	2	9	4
5	6	9	2	3	4	1	7	8
9	7	5	1	8	2	4	3	6
4	1	2	3	6	7	9	8	5
8	3	6	4	5	9	7	2	1

SOLUTION 251

8	9	6	7	3	5	1	2	4
7	5	1	9	2	4	3	6	8
3	2	4	6	1	8	7	5	9
6	8	7	1	5	2	9	4	3
1	4	5	8	9	3	2	7	6
9	3	2	4	6	7	8	1	5
4	7	3	5	8	1	6	9	2
2	1	9	3	4	6	5	8	7
5	6	8	2	7	9	4	3	1

SOLUTION 252

1. What should you do if you see an endangered animal eating an endangered plant?
2. Canadians are generally indistinguishable from Americans, and the surest way of telling the two apart is to make that observation to a Canadian.—Richard Staines
3. Ham and eggs: a day's work for a chicken, a lifetime commitment for a pig.
4. If you spread out all the sand in North Africa, it would cover the Sahara Desert.
5. I have friends who swear they dream in colour; I say it's just a pigment of their imagination.
6. I've decided to sell my vacuum cleaner . . . well, it was just collecting dust.—Tim Vine

SOLUTION 253

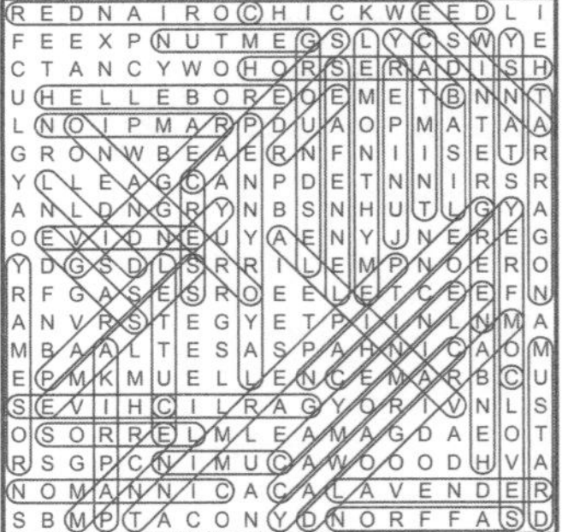

Hidden Phrase:

"Life expectancy would grow by leaps and bounds if green vegetables smelled as good as bacon"

SOLUTION 254

1. Bold move
2. Right wing
3. Pacing up and down
4. Short answer
5. Wide variety

SOLUTION 255

CON
CONE
CONQUER
CONQUERED
CORN
CORNED
CRONE
DEN
DENE
DERN
DON
DONE
DONEE
DRONE
DUN
DUNCE
DUNE
EDEN
ENCODE
ENCODER
ENCORE
END
ENDURE
EON
ERNE
NEE
NEED
NOD
NODE
NOR
NUDE
ONCE
ONE
OUNCE
QUEEN
REDONE
REND
ROUND
RUN
RUNE
UNDER
UNDO
URN

SOLUTION 256

C	H	O	R	D	■	F	A	N	■	A	P	T
L	I	V	E	R	■	A	C	E	■	P	R	O
I	M	A	G	O	■	E	C	O	■	H	I	T
■	■	■	A	P	P	R	E	N	T	I	C	E
L	U	L	L	■	R	I	P	■	I	D	E	M
E	R	A	■	B	E	E	T	L	E	■	■	■
U	N	C	L	A	D	■	A	I	R	M	A	N
■	■	■	O	R	I	E	N	T	■	A	L	E
S	L	U	G	■	S	A	C	■	I	D	L	E
W	I	D	E	S	P	R	E	A	D	■	■	■
E	N	D	■	L	O	T	■	C	E	A	S	E
A	G	E	■	A	S	H	■	R	A	D	A	R
T	O	R	■	B	E	Y	■	E	L	O	P	E

SOLUTION 257

S T E E D
T I A R A
E A G E R
E R E C T
D A R T S

SOLUTION 258

G I F T S
I D I O T
F I F T Y
T O T A L
S T Y L E

SOLUTION 259

ELF
FELT
FETISH
FIE
FILE
FILER
FILES
FILTER
FILTERS
FILTH
FIRE
FIRES
FIRS
FIRST
FIRTH
FISH
FISHER
FIST
FIT
FITS
FLESH
FLIES
FLIP
FLIPS
FLIT
FLITS
FLOE
FLOES
FLOP
FLOPS
FOE
FOES
FOIL
FOILS
FOIST
FOR
FORE
FOREST
FORT
FORTH
FORTIES
FORTS
FOSTER
FRESH
FRET
FRIES
FRO
FROST
FROTH
ITSELF
LEFT
LIFE
LIFT
LIFTERS
LIFTS
LOFT
LOFTIER
PROFILE
PROFILES
PROFIT
PROFITS
REFIT
RIFE
RIFLE
RIFLES
RIFT
SELF
SERF
SHELF
SHIFT
SHIFTER
SHOPLIFTER
SIFT
SOFT
SOFTER
STIFLE
STRIFE
THIEF
TRIFLE
TRIFLES

SOLUTION 260

1. Begin again
2. Catch of the day
3. All's well that ends well
4. Dragged through the mud
5. Lay it on the line

SOLUTION 261

5	6	9	8	7	3	2	1	4
3	2	1	4	5	6	7	9	8
7	4	8	2	1	9	6	5	3
8	3	5	7	9	1	4	6	2
6	1	4	5	3	2	8	7	9
9	7	2	6	4	8	1	3	5
4	9	6	1	2	5	3	8	7
1	5	7	3	8	4	9	2	6
2	8	3	9	6	7	5	4	1

SOLUTION 262

7	8	9	2	6	4	3	5	1
6	2	5	3	7	1	8	9	4
4	3	1	5	9	8	6	2	7
9	4	8	7	1	3	2	6	5
5	1	3	6	8	2	4	7	9
2	6	7	9	4	5	1	8	3
1	9	4	8	5	6	7	3	2
8	5	2	1	3	7	9	4	6
3	7	6	4	2	9	5	1	8

SOLUTION 263

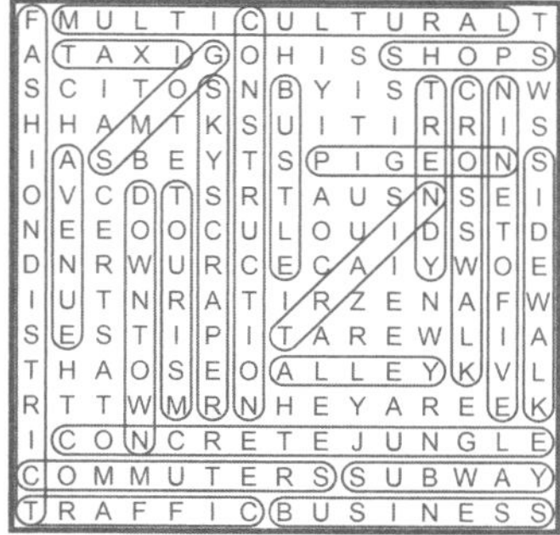

Hidden Phrase:

"This city is what it is because our citizens are what they are"

SOLUTION 264

1. BANANA
2. APPLE
3. PEACH
4. NECTARINE
5. AVOCADO
6. ORANGE
7. APRICOT
8. MANGO
9. CHERRY
10. GUAVA

SOLUTION 265

P	E	R	I	■	S	W	A	M	■	A	L	A	N	D
A	V	O	N	■	C	E	B	U	■	D	O	N	O	R
P	E	C	C	A	R	I	E	S	■	R	O	G	U	E
A	R	K	■	F	O	R	T	H	C	O	M	I	N	G
■	■	■	■	O	L	D	■	R	O	I	■	E	S	S
S	C	H	O	O	L	■	B	O	U	T	S	■	■	■
L	E	A	P	T	■	P	R	O	P	■	H	U	L	A
I	D	L	E	■	G	R	I	M	E	■	E	R	O	S
D	E	E	R	■	N	O	B	S	■	R	E	I	C	H
■	■	■	A	B	O	V	E	■	C	A	T	C	H	Y
H	E	B	■	E	M	I	■	P	E	T	■	■	■	■
E	A	R	T	H	E	N	W	A	R	E	■	V	I	S
S	T	O	R	E	■	C	H	R	I	S	T	I	N	A
S	E	O	U	L	■	E	A	T	S	■	A	N	D	Y
E	N	D	E	D	■	S	T	Y	E	■	B	O	Y	S

SOLUTION 266

P A S T E S
A M O U N T
S O O N E R
T U N D R A
E N E R G Y
S T R A Y S

SOLUTION 267

S C A R E D
C I N E M A
A N S W E R
R E W O R K
E M E R G E
D A R K E R

SOLUTION 268

MESSY
MISERY
MISTY
MOIETY
MOSSY
MUSTY
MYSTERIOUS
OYSTER
OYSTERS
ROSY
RUSTY
RYE
STOREY
STOREYS
STORMY
STORY
STY
STYMIE
SUEY
SYSTEM
TOY
TOYS
TRY
TYRE
TYRES
YES
YET
YETI
YETIS
YORE
YOU
YOUR
YOURS

SOLUTION 269

T	R	E	A		S	T	A	B		J	E	L	L	O
R	E	A	D		P	I	C	E		O	G	D	E	N
A	S	T	O	M	A	T	A	L		L	O	O	T	S
M	I	S	S	S	C	A	R	L	E	T		P	I	E
P	D	A		G	E	N	I	P	A			A	N	T
E	E	L		R	D	S		U	S	E	S			
D	S	O	S				P	L	E	I	O	N	E	
	I	N	T	H	E	B	A	L	L	R	O	O	M	
	N	E	A	T	N	I	K				N	A	P	A
			U	S	S	R		T	U	C		C	U	P
S	A	P			H	E	L	E	N	A		C	R	P
A	L	A		W	I	T	H	T	H	E	R	O	P	E
L	I	N	G	O		T	A	R	A	N	T	U	L	A
A	V	I	S	O		A	S	A	T		E	N	E	R
D	E	C	A	F		S	A	S	S		S	T	D	S

SOLUTION 270

C U B E D
U S A G E
B A D G E
E G G E D
D E E D S

SOLUTION 271

ADD
ADDLE
ADDLES
ADDS
ADO
AID
AIDE
AIDED
AIDES
AIDS
AND
ANODE
ASIDE
DAD
DADS
DALE
DALES
DANDELION
DANDELIONS
DEAD
DEAL
DEALS
DEAN
DEANS
DEN
DENIAL
DENIALS
DENS
DIAL
DIALS
DID
DIE
DIED
DIES
DIN
DINE
DINED
DINES
DIODE
DIODES
DOE
DOES
DOLE
DOLED
DON
DONE
DONNED
DONS
DOSE
DOSED
END
ENDS
IDEA
IDEAL
IDEALS
IDEAS
IDLE
IDLES
IDOL
IDOLS
INLAND
ISLAND
LAD
LADEN
LADIES
LADS
LAID
LAND
LANDED
LANDS
LEAD
LEADS
LED
LEND
LENDS
LID
LIDS
LIED
LINED
LOAD
LOADED
LOADS
LOANED
LODE
NAILED
NOD
NODAL
NODE
NODES
NODS
NOSED
ODD
ODDS
ODE
OILED
OLD
OLDEN
SAD
SADDLE
SAID
SAILED
SAND
SEND
SIDE
SIDED
SIDLED
SINNED
SLID
SLIDE
SNIDE
SOD
SODA
SODDEN
SOILED
SOLD
SOLID

SOLUTION 272

1. REPUTABLE
2. SOLITAIRE
3. INJUSTICE
4. PALATABLE
5. REDISPLAY
6. FURTHERED
7. CARPENTRY
8. PARTAKING
9. PARTITION
10. FORBIDDEN
11. SOPHISTRY
12. NUMERATOR

SOLUTION 273

BEL
BELFRY
BELT
BERYL
BLUE
BLUER
BLUEY
BLUR
BLURT
BURLEY
BURLY
BUTLER
BUTTERFLY
BUTYL
ELF
FELT
FLEURY
FLU
FLUE
FLUTE
FLUTTER
FLY
FLYER
FUEL
LEFT
LET
LETT
LEU
LEY
LURE
LUTE
LYE
LYRE
RELY
RULE
TRULY
TURTLE
UTTERLY
YULE

SOLUTION 274

8	7	9	3	6	4	1	5	2
3	5	2	1	9	8	6	7	4
6	1	4	5	2	7	8	3	9
5	3	7	8	4	6	2	9	1
9	2	6	7	3	1	4	8	5
1	4	8	9	5	2	3	6	7
4	8	1	6	7	9	5	2	3
7	6	3	2	1	5	9	4	8
2	9	5	4	8	3	7	1	6

SOLUTION 275

8	7	1	6	4	3	5	9	2
9	6	3	5	8	2	4	7	1
4	2	5	1	7	9	6	3	8
1	9	6	3	5	8	2	4	7
3	4	8	2	6	7	1	5	9
7	5	2	9	1	4	3	8	6
6	3	4	7	9	1	8	2	5
5	8	9	4	2	6	7	1	3
2	1	7	8	3	5	9	6	4

SOLUTION 276

A	B	A	B			G	U	A	M		G	R	A	B
N	A	N	O	S		O	N	N	A		R	O	M	O
E	D	I	C	T		S	T	O	M	P	E	D	I	N
W	A	T	E	R	L	O	O		M	I	N	I	N	G
			L	O	A	F		T	A	R	A	N	T	O
B	E	L	L	B	O	T	T	O	M	E	D			
O	L	D	I	E			H	O	I		A	B	B	A
G	E	L		S	A	L	I	N	A	S		R	E	L
S	C	S	I		S	O	S			E	B	A	T	E
			D	A	N	C	I	N	G	Q	U	E	E	N
C	A	R	O	L	E	S		A	Z	U	L			
A	D	E	L	L	E		F	I	R	E	L	A	N	E
R	A	D	I	O	D	I	A	L		N	I	N	O	N
I	N	E	Z		E	D	I	E		T	O	T	S	Y
B	A	S	E		D	O	R	R			N	A	H	A

SOLUTION 277

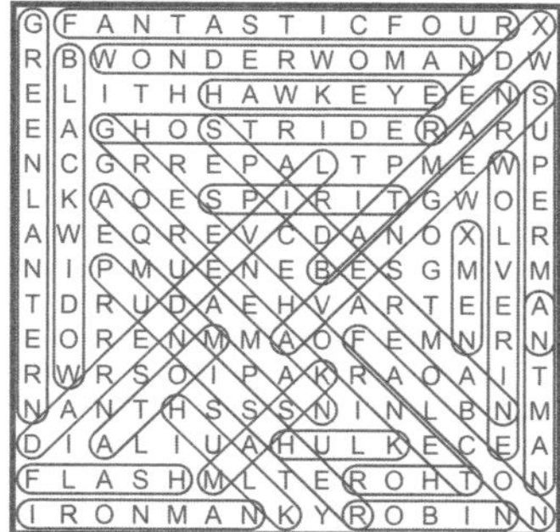

Hidden Phrase:
"With great power comes great responsibility"

SOLUTION 278

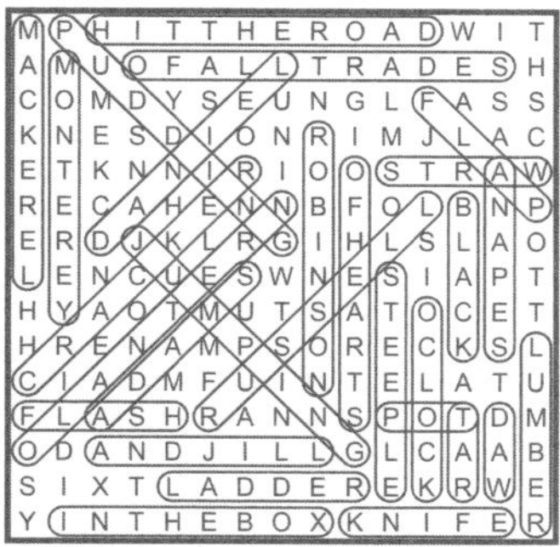

Hidden Phrase:
"With my sunglasses on I'm Jack Nicholson. Without them I'm fat and sixty"

SOLUTION 279

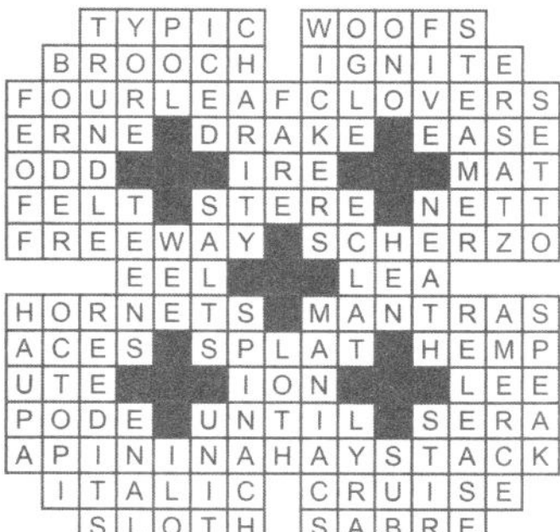

SOLUTION 280

1. Around the block
2. One in a million
3. Shadow of a doubt
4. Fortune favours the bold
5. Weakest link